Palestinian Youth Activism in the Internet Age

SOAS Palestine Studies

This book series aims at promoting innovative research in the study of Palestine, Palestinians and the Israel-Palestine conflict as a crucial component of Middle Eastern and world politics. The first ever Western academic series entirely dedicated to this topic, *SOAS Palestine Studies* draws from a variety of disciplinary fields, including history, politics, media, visual arts, social anthropology, and development studies. The series is published under the academic direction of the Centre for Palestine Studies (CPS) at the London Middle East Institute (LMEI) of SOAS, University of London.

Series Editor

Gilbert Achcar, Professor of Development Studies and International Relations at SOAS, Chair of the Centre for Palestine Studies

Board Advisor

Hassan Hakimian, Director of the London Middle East Institute at SOAS

Current and Forthcoming Titles

Palestine Ltd.: Neoliberalism and Nationalism in the Occupied Territory, Toufic Haddad
Palestinian Literature in Exile: Gender, Aesthetics and Resistance in the Short Story, Joseph R. Farag
Palestinian Citizens of Israel: Power, Resistance and the Struggle for Space, Sharri Plonski

Palestinian Youth Activism in the Internet Age

Online and Offline Social Networks after the Arab Spring

Albana S. Dwonch

I.B. TAURIS

LONDON · NEW YORK · OXFORD · NEW DELHI · SYDNEY

I.B. TAURIS
Bloomsbury Publishing Plc
50 Bedford Square, London, WC1B 3DP, UK
1385 Broadway, New York, NY 10018, USA
29 Earlsfort Terrace, Dublin 2, Ireland

BLOOMSBURY, I.B. TAURIS and the I.B. Tauris logo
are trademarks of Bloomsbury Publishing Plc

First published in Great Britain 2020
Paperback edition first published 2021

Cover design: Simon Levy
Cover image: Mural of the jailed Palestinian teen, Ahed al-Tamimi, on the
separation barrier, in Bethlehem, West Bank, July 29, 2018.
(© Wisam Hashlamoun/Anadolu Agency/Getty Images)

A catalogue record for this book is available from the British Library.

A catalog record for this book is available from the Library of Congress.

ISBN: HB: 978-1-8386-0063-1
       PB: 978-0-7556-4376-9
       ePDF: 978-1-8386-0064-8
       eBook: 978-1-8386-0066-2

Series: SOAS Palestine Studies

Typeset by Deanta Global Publishing Services, Chennai, India

To find out more about our authors and books visit
www.bloomsbury.com and sign up for our newsletters.

To my Mom and Dad,
with love and gratitude.

Contents

Abbreviations

ADALAH	The Legal Center for Arab Minority Rights in Israel
AFCR	Association for Civil Rights in Israel
FGM	Free Gaza Movement
GYBO	Gaza Youth Breaks Out
HFR	Hungry for Freedom
ISM	International Solidarity Movement
PA	Palestinian Authority
PCPSR	Palestinian Center for Policy and Survey Research
PFD	Palestinians for Dignity
PLC	Palestinian Legislative Council
PRDP	Palestinian Reforms and Development Plan
PSF	Palestinian Security Forces
SMN	Social media Networks

Acknowledgments

I would like to express my gratitude and appreciation to the many people who have inspired and supported me in this project. While parts of this writing journey were grueling and lonely, others were reassuring, enlightening, and invigorating, particularly those times when I felt the presence of an incredible team of people supporting me, in so many different ways. I want to acknowledge my deep gratitude and thanks to many of them for their support while I labored through this study.

First, this book would not have been written or even conceived of, were it not for the many activists in Gaza, the West Bank, East Jerusalem, and inside of Israel who gave willingly of their time and insights for the many questions and topics that this study sought to address. Some of them asked that I not mention their names here, but they know who they are. They supported me every time I asked for help, doing interviews and encouraging others to do them for their sake. I particularly want to thank Jehane El Farra, Heba Hayek, and Reem Omran. Their help with collecting data about patterns of Palestinian youth engagement online was crucial to get me started. Moheeb Shaath, in Gaza, was an incredible source of support while writing the Gaza chapter. Issa Amro in Hebron, with his passion for Palestinian human rights and his life dedicated to nonviolent resistance, remained inspirational throughout my fieldwork in Israel and Palestine. Their willingness to extend their personal and work connections to me allowed me to conduct interviews with some activists I did not know personally, but who proved very important to my writing afterward. This book is really about efforts of people like these named and other unnamed individuals, who, despite the difficulties in their own lives, when given the chance, did what they thought was right—for themselves and their community. I hope that one day I will be able to return the gesture of friendship and kindness that each has shown to me.

When I decided to alter the professional trajectory of my life, switching from the NGO world and leaving behind a career I was passionate about, to enter the world of academia, no one warned me about the dangers that come with such "Leaps of Faith." I am grateful to my previous organization, Mercy Corps, and its people, which offered me opportunities to travel the world and observe, in person, the realities of youth growing up in a highly unstable region, the Middle East. Along that journey, I made long-lasting friendships and learned a great deal. Above all, the most valuable NGO lesson that served me in this writing endeavor is that the projects, ideas, and plans that you passionately write up on paper take on a life of their own when implementing them on the ground. You can only take it a day at a time and do your best with and for the people that happen to be with you on that particular journey. I owe my special thanks to David Holdridge, who has supported me from day one, when we first met in Iraq, and who has since become a mentor and good friend.

I want to take this opportunity to thank each of my committee members at the University of Washington, for allowing me to find my own way to combine all these separate strands of my life into a meaningful scholarly work. Joel Migdal has been an inspiring force in this journey, as a scholar, a teacher, and my closest advisor. His unique way of expecting high standards of academic work, while demonstrating empathy, patience, and respect for his students and their work, has had a significant impact on the professor I hope to one day become. Though his scholarly work influenced the way I approached my research, he never pushed me one way or another in writing of this book. Instead, he let me follow my own instincts and passion to guide my research focus. Particularly, during my fieldwork in Israel and Palestine, his ability to help me sort through a myriad of interesting facts and fascinating interviews helped me create a meaningful thesis.

I owe a particular debt of gratitude to Philip Howard, whose writing and literature advice helped shape the theoretical framework of my thesis. Phil believed in my ability to get this book written and encouraged me even in the moments when I most doubted myself. My Skype meetings with him have been crucial in helping me see and appreciate my own accomplishments and in encouraging me to look at the bigger picture when I was stuck in the weeds. Sabine Lang has been a friend and a close confidante in this journey. I have come to admire and deeply respect her natural ability for equal relations that are both highly professional and mutually respectful and trustworthy with her colleagues and graduate students. Resat Kasaba has always shown keen interest and candid support to my work. He embraced my background and my combination of experiences and aspirations from our very first meeting together. Ali Jarbawi has been a consistent source of support, every time I asked for help or advice, during and particularly after my fieldwork in Palestine. My time as a visiting researcher at Ibrahim Abu Lughod Institute of International Studies, at Birzeit University, was invaluable. In Jerusalem, I was affiliated with PASSIA (The Palestinian Academic Society for the Study of International Affairs) which opened its door, library, academic advice and support on a regular basis during my stay in the country. Thank you all for your wonderful support and partnership on this journey!

I also wanted to thank a group of friends and fellow PhD students who helped me with different forms of support, including reading chapters and providing valuable suggestions and comments: Jim Rzegocki, Michael Degerald, Ayse Nal, Filiz Kahraman, Jessica Beyer, and Jean Rogers.

Last, but not least, I would like to thank my amazing husband, Andy, my first reader and editor, my most loyal friend, with whom I lived both through the disappointments and anxieties of some battles lost and through the love and gratitude of others that were won. I could not have finished a demanding PhD course of study and written a book without his never-ending emotional and intellectual support. Throughout this journey, he has been the first to show belief in my ability and the first to assure me that no matter what, at the end of the race, he would be there with me. My children, Emma and Josh, have been my daily reminder of what truly matters in life. Every day they have asked with sincerity and concern about my studies and my writing. The curiosity, joy and enthusiasm, with which they live every day, have helped me learn and grow more than writing this book could ever have. For that, I will be forever grateful!

East Jerusalem
January 2019

Preface

Just after US president Donald Trump officially recognized Jerusalem as the capital of Israel,[1] two major developments took place in the West Bank and Gaza that speak directly to the topic of this book: the dynamics of Palestinian youth activism at the intersection of online activism and on-the-ground mobilizations and more broadly the evolving role of social media networks for youth activism in the Palestinian context. The first was the viral spread of a YouTube video from Nabi Saleh village in the West Bank and the rise of Ahed Tamimi as an online symbol of the Palestinian youth resistance against the occupation. The second was the beginning of the so-called Great March of Return protests in the Gaza Strip.

As these events were still unfolding, I concluded a series of follow-up interviews with Palestinian activists directly involved in the Palestinian youth mobilizations of 2011.[2] These interviews were structured to capture information about how the online and on-the-ground conditions for Palestinian youth activism had changed since 2011–13, the primary period under analysis in this book.[3] But since these two events are still unfolding at the time of writing this book, I decided to start with a brief narrative of each event and explain why and how they speak to the main topic: the evolving dynamics of online activism and on-the-ground mobilizations by Palestinian youth activists in the Internet Age.

Gaza, January 7, 2018: A social media activist and independent journalist from Gaza posted this message on his Facebook wall:

> What if two hundred thousand demonstrators marched peacefully and broke into the barbed wire, East of Gaza, and accompanied by the international media, pitched tents inside, established a city there, and called it Bab al Shams? What if thousands of Palestinians insisted on staying there peacefully without using any form of violence? What can a heavily-armed occupation do to such a peaceful human crowd?

The author of this post, Ahmed Abu Artema, refers to this message as the first online call that turned into a massive, weekly Palestinian protest called

"The Great March of Return."⁴ Before examining the meaning of these most recent mass protests in Gaza, it is worth focusing briefly on the content of the post, its author, the type of new protest he called for via Facebook, and the type of mobilizations that actually took place subsequently in the Gaza Strip.

First, the wording of this text sounded remarkably similar to another message posted on January 14, 2011: "If 100,000 take to the streets, no one can stop us. I wonder if we can." This was the first online call for the January 25 revolution by Wael Ghonim, whose digital activism at the time propelled him forward as the symbol of the 2011 Egyptian revolution. Like Ghonim, Abu Artema chose to construct and share his message via social media networks, bypassing coordination, authority approval, or organizational support by the traditional political parties.

Second, the type of peaceful protest, titled "Bab al-Shams" (literally translated as "the Gate of the Sun") and promoted in Abu Artema's Facebook wall as a possible alternative for the Palestinians of Gaza to resist, had been implemented first in the West Bank. "Bab al-Shams" was one of the most successful and creative forms of nonviolent grassroots activism in the West Bank. (The reader of this book can find more information about this protest in Chapter 4.) It took place on January 11, 2013, when a few hundred activists, some of them participants and organizers of the protests analyzed in this book, erected tents on a piece of land in the West Bank, next to a major Israeli settlement (Ma'ale Adumim).

These activists announced the establishment of a Palestinian village called "Bab al-Shams." The nonviolent protest was covered by many international news outlets, was spread online via networks of social activism, and was ultimately replicated through a series of other campaigns, even before it was in Gaza. Still the type of protests that ultimately became known as the "Great March of Return" took another turn and a very different trajectory in Gaza.

The last piece of information that is important to mention here is that the author of the message, Ahmed Abu Artema, was also involved in the mobilizations of 2011–13—the main period under analysis in this book. Like his fellow organizers of the mobilizations, he defines himself as an independent activist. Even today, Ahmed remains critical of Palestinian factional rivalries and resents the deepening division between the two main Palestinian parties. Still, seven years later, he initially played a central role in a very different type of mobilization that ultimately evolved in an unlikely and very different way than the Bab al-Shams protests in the West Bank did. Despite similarities in the ways these movements were first initiated online and the creative form of activism Abu Artema sought to replicate in Gaza, the ongoing weekly protests took a very different trajectory.

After a gathering of several leaders of the Palestinian factions, which Abu Artema attended, it was agreed to organize a massive nonviolent protest with the organizational support and resources of the Palestinian factions in Gaza including the ruling authority: Hamas. As a result of this decision, from a movement that was initiated in the digital networks and sought to try something new and previously successful in the West Bank, the "Great March of Return" turned into a collective action organized by the political parties— using the same forms of traditionally organized activism: top-down mobilizing modes and strong formal party leadership with organizational resources and politically affiliated activists.[5]

Beginning on March 30,[6] 2018, and every Friday until May 14, 2018,[7] thousands of Palestinians sought to breach the "Security Fence" as the Israelis call it or the "Apartheid Wall" as Palestinians do. They brought their families along to sit in tents that had been constructed close to the border. In particular, the demonstrations in Gaza on the 14th of May were unlike any demonstration before in the "Great March of Return" Friday's protests. This particular demonstration sought to gain momentum and attract global attention by the date of the opening of the US embassy to Israel in Jerusalem.[8] There have been different claims on the origin, strategy and scope of this movement still developing at the time of this writing. A debate has also enveloped the "Great March of Return": whether it was an orchestrated effort by the ruling authority in Gaza, Hamas, together with other factions to transform the idea of totally nonviolent action in another tactic for violent confrontation with Israel.[9] Discussion on this point is beyond the scope and analysis that this book offers.

The Great March of Return revealed however, a different aspect of the mobilizing dynamics that this book studies: What happens when activists who used the digital networks to broadcast their calls for new forms of activism face a completely different reality such as the context in Gaza? How do these constraints influence the transformation of their online calls for action into offline mobilizations? While the search for new alternatives for organizing is ongoing, what this movement demonstrated was that when creative ideas involving digital networks and new forms of activism are forced into the older mold of top-down traditional activism, with large organizational resources, strong leadership, and rigid ideology, these dynamics completely change. Ultimately, under such conditions, movements often do not achieve the same positive impact as others have, and the online and offline space for creative forms of nonviolent activism significantly shrinks.

Yet, for activist Abu Artema, a strong believer that peaceful resistance is the only way to strengthen moral legitimacy and to develop a strong global advocacy for the Palestinian cause, this is just the beginning. New ways to resist, according to him, using social media networks and empowering nonviolent grassroots activism can be accomplished even in a challenging Gaza context.

Nabi Saleh, December 19, 2017: The second event worth noticing in this preface starts from a YouTube video showing Ahed Tamimi, a sixteen-year-old girl from Nabi Saleh village in the West Bank, fearlessly slapping a heavily armed Israeli soldier and shouting at him to leave the courtyard of her home.[10] A few days after the video went viral, fueling the digital networks of millions of Palestinians and supporters, Ahed was arrested in the middle of the night by the Israeli military.

Simultaneously, her mother and cousin were also arrested and charged with "online incitement" for uploading the video and distributing it on social media networks.[11] A short time later, Twitter suspended Ahed's account and her father's Facebook page was hacked.[12] On January 1, twelve charges were laid against Ahed Tamimi, including "online incitement" and "throwing stones," offenses punishable under Israeli military law by several years in prison.[13]

The instant global response to the arrest of Ahed Tamimi transformed the sixteen-year old into a vision of hope and rebellion against Israel's military occupation of the Palestinian territories. An online campaign demanded Ahed's release, while the hash tag #AhedTamimi trended all over social media.[14] An impressive mural of the jailed Palestinian teenager was painted in the separation wall in Bethlehem in the West Bank.[15] Hailed as a Palestinian Rosa Parks, another Malala Yousafzai, and a fearless Joan of Arc of the West Bank, Ahed served eight months in the Israeli prison before being released. Today, she is considered a living icon of Palestinian resistance and youth mobilization in the Internet Age.

Ahed Tamimi and her video unexpectedly directed the online attention from the status of Jerusalem toward the weekly popular protests that the villagers of Nabi Saleh in the West Bank have conducted each Friday for the last decade. The current online fame of Ahed may seem temporary, but the exposure of the environment where she grew up, in the village of Nabi Saleh, is anything but that.

The Tamimi family and Nabi Saleh are well known as leaders of resistance and the location of frequent protests against the occupation over the last decade. They have also been highly active in the use of social media and particularly Facebook and YouTube videos, to expose their side of the conflict with Israel's occupation represented by the struggle of villagers in Nabi Saleh through their weekly unarmed confrontations against Israel's military forces. Taken together, these videos seek to give to the world a glimpse into the life of every day Palestinians and their ongoing protest movements resisting the occupation on the ground.

Bassem Tamimi, Ahed's father, has been a key figure in Palestinian popular resistance dating back to the First Intifada. His story of activism is included in details in Chapter 6 of this book. At the time of this interview while his daughter was still in jail, he stated his belief that Ahed has become a new symbol for the new generation and that they will not be held captive by the old ideologies as represented by the Palestinian parties.

> I think this generation should lead the way ahead for a new and renewed vision for the Palestinian struggle. These younger Palestinians are searching for freedom, justice and rights, not for a State or "authority" and not for the liberation of the country. I believe this generation thinks more of the human value and human dignity in this struggle. All the Palestinian parties seek and demand authority—while this new generation demands justice and dignity, and fights for equal rights. We should follow them. (Personal Communication, January 2018)

Tamimi's quote exemplifies the ongoing rupture between organized activism as represented by the Palestinian parties and new forms of grassroots resistance and online youth activism that empowers leaders on the ground. He believes that social media plays a great facilitating role and hopes that one day the web resistance signals from Nabi Saleh will spread across the world, will wake everyone up, and will bring dignity and justice to Palestinians, young and old.

Hebron, January 7, 2018: Nothing seems to shock any longer Issa Amro a leading Palestinian human rights activist, often referred to as the "Palestinian Gandhi."[16] Not Trump's declaration, not the legitimacy crises of the Palestinian leadership, nor the continuing efforts by both Israeli and

Palestinian authorities to co-opt or crush any form of dissent on the ground, and not even their increased Internet surveillance of any form of online activism that seem to threaten their authority. "This is the daily reality in which we live, breathe and act," he said as he started talking about the impact of Trump's declaration for online and on-the-ground broad-based youth mobilizations. Issa himself is no stranger to arrest and detainment, by both the Palestinian and Israeli authorities. In December 2016, he had just been released after being detained by the Israeli military.[17] In 2017, he had been arrested and detained again, this time by the Palestinian Authority. This arrest was due to a post he made on his Facebook page demanding the release of a Palestinian journalist arrested by the Palestinian Authority for criticizing them and the Palestinian president, Mahmoud Abbas. Issa was charged with "online incitement" and "causing division among young Palestinians by criticizing the Palestinian leadership."[18]

As he spoke about the online and on-the-ground conditions for Palestinian youth mobilizations—surveillance, arrests, occupation, and internal Palestinian division—Issa was nevertheless upbeat and active. In one of the rooms of the "Youth Against Settlements" center, a group of young people are monitoring and reporting online the reactions of Jewish settlers in Hebron to Trump's declaration. Simultaneously, he is constantly checking his phone and making sure that he keeps up his participation in the latest tweet storm, under the hash tag #FreeAhed. "Yes, there is online surveillance and censorship on one side—but there is also global attention, solidarity and support for Ahed and for what she represents to the young Palestinians seeking new ways to mobilize on the ground."

These two still-developing stories of Nabi Saleh and Gaza's ongoing protests as well as the personal stories of activists like Ahed and her father Bassem Tamimi, Issa Amro in Hebron, and Ahmed Abu Artema in Gaza are important. First, the online and offline evolution of their activism speaks to the main theme of this book: studying the dynamics of Palestinian youth activism at the intersection of online activism and on-the-ground mobilizations. It is important to note here that each of these activists, representing three different generations of Palestinian activism, were directly or indirectly involved in organizing and leading the networked movements of 2011 that form the empirical base of this study. Moreover, the leaderless and Internet savvy youth groups that were at the core of the networked mobilizations of 2011–13 were crucial in getting Nabi Saleh fully online, back in 2008.

Second, each of the activists who shared their stories with me have, at some point, been arrested or detained and also systematically surveilled or censored online by both the Palestinian Authority and Israeli intelligence. This reveals the broader context and the major limitations that young Palestinians face in their day-to-day lives marked by segregation walls and territorial fragmentation, military borders and checkpoints, internal Palestinian political division, and increased online surveillance and censorship. Taken together, these activists seek to expose, via digital networks, the reality of these young people's day-to-day lives and how it affects their choices and modes of mobilization.

Third, while these stories may appear as erratic online episodes of mobilizations, they manifest a certain set of characteristics, analyzed in detail in this book in relation to the Palestinian youth mobilizations of 2011: they first occurred online where people shared the emotions of outrage and despair over an event that resonated deeply with them. Increasingly, the evolving mobilizations on the ground materialize as decentralized and leaderless cycles of protests or confrontations that persistently take place outside of the official mobilizing structures as represented by the Palestinian parties.

Finally, the online and offline stories of these activists challenge the overwhelming narrative of diminished or declining Palestinian youth activism and indicate that, far from sitting on the sidelines, youth are indeed involved in a variety of different protests and confrontations while constantly seeking new ways to mobilize outside of the traditional mobilizing structures of their parties. The still evolving story of Ahed—as a vision of youth and hope—the ongoing search for new forms of activism as evident in the personal quest of activist Ahmed Abu Artema in Gaza, and the example of Issa as a human rights activist and champion of nonviolent resistance and civil disobedience speak more broadly to the central argument of this book: that the online campaigns and offline protests of 2011 represent a major turning point for Palestinian youth activism in the Internet Age.

This book was written at a time when, in spite of the fact that inspirational images of the Arab Spring were quick to spread across the globe, the Palestinian expectations for any form of a sustained wave of mobilizations were depressingly low. Even when the Palestinian mobilizations of 2011 and the rise of a new group of tenacious actors with new ways of organizing were evolving on the ground, they were somewhat overlooked, fading instead in the background of bigger mobilizations across the region, particularly the Tunisian and Egyptian Uprisings. For that reason, and in the wake of these most recent events, this study seeks to focus on Palestinian protests and individual voices, previously absent in the overall narrative of the Arab Spring and still easily neglected in the larger field of the Palestinian-Israeli conflict.

While most of the current circumstances speak of dark times ahead for Palestinian youth activism, the analysis of this book cautions against seeing the Palestinian youth as powerless and without any agency to act. As my assessment of the 2011–13 Palestinian networked mobilizations indicates, despite the existing data on the massive exit of Palestinian youth from formal politics, a series of protests erupted nevertheless across Palestine on the cusps of the Arab Spring. This book contends that these protests should be seen as recurrent cycles of protest and rebellion signaling a turning point in Palestinian youth mobilizations.

These most recent stories of activism in the digital age from Nabi Saleh to Gaza and Hebron reveal new opportunities as well as significant limitations presented by increased social media use and social media literacy of Palestinian activists. They call for more attention to capturing and discussing evolving conditions that enable the transformation of sentiments of hope or despair that energize the social media networks into the next movement for change in the Palestinian context.

Series Foreword

The question of Palestine—with its corollaries, the Israel-Palestine and Arab-Israeli conflicts—has been a key issue of world politics and a major source of world tension since the 1917 Balfour Declaration. Few global issues have attracted so much attention over such a long period of time. As a result, despite its small territorial size, Palestine has become a key component of Middle East studies in the academic community as well as a field of study in its own right, in the same way that France or Germany are each the subject of individual study while being part of European Studies. This "disproportionate" status of the Palestine topic is due to several factors.

First is the strategic location of Palestine at the Mediterranean door of the Middle East and the "East of Suez" world. This strategic position—the source of British interest in Palestine at the beginning of the twentieth century—has been enhanced by the greater importance of the broader Middle East in global affairs as manifested by the high frequency of wars and conflicts in the region since World War II, and even more since the end of the Cold War.

Secondly is the very particular fact of what has been described as a "settler-colonial" project in Palestine that was boosted by the huge human tragedy of the Nazi genocide of European Jews in 1941–5. The result has been a complex mingling of the Holocaust, which the Zionist movement claims as legitimizing its actions, with what Palestinians call the *Nakba*, or "catastrophe," which describes the "ethnic cleansing" of Arab Palestinians from great swathes of Palestine in 1948 by the Zionist drive toward the creation of Israel.

Thirdly is the sheer complexity of the Palestine question engendered by the *Nakba* and the subsequent occupation by the state of Israel of the West Bank and Gaza following the Six-Day War in 1967. As a result of these, the Palestinian people today are living under very different conditions and legal regimes: they encompass those who remained in Israel after the state's establishment in 1948; those, including refugees, under direct Israeli occupation or indirect Israeli control in the West Bank and Gaza; those displaced by the wars of 1948 and 1967 to the eastern bank of the Jordan River, some of them still living in camps, and most of whom became Jordanian citizens; those living in the refugee camps of Lebanon and Syria; those of the diaspora living in other Arab countries; and those of the global diaspora.

Finally, the question of Palestine plays such a major role in Arab politics in general and represents such a major trauma in collective Arab memory that it has been the focus of prolific artistic and literary energy, a drive that goes beyond Palestinians to include creative minds and talents from all Arabic-speaking countries.

This complexity and the unparalleled diversity of contemporary Palestinian locations and situations help to explain Palestine's "disproportionate" status and account for the abundance of publications on Palestine and its people. And yet, surprisingly, there has until now been no university-based English-language book series specifically dedicated to Palestine Studies. The SOAS Palestine Studies series, published by I.B. Tauris in collaboration with the SOAS Centre for Palestine Studies (CPS) at the London Middle East Institute (LMEI), seeks to fill this gap. This series is dedicated to the contemporary history, politics, economy, society and culture of Palestine and the historiographic quarrels associated with its past.

The subject of Palestine has aroused intense passions over several decades. On such a topic it is very difficult to exclude passion, and the pretension to be "neutral" is often disqualified by both sides. But we will make sure that none of our books stray beyond the realms of intellectual integrity and scholarly rigor. With the Palestine Studies series we hope to make an important contribution towards a better understanding of this most complex topic.

Professor Gilbert Achcar, Editor Chair of the Centre of Palestine
Studies, SOAS, University of London

1

Introduction

No one expected or saw their protests coming. Nobody warned them how rocky and messy it would get once they plunged from the safety of their social media networks into the streets of Gaza and the West Bank and even inside Israel. Despite the rapid diffusion of the inspiring images of the Arab Uprisings in 2011, in a fast-paced world networked by the Internet, Palestinian expectations of any form of massive youth revolts seemed depressingly low. One way or another, their odds to come together and protest were close to none.

Overwhelmingly, in this period, the "Oslo generation"—young Palestinians born around the historical period of the Oslo Accords of 1993—appeared depoliticized, demobilized, fragmented, politically alienated, and economically marginalized (Sayre and Botmeh, 2010; Dhillon and Yousef, 2009; Khalaf and Khalaf, 2011; Christophersen, Høigilt, and Tiltnes, 2012; Hoigilt, 2013, 2015; Dana, 2015; Casati, 2016). Consistently, these studies highlighted the cynicism, despair, and hopelessness of these young Palestinians, locked in their segregated geographic areas and trapped between Israel's military occupying regime and the deepening division between Palestinian factions in the West Bank and Gaza. Endless and ominous studies and surveys conducted between 2009 and 2013 pointed to the gloomy prospects of a disillusioned group of youth, whose emotional bond with their traditional leaders was dissipated and replaced instead with a bitter sense of betrayal by their authoritarian parties and formal political movements (Sharek, 2009, 2011, 2013; al-Shabaka, 2011, 2015, 2018, 2019; FAFO, 2012, 2013; AWRAD, 2012, 2015, 2016; ASDA'A Burson-Marsteller, 2017).

Notwithstanding this bleak political background and loads of insurmountable contextual constraints, a rising tide of Palestinian youth-led activism and protests surged in the Palestinian territories and inside Israel between 2011 and 2013. It first started on their social media networks (SMNs), where groups of young Palestinians, inspired by the Tunisian and Egyptian revolutions, shared their own great expectations online. They called on their peers to join them in their Palestinian revolution against the division of the two main Palestinian political parties, Fatah in the West Bank and Hamas in Gaza.

On March 15, 2011, at various sites in the West Bank, in the Gaza Strip, and even inside Israel, vast numbers of young Palestinians took to the streets with a core demand, never embraced so publicly before: "The people want the end of the division," referring to the political division of the West Bank, ruled by Fatah, and the Gaza Strip, controlled by Hamas. From there, a sustained series of seemingly isolated protests followed: In November 2011, young activists of the West Bank were the coordinators of another successful campaign, "Palestinian Freedom Rides," whose images were instantly diffused via the Internet across global networks, exposing the expansion of the Israeli settlements in the West Bank and the military checkpoints that prevent West Bank Palestinians from crossing into Jerusalem. In September 2012, a growing network of activists coordinated massive protests in Ramallah, Hebron, and Nablus against Palestinian Authority (PA) economic policies. Images of Palestinian Security Forces (PSF) violently beating and cracking down on activists went viral. In January 2013, the initiative of Bab al-Shams (Gate of the Sun), wherein young Palestinians erected tents and caravans, simulating Palestinian settlement on Israeli-occupied land, caught the Israeli authorities by surprise. It took them three days to dismantle the tents and arrest the activists, but by that time this activity was hailed as the most creative youth initiative seen in the past decade.

Lastly, in June to July 2013, thousands of young Palestinian-Israeli citizens living inside Israel, waving Palestinian flags, and wearing checkered black and white *keffiyeh* rose up to protest Israel's government plan to remove about 40,000 Bedouins from their lands in the Negev desert. Through coordination via digital networks, solidarity protests were simultaneously organized in Gaza, the West Bank, and East Jerusalem. Similarly, images of Israeli police brutally cracking down on activists were posted and shared instantly through social media pages of the activists participating in the demonstrations.

Against a predominantly dark narrative of Palestinian youth activism in the past decade, this persistent wave of youth protests and new forms of activism are quite striking. Even more remarkable is the fact that these politically unaffiliated activists willingly exposed themselves to tear gas, rubber-coated bullets, skunk water, severe beating, and imprisonment in both Israeli and Palestinian jails.

In this book, I aim to explain this paradox of supposedly depoliticized, distressed, and demobilized Palestinian youth rising up in demonstrations. While examining the dynamics of these youth demonstrations and protests, I ask this central question: In the face of these seemingly insurmountable obstacles and to the detriment of their own personal safety, why and how did these young groups come together to effect change in their lives, as is evident in a sustained chain of protests? This book answers this question by studying their mobilization modes and the practical and concrete ways that digital networks such as Facebook, Twitter, YouTube, and blogs affected their new forms of activism. A series of online and offline protests that seemed both chaotic and unorganized and yet somehow recurring frequently, with similar protesting themes and venues, were coordinated by a consistent network of activists. These actors and these movements surprised those who praised them for injecting hope, enthusiasm, and novelty in the fatigued modes of Palestinian mobilizations as well as those who criticized them for their various shortcomings, most obvious of which is the lack of results and a long-term strategy.

This study addresses this question, through a bottom-up analysis of the online and offline evolution of a series of Palestinian youth protests, led by leaderless and independent Palestinian youth groups between 2011 and 2013 in the occupied Palestinian territories and in Israel. These mobilizations were coordinated and announced primarily on social media networks (Facebook, Twitter, and blogs) and then materialized into street protests. They were led by masses of youth unaffiliated with established political parties who were distrustful of their current leadership. I initially focused on such movements, because despite their similarity and their occurrence in tandem with other protest movements in the Middle East at the time, they barely left a mark on the ongoing narrative of the historic period widely known as the "Arab Spring."

However, when moving beyond the online content analysis of this collection of protests between 2011 and 2013 and tracing the offline evolvement in their separated geographic areas in the Palestinian territories, my attention quickly shifted beyond the context of the Arab Spring where these movements originated. My attention was drawn to the compelling and courageous stories of the activists involved in these protests, their new forms of activism initiated on their digital networks, such as Facebook and Twitter, and the formational dynamics of the Palestinian youth movements in the age of the Internet. By "formational dynamics," I mean a detailed account of the online and offline actions of these activists and their evolving experiences from the digital networks, where they first expressed dissent, to the offline challenges of street protests where they demanded change; from the easy start and instant success in creation of small groups and opening their group Facebook pages to the long struggle to agree on one common demand and then breaking up their groups again; from the multitudes of young Palestinians "liking" and "sharing" ideas and stories of activism in their digital platforms to the real numbers of young Palestinians taking to the streets to protest oppression, occupation and injustice. Such stories of online and offline activism appear unconnected on the surface, but when studied more closely show that they are actually intertwined in a myriad of unexpected ways. Together they give us a glimpse of the complex realities of the everyday political organizing of these Palestinian youth groups in the age of the Internet. These dynamics between online and offline contexts constitute, I believe, one of the central fields for social movement studies in the coming decades.

Research questions

This book zooms in on the interplay between the personal life stories of these individual activists, the digital networks that connected them across territorial fragmentations and military borders and the contentious political realities that shaped their mobilization processes and influenced the evolution of these protests in Gaza and the West Bank in Israel. It sheds light on the motivations that led groups of Palestinian youth to search for alternative ways of mobilizing, while simultaneously tracing the pathways that led to disconnect from Palestinian governance, and on the challenges of influencing the course of the Palestinian-Israeli conflict.

The study answers these three empirical questions: (1) What internal and external factors determined the transformation of certain actions initiated on digital networks into street protests led by these youth groups in Palestine and Israel? (2) To what degree did these youth networks and their newer forms of activism affect the more traditional mobilization modes, as implemented by official parties and conventional organizations in each separate geographic area? (3) What prevented these activists from moving beyond specific events and initiatives and from developing a sense of a common purpose and shared commitment in order to affect longer-term political change? These questions intersect closely with literature in the fields of communications and social movements, which I will review below, after I proceed with an outline of case selection, methodology, and chapter organization.

The book contends that the series of social media-fueled protests in the period of 2011–13 signaled a turning point for Palestinian youth activism, from collective uprisings affiliated with official parties to a multiplicity of leaderless movements developing outside of the mobilizing structures of formal political organizations. Unlike the historic activism of Palestinian youth in the first and second intifadas, these new and networked movements occur as cycles of confrontations with both the current political systems in the West Bank and Gaza and Israel's military occupation of the Palestinian territory.

The book demonstrates that the decade-long crippling division between the two main Palestinian factions, Hamas and Fatah, further deepened the disconnect and significantly accelerated the pace of withdrawal of youth from party-affiliated activism. This rupture became publicly visible in the aftermath of the 15 March movement, wherein young independent Palestinians rose against the ongoing bitter political rivalry between the two main Palestinian factions, Fatah and Hamas. In response, both parties used similar tactics to infiltrate, co-opt, and arrest these youth crowds, demonstrating the common repressive nature of both political systems in the West Bank and Gaza.

A second common theme of the mobilizations analyzed here, is a search for a renewed strategy of non-violent resistance against the Israeli occupation. This search hinges on the fusion of online youth activism networks and offline grassroots movements. Such an approach seeks to rebuild community trust and empower leaders of a variety of forms or movements on the ground, as opposed to the traditional leaders sitting in their offices. In their quest for an alternative path of freedom, justice, and dignity, these activists have abandoned the grand formal strategy for national liberation as represented by their parties and replaced it instead with intentionally quick and disuptive cycles of protests that are aimed at unsettling both Israel's military control and the domination of repressive Palestinian factions. This dramatic shift in the targets of their protests is tied to the influence of the Arab Spring in the political aspirations of these young activists. The way young Arabs rose against their corrupt institutions and authoritarian regimes, demanding political change, left a deep impression on the young Palestinians' hearts and minds. For the first time in the rich history of Palestinian youth activism, young Palestinians publicly rebelled against their own political parties. By turning against their divided leadership, while simultaneously resisting Israel's occupation, they introduced the notion that the Palestinian endeavor must be engaged on two parallel fronts: internal and external.

My second argument is that despite Palestinians' everyday experience marked by territorial fragmentation, military borders, and internal political divisions, social media played a crucial role in allowing youth to overcome these obstacles, connect online, share information, tips, and specific time frames in simultaneously organizing these impressive youth mobilizations across borders. A significant majority of my interviews with activists directly involved confirmed this conclusion. They were able to share content and information about their actions instantly and raise awareness about their protests through their ties with global networks of action. Through their digital networks, they were able to expand, maintain, and strengthen ties across borders and lines of division in Israel and Palestine. SMNs and increased social media literacy among Palestinian youths enabled these protest movements to move from the margins of Palestinian society to its center. As we will see over the course of this book, uses of social media among Palestinian activists are almost as distinct as their venues and modes of mobilizations in their separate geographic territories in Gaza, the West Bank, East Jerusalem, or Israel. However, when authoritarian actors attempt to appropriate these new forms of activism and execute them using existing modes or top-down leadership and heavy organizational resources, the dynamics of these movements change and their impact on new forms of youth mobilizations diminishes.

It is true that, to date, most of these forms of actions have been contained and have not managed to change the internal political systems of the parties, nor have they altered the broader dynamics of Palestinian politics or the Palestinian-Israeli conflict.

Nevertheless, despite their failure to visibly affect the broader dynamics of these politics, my findings lead me to believe that this series of youth-led protests marked the onset of an independent and effective network of activists, increasingly aware of their power to organize outside of their controlling structures. As a result, a growing and experienced pool of leaders may be able to transfer their successful examples and experiences from these waves of protest from their informal youth networks to larger and more visible networks of actions, such as the non-violent popular resistance in many villages across the West Bank and the BDS (Boycott, Divestment, Sanctions) movement.

Finally, issues of researcher's objectivity may come into question and are discussed in the methodology section of this book. However, it should be noted here that my academic interests regarding new social movements (NSMs) and new forms of youth activism in the era of the Internet emerged in the context of my previous work career in the international development field in the Middle East, between 2003 and 2010. During one of the periods analyzed in this book, between 2006 and 2011, I was living and working in Israel and Palestine. During this period, through my work as a youth mobilizer for an international humanitarian organization (Mercy Corps) and as a result of frequent work travels to Gaza and across the West Bank, I had close contacts with some of the activists that participated in these movements. Upon my arrival in Israel and Palestine to conduct fieldwork for the purposes of my doctoral dissertation, they were crucial to network me with a new generation of activists whom I did not know personally.

Case studies

Gaza Strip: The forgotten revolution

No one predicted the explosive outcome of a seemingly random and insignificant event in the Gaza Strip in November 2009. The event was the closure by Hamas, the ruling authority of the Gaza Strip, of "Sharek," a local and small independent youth organization. Analysts and researchers lightly referred to it as an example of the increasing restriction on Gaza's civil society and the ongoing political rivalry between the two main Palestinian factions, Hamas in Gaza and Fatah in the West Bank (Sayigh, 2010; Brown, 2010; Salem, 2012).

But, if not a noteworthy development in the broader geopolitical reality of the Gaza Strip, the closure of Sharek had a dramatic effect in the daily lives of a small group of university students, regular participants in Sharek's youth programs. Eight outraged university students formed a group called "Gaza Youth Breaks Out" (GYBO) and decided to pour out their immense frustration straight from the depths of their troubled young hearts on their Facebook pages. Using a confrontational language, they wrote a shocking message, which they called as "Gazan Youth's Manifesto for Change." For the very first time, their online statement contained a personalized insult and in defiance of Hamas's four-year rule in Gaza. To their surprise, the manifesto went viral almost instantly—translated into various foreign languages, shared in global online youth and social activism networks, and was covered by major international media outlets.[1]

While this episode was widely covered as a fragment of the online experience and realities of Gazan youth, little was said about what happened afterward to the youth group that wrote the manifesto. There was no link between that fearful November morning and the events of March 15, 2011, when many members of GYBO group helped to organize one of the largest youth-led protests in Gaza in at least the last decade: the 15 March movement.

Going beyond a content analysis of their online manifesto and bringing the stories of their involvement into these protests, as well as the trajectory of the movement itself in Gaza, it is critical to understand how these youth connected with other scattered youth groups inside Gaza and the West Bank helped transform viral online activism into massive on-the-ground protests. This is especially true in light of the fact that the 15 March movement is primarily referred to and analyzed as a case of West Bank youth activism. This is even more puzzling, given the fact that the number of youth who took to the streets in Gaza was reportedly much larger than that in the West Bank. In addition, the way that Hamas forces crushed this nascent movement and violently attacked the protesters was much harsher than the way the PA responded to the same movement in the West Bank. To my knowledge, at the time of writing this book, this aspect of the 15 March movement has not been previously analyzed.

"An open air prison" is the most widely used metaphor when referring to Gaza: a tiny strip of land, only 365 km square, surrounded by a tall concrete wall and a barbed wire barrier separating it on the south from Egypt and on the east and north from Israel. To the west of Gaza lies the Mediterranean Sea, access to which is also controlled by Israel. Comprising only one-sixth of the occupied Palestinian territories, Gaza contains more than one-third of the entire population. Nearly 2 million people live in Gaza, 67 percent of whom are '48 refugees.[2] Unlike the ongoing military presence and expansion of Israeli settlements in the West Bank, Gaza presents a different reality. In September

2005, the government of Ariel Sharon disengaged the Israel Defense Forces (IDF) from the Gaza Strip, withdrawing the Israeli settlers and troops back to the borders. Nevertheless, because the State of Israel maintains control over its borders, maritime, and airspace, the United Nations Security Council and most countries and humanitarian organizations consider that the Gaza Strip continues to be occupied and blockaded by Israel (Scobbie, 2007; Darcy and Reynolds, 2010).

The West Bank: Palestinians for dignity after the 15 March movement

Here are examined a wave of protests that took place in the West Bank between 2011 and 2013, organized by a youth group called "Palestinians for Dignity" (PFD). Notwithstanding Israel's military checkpoints across the West Bank and the PA's police brutality in crushing their initiatives, the activists of the PFD led an impressive and sustained number of online and offline protests for almost three years. Then they decided to break up and return to their informal ties and digital networks. This chapter seeks to explain "why," despite the success of their protests, was this youth group unable to expand their attempt to affect social change. To answer this question, this study examines the formational dynamics of "Palestinians for Dignity," created in the aftermath of the 15 March movement in the West Bank.

The attention that the 15 March movement received as a Ramallah-based movement is partially explained by the focus of researchers in the urban culture of Ramallah, shaped primarily by the neoliberal policies of the PA and the NGO-ized local and international communities (Hanafi and Tabar, 2005; Challand, 2009; Merz, 2012; Lang, 2013; Dana, 2015). Yet, focusing on Ramallah alone as representative of youth activism across the entire Palestinian territory may lead to a disconnect from the realities in the rest of the Palestinian areas.

The Palestinian youth activists involved in these movements come from various towns and villages across the West Bank, and youth organizing occurs in multiple locations where young people have been involved in ongoing resistance against the wall and the settlements. For the purpose of this study, after just several interviews conducted in coffee shops in Ramallah, the remainder of interviews were conducted in towns and villages across the West

Bank where the majority of leading activists directly involved in a series of protests in the West Bank following the 15 March movement reside.

The West Bank is the largest area of the Palestinian territories that make up the contested State of Palestine. It has been occupied by Israel since the 1967 Six-Day War. It is located on the West bank of the Jordan River with Jordan directly to the east and Israel flanking it on all other sides. Today, according to the Palestinian Central Bureau of Statistics (PCBS, 2016), around 2.93 million Palestinians live in the occupied West Bank.[3] Military violence, checkpoints, Israeli settlements, a security wall, as described by the Israelis, or an apartheid wall, by the Palestinians, marks the overall context of the West Bank.

Without exaggeration, research under occupation and periodic violence was unpredictable. For example, as soon as I arrived during the first period of my fieldwork, October 2015 to February 2016, a wave of protests and youth violence exploded in Jerusalem and the West Bank, sparked by an initial event in the Old City of Jerusalem. This period was characterized by a series of "lone-wolf" attacks in the streets of Jerusalem, the West Bank, and Israel.

As these events accelerated, so too did tweet storms fueled by Palestinian youth about the beginning of a potential "Third Intifada." East Jerusalem was divided by military checkpoints and was effectively closed off from the rest of the West Bank as the Israeli security forces tried to contain the situation.

It should be noted here that this wave of lone-wolf attacks is not analyzed in this book. Having just arrived in Israel and Palestine and based in East Jerusalem, while traveling across the West Bank and Israel gathering data for the Palestinian Youth mobilizations of 2011, I did not have sufficient time and resources to cover this cycle of leaderless and decentralized Palestinian confrontations of 2015. However, the implications of this wave of attacks on the role of social media for new and multiple forms of Palestinian youth activism in the Internet age were widely debated in both media and scholarly accounts. Understanding the nature of the differences between this wave of attacks and previous confrontations between Israeli and Palestinians hinged on the specific role that social media played in this new cycle of Palestinian youth confrontations with Israelis (Chorev, 2017). Many viewed social media as a tool for incitement and radicalization of Palestinian youth. In contrast, others analyzed it as a new and powerful tool for Israeli surveillance of Palestinian political activism (al-Shabaka, 2017, October). Once again these polarized accounts offered a somewhat essentialist vision of the role of social media for youth activism by focusing primarily on the tools as either good or bad for youth mobilizations. Lacking in-depth context analysis, such an approach missed examining the particular ways in which SMNs affect the mobilization modes of young Palestinians of East Jerusalem and why they differ from the mobilization modes, formats, and venues of Palestinians in the West Bank, Gaza, and Israel.

I resumed more intensive fieldwork in the West Bank during the entire year of 2016. Traveling for the purposes of this research was not limited to sites in Ramallah, but includes those in other cities such as Hebron, Bethlehem, and Nablus and villages around Gush Etzyon in the southern West Bank. Frequent visits were also made to the enormous student campus at Bir Zeit University near Ramallah and to the smaller, but no less noisy one at Bethlehem University. Interviews and informal conversations over these events and the questions of my research were also conducted during this time frame with Palestinian public intellectual figures, academics, policy influencers, and media pundits. I consulted surveys conducted by the Palestinian Center for Policy and Survey Research (PCPSR) and polls on youth activism by various independent youth NGOs such as Sharek Youth Forum. To understand the breadth, range, and reach of youth protests, I also referred to a combination of news reports on the events, as well as youth's own personalized accounts via social media (Twitter and Facebook) pages and their blogs.

As a result of these various research efforts and interviews, the focus of this research shifted significantly: from the online dynamics of the 15 March movement in the West Bank to the offline stories of the activists involved and the evolution of their actions. This study goes beyond an online analysis of activism and shines a spotlight on the story of formation, evolution, and breakup of one of the youth groups that was at the heart of this movement: the "Palestinians for Dignity." Most importantly the book highlights the conditions that brought about the formation and dissolution of this group while simultaneously discovering hidden connections between a network of activists with this youth group at its core and a cycle of seemingly isolated activities and protests that happened after, in the period of 2011–13.

Israel: Stop the Prawer Plan Youth Movement—a case of Cross-Green Line activism

The Prawer Plan aimed at relocating at least 40,000 Bedouins from the southern arid region of Israel, known as Negev in Hebrew or Naqab in Arabic, into designated state locations for the Bedouin population. While the movement by itself, as well as its forms of protests, was new, the Bedouin issue, which the Prawer Plan promised to solve, was not. To oppose this plan, loose and leaderless networks of young Palestinians of Israel first took to their online social networks with hashtags and tweets "Stop the Prawer Plan" and Facebook groups calling for protests. As a result, from the period of June to July 2013, "Days of Rage," in the form of massive youth protests, took place in Southern and Northern Israel. These protests culminated on November 30, 2013, where Palestinians of Israel, together with Palestinians of the West Bank, Gaza, and East Jerusalem, synchronized their protests by organizing separate demonstrations on the same day within their geographic areas and shared their protests online via their digital networks. On December 12, 2013, the Government of Israel decided to drop the Prawer bill—at least temporarily.

The focus on this particular case study of youth activism of Palestinians living inside Israel changed several times during my fieldwork in 2016. Initially, several interviews were scheduled with a number of youth activists who had been directly involved and engaged in an online campaign and solidarity sit-in on the streets of Haifa. The campaign was called "Hungry for Freedom" and was organized in response to a hunger strike held by 100 Palestinian political prisoners in Israeli jails.

During interviews with some of these activists regarding this campaign, other stories of their involvement in earlier similar protests were also shared. This meant that "Hungry for Freedom" was neither the first nor the last campaign they had organized. On the contrary, groups of Palestinian activists in Israel were also active and involved in the mobilizations of their young peers in the West Bank and Gaza during 2011–13.

Back in January 2011, they had organized demonstrations in Jaffa, Haifa, and Tel Aviv, in solidarity with the Tunisian and Egyptian revolutions. Furthermore, the same activists had organized and participated in their own 15 March movements in Haifa and Jaffa, while others had joined their Palestinian peers beyond the Green Line, in the West Bank. During this time, social media had played a crucial role in linking these activists with various

Palestinian digital networks across borders through sharing their activities online and forging new connections.

By tracing their participation in these events, an outline of the conditions that enabled these forms of activism for young Palestinians of Israel is also compiled: They came from both Northern and Southern Israel, were unaffiliated with political parties, and represented various segments of the Palestinian citizens of Israel, including the Druze, Bedouins, Christians, and Muslims. The "Stop the Prawer Plan" movement, which became the focus of my study, had been primarily studied through the lenses of Bedouin indigenous rights within Israel. I noticed that scholars tend to focus on either the Israeli Jewish youth protests movements during this period of 2011 (Alimi, 2012; Allweil, 2013; Grinberg, 2013; Shechter, 2013; Amram, 2013; Marom, 2013; Schipper, 2015) or Palestinian youth movements in the context of the occupied Palestinian territories (al-Shabaka, 2011; Casati, 2016; Christophersen, Høigilt, and Tiltnes, 2012; ACRPS, 2012; Farsakh, 2012; Hilal, 2011; Hoigilt, 2013, 2015; Maira, 2013). As a result, research on the protest movements led by Palestinian youth of Israel and the impact of social media in their communication patters and mobilizing modes was not conducted.

This indicated not only the scarce attention that the protests of young Palestinians of Israel in the wake of the Arab Spring had received but also how much these seemingly separate protest movements were actually connected through a core network of activists across the geographically fragmented and military borders of the Palestinian territories. Their frequent involvement in a series of protests was evidence of a growing network of activists whose ties were forged at the sites of these protests and in their digital networks with activists from Gaza and the West Bank. Consequently, by the time the biggest "Stop the Prawer Plan" youth mobilizations in Israel took place, this youth network, active since 2011, was already well positioned and experienced to organize and mobilize such massive numbers of youth.

While the learning curve was steep, most of the interviews conducted with the activists directly involved in this movement were contacts made thanks to introductions from other activists in the West Bank and Gaza. Often calls to various activists in the West Bank and Gaza would bring new contacts, suggestions for new interviews, and sometimes personal accounts of their involvement in the Prawer Movement.

The Palestinian activists in Israel interviewed here often referred to themselves as "48-ers." This definition of the Palestinians of Israel is a symbolic marker of the year, 1948, where the foundation for two sharply contrasted narratives lays: For the Jewish Israeli people, the historic year marks the creation and declaration of independence by the State of Israel. For the Palestinian people, the year marks the beginning of a tragic narrative known in the national memory as the year of Nakbah (the "catastrophe" in Arabic).

To collect current data about Palestinian youth of Israel, several Israeli and Palestinian resources, such as recent surveys and statistics published by the Galilee Society: The Arab National Society for Health Research and Services, youth studies conducted by Baladna—the largest Arab youth organization within Israel—as well as statistical data drawn from the Israeli Central Bureau of Statistics, were consulted.

Today, one-fifth of Israel's population are of Palestinian-Arab origin, totaling more than 1.6 million citizens. Of these, 82 percent are Muslims, 9 percent are Christians, and 9 percent are Druze. In addition, around 200,000 of this population are Arab Bedouin citizens, members of the indigenous Palestinian community who remained on their lands in the Negev (Naqab) region of the country. Youth constitute more than half of the Palestinian society in Israel, with the age group ranging between zero and twenty-nine making up 62 percent of the population.[4] A further 36.0 percent of the population is at or under the age of fourteen, and the median age of Palestinians in Northern Israel is twenty-two and just fifteen in Southern Israel.[5]

Similar to the case studies in Gaza and the West Bank, this too illustrates how this book started as an attempt to analyze the reach and span of three different campaigns and protests organized by small groups and loosely networked Palestinian youth. However, upon further fieldwork and research during 2015–16, this study took a different turn. It focused less on the separate online chronicles of these protests and more on their offline evolution, the stories of individuals involved in them, their motivations, and their preferred mobilizing ways.

More and more, the activists interviewed resembled a network with ties particularly strengthened at the sites of these protests. While the groups that they would create would quickly break up after completing a particular campaign, the core members would regroup in different formations and be involved in different forms of protests and campaigns. From their perspective, being independent implied opening up a space for expressions around issues that pertained to their daily lives. According to them, issues that were not priorities in the parties' ideological agendas were the ones that brought together young people from different groups within the Palestinian society.

Another surprising fact was the intentional breakup or dissolution of certain youth groups after merely one campaign. After the 15 March movement, these activists had understood that every group that extends its life beyond the goal of the campaign will sooner or later run into conflict with other existing groups/organizations/parties and will be crushed. While the activists continued their protests, they left behind their fixed groups, preferring instead loose networks on digital platforms. All of these factors, as they were revealed in the everyday political realities of the occupied Palestinian territories and Israel, shaped the different ways these movements evolved in these three different contexts

Research design and methodology

This book relied on a set of mixed approaches with primary reliance on qualitative methods and secondarily on quantitative methods. As primary methods for qualitative research, I relied on in-depth interviews with sixty-eight Palestinian social media activists: forty of them are included in the appendix of this book, while twenty-eight spoke only on conditions of anonymity. Most of the interviews were recorded; others who did not want the sessions to be recorded allowed me to take notes instead. Activists such as Yusuf Jamal, Asmaa Al Goul from Gaza, Fadi Quran, Huwaida Arraf from Ramallah, Bassem Tamimi from Nabi Saleh, Badia Dwaik and Isa Amro from Hebron, and Majd Kajal and Maysan Hamdan from Haifa are among those whom I conducted the most in-depth interviews with, and they agreed that I reveal their identities. International newspapers and TV networks have as such also regularly published their stories as political activists. These include *Al Jazeera*, *BBC*, *The Guardian*, and many more news agencies across Europe and the United States.

Other activists who preferred that I not reveal their identities were directly involved in a series of youth movements, protests, and campaigns, mostly recognized in their organizing efforts, which culminated in the 15 March movement. The actions of all the activists interviewed for this book have been met with a similar set of consequences: they have been arrested, jailed, or regularly threatened by both Palestinian and Israeli authorities in the West Bank, Gaza, and Israel. For example, Asmaa Al Ghoul was threatened by Hamas authorities for her online blogs; Fadi Quran was arrested by the Israeli authorities for his organizing and participating in various protests, targeting both Israel's occupation of the Palestinian territories, and by the PA security forces for protesting the PA's repressive practices and harassment of youth activists in Ramallah. During 2016 Issa Amro was arrested and released several times by the Israeli authorities. In 2017, he was arrested and jailed by the PA in the West Bank, only to be released a few days later. These are all facts, documented in the local, regional, and international media.

The relevance of these activists for this research was crucial, because of their direct involvement in these protests, as well as their familiarity with both online and offline activism in my focal geographies. They pinpointed from their perspectives major points of friction with more formally organized movements. Through these interviews, I gained a deeper understanding of their strategies and tactics and experiences and motivations for their preferred choices of activism.

The next set of in-depth interviews were conducted with a number of Palestinian scholars, NGO executives, and public intellectuals, such as Mohib Shaath in Gaza, Sam Bahour, Professor Khalil Shikaki in Ramallah, Professor Mazin Qumsyeh and Sami Awad in Bethlehem, Khaled Faraj in East Jerusalem, and Nadim Nashif in Haifa. The goal of these interviews was not only to establish their perspective on my overall research questions but also to debate with them about the disconnect between today's youth activists and the Palestinian political movements and their leadership. A complete list with the names of the individuals who agreed that I use their real names and identities for the interviews is also added as an appendix at the end of this book.

As a primary source for my online part of this study, I employ the results of a broad online content analysis of online Palestinian youth engagement patterns, through their production and consumption of online content between 2011 and 2012. This survey in the form of content analysis of youth actions, as shared by members in online forums and social media, was conducted during my PhD training years at the University of Washington, between 2012 and 2013. By the time I had studied three years of Modern Standard Arabic at the University of Washington. My advanced writing and reading comprehension in Arabic enabled me to conduct the analysis of these social media sites and posts in Arabic as well as in English. For interviews conducted in Palestinian spoken Arabic, I relied on assistance from native speakers of Arabic.

Roughly 1 million (78 percent of West Bank youth as a demographic group) of Palestinian youth were active Internet users at the time when Arab youth began using Facebook and Twitter as organizing tools for political change. Facebook penetration by Palestinian users reached 1 million in 2012, with users aged from eighteen to twenty-four being the largest age group (487,280 users), followed by twenty-five- to thirty-four-year olds. At the time of writing this book, this number has almost doubled, with 1.8 million young Palestinians being active users of Facebook and other SMNs. I tried to make sense of these numbers by engaging in an online content analysis of the engagement patterns of this entire group of Palestinian Internet users.

Before I delve further into this data set, and as tempting as it is to search for large data sets and broad statistics, I must admit the serious challenges a researcher faces, in the Palestinian case. Presenting solid data collection on Palestinian usage of Internet can be deceptive, since it requires that Palestine be presented as a single unit, when in reality it is not (Aouragh, 2012). On the one hand, the '48 Palestinians (Palestinians who live in Israel and hold Israeli citizenship) receive all communication services from Israeli service providers.

On the other hand, Palestinians in the '67 areas (the Palestinian territories occupied by Israel in 1967) are further divided into three groups: The first and largest group lives in the West Bank, the second in the Gaza Strip, and the third in East Jerusalem. The Palestinians of the West Bank receive most communication services from Palestinian telecommunication companies. Some, however, receive services from Israeli companies, as a result of the West Bank's economic dependency on Israel's economy and the fact that Israeli telecommunication companies also serve settlers and Palestinians living in the West Bank. Palestinians in the Gaza Strip also hold PA identity cards and receive their communication services from Palestinian telecommunication companies.

Palestinians from East Jerusalem receive communication services from both Israeli and Palestinian telecommunication companies. Because each of the distinct segments of the Palestinian population is served by a combination of service providers and since Israeli population is served by some of the same providers, it is quite difficult to find accurate data about the exact numbers of Palestinians online and on social media.

This is why determining the accurate figures of the percentage of Internet usage among Palestinians across borders is very complicated, and only approximations are possible. Still, understanding the online patterns of Palestinian youth engagement, how they have evolved over time, how the statistics and patterns relate to various youth mobilizations and grassroots movements in the Palestinian territory, and to what degree social media has influenced their communication and mobilizing patterns remains crucial in my study. So, I worked with the available data in spite of its imperfect nature and limitations.[6]

The initial resurvey conducted online, and prior to my fieldwork, included evaluation of about 400 online sources (200 Facebook pages, 200 blogs/ Twitter pages of Palestinian youth, mostly in Arabic, with some in English too, reaching an audience of about 400,000 Palestinian users). The main objective that underpinned this survey was the following: to understand how the new communication technologies affected the ability of Palestinian youth to consume and produce information online. Primary focus of the survey at that time was on two digital platforms: Facebook and blogs. The owners of these Facebook pages and blogs were from both the West Bank and Gaza, and their age ranged from eighteen to twenty-four.

Two conclusions came out of this content analysis on Palestinian digital communication patterns. The first was that, thanks to the growing regional information technology infrastructure and the large growth of users coming online, Palestinian youth skills to consume and produce content online also grew significantly. The second conclusion that I reached was that the particular effect of the blogosphere on the ability of young Palestinians to find and express their own political voice through alternative mediums of expression was immense. The bloggers were interconnected; speakers of Arabic and English; promoting issues they felt passionate about; and creating, sharing, and consuming information, both political and personal.

These blogs, Facebook comments, and narratives posted on various digital platforms from social media activists provided an ideal jumping-off point for understanding the role of the new technologies for youth activism in the Palestinian territories. During my fieldwork in 2015, interviews were conducted with some bloggers that were part of the online survey I had conducted in 2011–13. For some time now, they were personalizing their grievances primarily online, the most acute one being the disavowal of their emotional bonds with their current ruling elites and dismissal of rigid ideological frames in which they have no say.

In short, this quantitative part of my research indicated that an emerging network of Palestinian youth was just finding each other online. When the torrent of the events of the Arab Spring exploded, the political demands of their Arab peers offered an outlet for these youth groups to stir something deeply missing in the political foundation of Palestinian national bodies, participatory democratic mobilization (Khalil, 2013; Herrera, 2014). The decentralized nature of new technologies enabled youth groups to create and share their own narrative and their original voices with a local and international audience.

Lastly, I bring into this analysis a collection of about 250 news articles, published in mainstream media outlets, such as *The New York Times, Al Jazeera, The Atlantic, The Guardian, Al Monitor,* Ma'an, and so on. However, what proved particularly important was my daily subscription and follow-up of news from a selected group of online news networks, particularly focused on Palestinian-Israeli events such as Mondoweiss,[7] *Electronic Intifada,*[8] *+972,*[9] and so on. These sources proved extremely valuable for two reasons: some of the activists that were interviewed for this study wrote and reported directly for these news sites and sometimes from the location of their protests. Others were interviewed directly about their involvement and the dynamics of their participation in the events that I analyze in this study.

Finally, despite the combined approach of online and offline methods, as well as various stages of fieldwork, some limitations are also worth mentioning here. While the Palestinians of Gaza, the West Bank, and Israel are the main focus of this study, the diaspora Palestinians are not included here. For reasons of time, resources, and contacts, this study is limited to only the youth groups in their own contextual realities of Gaza, the West Bank, and Palestinians of Israel (and in particular Haifa). These youth groups do not represent all of the youth of Palestine, or all forms of youth movements in Palestine.

In addition, the geographical separations are present in multiple and intertwined groups and categories of Palestinians: Palestinians within the Palestinian territories, Palestinians of the Diaspora and Palestinians of Israel. While I describe some of these nuances in separate chapters, I would like to clarify that this study is not intended to explain substantially the legal, geographic, and political status of a nation without a state, such as Palestine.

Outline

Chapter 1 explains the theoretical underpinnings of this study. It explains the significance of these digital networks for these new forms of protests as well as the theoretical criticism about its impact for long-term political change. The second chapter serves to position the Palestinian youth mobilizations in the historic events of the Arab Spring. It examines early scholarly accounts on the Arab Spring and points out their essentialist approaches on the role of social media for political mobilization. In addition it brings theoretical insights from recent publications that speak more closely to the broader topic of this book: the impact of Internet and networks for NSMs and networked mobilizations in the Middle East.

The central question of Chapter 3 is why and how did members of four youth groups negotiate and agree on the core demand: "People want the end of the division" (between the two main Palestinian political factions, Fatah in the West Bank and Hamas in Gaza), in what is now widely referred to as the 15 March youth movement (2011). With a primary focus on the formation and dissolution of GYBO, this chapter reveals how the first public rejection of the ruling authority of Gaza, Hamas, since its election in 2006, happened online through the viral spread of a scathing online document posted by GYBO. Next, beyond the online ripples that this document caused, the focus shifts to the effect it had afterward on the daily lives of the activists who wrote the text and their involvement in the 15 March movement. A detailed series of actions and reactions are embedded within a sequence of internal and external events between 2006—the electoral victory of Hamas in Gaza—and 2011—the heyday of the Arab Uprisings. The chapter concludes that employing a strategy of rejecting their political actors online and raising a network of young activists offline stripped away their own political affiliations.

Chapter 4 examines a wave of youth-led protests that took place in the West Bank between 2011 and 2013, organized by a youth group called "Palestinians for Dignity." Notwithstanding Israel's military checkpoints across the West Bank and the PA's police brutality in crushing their initiatives, the activists of the PFD led an impressive and sustained number of online and offline protests for almost three years. Then they decided to break up and return to their informal ties and digital networks. This chapter seeks to explain "why?"

despite the success of their protests, were these youth groups not able to move beyond issue-specific initiatives and develop a common purpose and strategy, which could have led to longer-term consequences in their attempt to affect social change.

To answer this question, this chapter examines the formational dynamics of the "Palestinians for Dignity," created in the aftermath of the 15 March movement in the West Bank. It concludes that, through their repeated cycles of protests, the PFD forged a new strategy of resistance, shifting targets of protest and alternating between Israeli and Palestinian controlling structures. I also conclude in this chapter that the ideas, campaigns, and protests of the PFD marked a return to a more creative phase of popular resistance in the West Bank.

Chapter 5 deals with the mobilizing dynamics of the "Prawer Plan Movement"—a series of online and massive offline youth mobilizations against the Prawer Plan led by young Palestinians of Israel in 2013. The central objective of this chapter is to understand why and how a protest campaign demanding Bedouin rights within Israel became a cross-border Palestinian youth movement demanding Palestinian national rights.

The chapter argues that the impressive youth mobilizations of July to November 2013 were a turning point for the political awareness of young Palestinians of Israel. It revealed the ongoing evolution of the mobilizing modes and strengthening of ties of a growing network of Palestinian activists across borders. It signified their evolving attempts to forge new connections through their digital networks and new strategies for resistance, as inspired by the demands of their own communities. My findings in this chapter also indicate that the Arab Spring created a moment in time where the hopes of Palestinians in Israel about their level of citizenship aligned with the national aspirations of the young Palestinians across the Green Line. This movement also exposed the vast political potential of a network of Palestinians able to unite efforts across the fragmented segments of Palestinian society into one broad-based movement.

Chapter 6 summarizes some of the main conclusions of this book and final thoughts on the meaning and impact of these movements in the arena of Palestinian youth activism, as well as its impact in the larger field of the Israeli-Palestinian conflict.

2

New Social Movements in the Internet Age

The study of digital networks (from now on "social media networks" or "SMNs") for NSMs is increasingly becoming a critical subject for communication scholars and social movement scholars alike (Castells, 1996, 2009, 2012; Mason, 2012; Juris, 2008, 2012; Anduiza, Jensen, and Jorba, 2012; Postill, 2011; Bennett and Segerberg, 2013; Chadwick, 2013). Most of the scholarship produced in the recent years highlights the significance of these networks in contemporary society and activism in particular, associating them with faster political mobilization, accelerated cycles of protests, and new forms of collective actions. In this chapter I explain some of these theories and their effects on our understanding of social movements in general and contemporary forms of youth activism in more specifics.

Manuel Castells's important work in communication is perhaps the most referred to by scholars representing a broad array of academic disciplines and engaged in crosscutting fields of research on state and society, social movements, and networked youth activism in authoritarian regimes, as well as democratic societies. He is particularly influential with regard to his concept of the network society as the new social structure of the twenty-first century. It is not just the information tools that have changed over the last decade, argues Castells, but also its very structure of organization. Networks, according to Castells, provide a new structure that connect people across old boundaries, as well as serve to redistribute resources more generally. Tracking the flow of communication and the construction of meaning within and across these networks is fundamental to his theoretical approach. Ultimately, what activates these networks, argues Castells, are the same human emotions that run at the very foundation of social movements: either enthusiasm or hope or fear and resentment. Mass-self communication is a phenomenon that seeks to capture how the use of Internet has caused a fundamental change in the realms of communication. In his authoritative book, *The Rise of the Network Society* (1996, 2010), Castells concluded that an essential implication of network society has been the way in which politics is leaving the sphere of formal institutions, moving away from rigid hierarchical structures and strong charismatic leaders, toward the alliances by the multitudes in the network society. Thus, the rise of network society has come to affect all forms of social relations, in particular the organization and the production of power relationships.

Castells challenged the predominant understanding of the overwhelming power of the state over the society. He questioned whether the power to produce and control information resides exclusively with the institutions of the state or formal non-state actors. States, argued Castells in his book *Communication Power* (2009), can no longer monopolize information. On the contrary, a substantial bulk of economic, political, and cultural power has shifted from the top-down structures of the state to the horizontal media networks. Grounded in these key theoretical concepts of power networks and the rise of mass-self communication society, Castells has thus concluded that the array of protest movements across diverse political contexts, culminating in the events of the Arab Uprisings of 2011, represent the NSMs of the network society.

Castells's theoretical conclusions in conjunction with an ongoing global explosion of revolts (Mason, 2012, p. 43) increasingly starting on digital networks exposed the undercurrents of an ongoing scholarly debate intersecting the fields of social movements and communication (Bimber, Flanagan, and Stohl, 2005, 2012; Hardt and Negri, 2005; Langman, 2005; Tilly, 2005; Shirky, 2008; Bauerlein, 2011; Earl and Import, 2011; Bennet and Segerberg, 2013; Della Porta and Diani, 2006). At the core of this debate lay a very intriguing, yet still contested, theoretical question: Could older theories about collective action and social movements still explain these newer forms of protests?

Formulated slightly differently when raised by social movement scholars, the question still hinges on the one subject that has been common and prevalent in other distinct scholarly fields such as communication: the role of the Internet and new digital tools for collective action. Ultimately, most empirical questions that initially searched for a comprehensive theoretical approach to reconcile the debate between new and old forms of activism emerged from a reality where movements were initiated primarily online and then followed by different cycles of street protests. The increased frequency of such questions zoomed in on the urgency to reflect on concrete and practical ways to capture and explain the impact of Internet and SMNs for social movements in the social media age.

"The Tectonic Shift": The impact of digital networks on collective action

Social media theorist Clay Shirky defined such an impact as a "tectonic shift"—a term he borrowed from George W. S Trow, through which he went on to explain how the social effects of the new technologies affected the traditional institutions and other more conventional organizations. He maintained that while most of the institutions that we have today we will still have tomorrow, these institutions, however, are not as irreplaceable as they used to be. Increased competition caused by constant innovation on social media tools—increasing multiplicity of group formation and decreasing cost of activity—continuously competes with traditional institutional forms for getting things done, thus rendering their hold on public life weaker. One implication from the multiple formations of small groups via social media is that it made it simpler to integrate young people's ideas that do not need to be sought out for approval from institutions (Shirky, 2008). Some of these ideas borrowed from Shirky's work and as this book will later demonstrate, were critical to the initial uses of social media for political mobilization in the case of Palestinian youth activism.

Bimber, Flanagan, and Stohl avoided altogether the approach of listing the pros and cons of the collective action versus new forms of contemporary activism primarily initiated online. Instead, they reframed collective action as a set of communication processes involving the crossing of boundaries between private and public life. They concluded that boundary-crossing phenomena lie at the heart of new forms of technology-based collective action—another theoretical insight that I will further explore in the case studies analyzed in this book.

Bennett and Segerberg (2013) offered a more distinct and detailed account of digital networks and collective action in order to explain the new array of ongoing protest across the globe. Contributing significantly to an emerging literature on a general theory of such movements, they argued that digital networks or as they call them "social media platforms" offer a new logic of "connective" action, distinct from the logic of "collective action." This distinction, they concluded, derived from the personalized nature of the communication technologies. SMNs, these scholars maintained, were not merely technological tools that accelerated these protests, but organizing *agents* that enabled them. In other words, the authors suggest moving away from seeing people as "agents" and technologies as "tools." They propose instead to look at the mobilizing tools, or social media networks as indivisible from the users and the evolution of their mobilizing platforms.

In addition, and drawing mostly from anti-globalization protests in the United States or the United Kingdom (Seattle protests in 1999; the WTO global activities, Occupy Wall Street Movement, Put People First Campaign, and We Are The 99%), Bennett (2012); Della Porta and Diani (2006) and others identified neoliberal globalization as a structural condition, shaping the emergence of these newer mobilizations against global poverty, rising inequality and global warming (Bennett, 1998; Beck, 2006; Giddens, 1991; Castells, 1996; Benkler, 2007; Langman, 2005).

This group of scholars captured accurately the significance of these digital networks for these new forms of protests. Although their individual approaches may diverge on the degree to which these digital networks have altered the fundamental conditions of politics, analytically, their works concur when they point to the strained explanatory capacity of the older social movement theories to explain these contemporary movements. Taken together, this emerging body of literature represents a significant scholarly search for a new theory that seeks to explain this array of mobilizations as the NSMs of the digital age.

The scholarly contributions that I discussed thus far establish the significance of the digital networks in contemporary forms of activism. This emerging literature on global networked social movements led by Castells is central in my study. Of particular interest for my own analysis in this book is the role that these networks play in mobilizing diverse and unconnected youth groups in authoritarian contexts. The case studies that I analyze in this book indicate how more and more, rebelling youth prefer to coordinate through a web of layers of SMNs bypassing strong leaders and ruthless factional rivalries as well as rigid ideological directions.

The ways that these networks have affected the mobilizing modes and structures of formal traditional parties are also very important in my analysis of the relations between the youth groups involved in these movements and their authoritarian ruling parties or organizations in a Palestinian context. Though the diminished role of Palestinian parties in inspiring and mobilizing their youth follows a different trajectory, which this study explores in depth, they are not, however, an exception to this general rule or assumption. I demonstrate in this study how these formal Palestinian Parties and traditional social movement organizations have been losing their hold over the young and are referred to as declining sites of youth mobilization. As I show in this book, Palestinian youth too have taken it on them to seek out alternative forms of engagement through more informal, horizontal, and globally informed networks.

The relevance of these theoretical insights became crucial, particularly when I started noticing an analytical trend in a handful of existing studies of these newer Palestinian protests at the wake of the Arab Spring (Hilal, 2011; al-Shabaka, 2011; Christophersen, Hoigilt, and Tiltnes, 2012; Hoigilt, 2013, 2015; Burton, 2017). As I will demonstrate later, this trend consisted of insulating these protests from the unfolding regional events in 2011 and examining them primarily in the Palestinian historical context of collective youth mobilization against Israel's occupation. When studied through the lenses of the first and second intifadas (1987 and 2000), the online and offline mobilizations patterns of the activists that led the protest movements of 2011 appeared as rather erratic, short-lived, and inconsequential. Also, in sharp contrast with the characterization of the generation intifada presented as heroic, unified, patriotic, and highly politicized, the general labels of the Oslo generation that led these protest movements are "cynical," "depoliticized," and "demobilized" (Sayre and Botmeh, 2010; Dhillon and Yousef, 2009; Christophersen, Høigilt, and Tiltnes, 2012; Hoigilt, 2013, 2015; Dana, 2015; Casati, 2016).

Such an emphasis on youth mobilization modes and collective action in these historic Palestinian popular movements left unexplored the emerging Palestinian mobilizing trends in their contemporary context of social movements in the Internet age. Mindful of such analytical pitfalls, Earl and Kimport warned in their book *Digitally Enabled Social Change*: "We will have to think of ourselves as scholars of protest rather than as scholars of social movements" (Earl and Kimport, 2011, p. 186). The case studies analyzed in this book indicate that some of the characteristics of the younger Palestinian generation, their online tactics, and offline protests were remarkably similar to those of their global peers and their protest movements: determined to remain unaffiliated with any political party; their decentralized and leaderless networks of action; their reliance on social media networks as their primary coordinating and communicating tool; and the "occupation" of the public streets and main squares as their sites of protest (Bennett, 2008; Bennet and Segerberg, 2013).

I am not suggesting here that the analysis of these Palestinian protests of 2011 should be done without considering the particular historical context as well as the political and social conditions that enabled these types of networks. In fact, grounding these protests in the Palestinian context as a nation without a state, territorially fragmented and under the military occupation by Israel is central to my study. I'm merely proposing that the former (mobilization modes within a Palestinian context) should not be omitted at the expense of the latter (global expansion of similar revolts and changing mobilization processes in this digital age).

Theoretical criticism

Some scholars have critically examined the role of digital networks for NSMs and more generally, political change in recent mobilizations across diverse political and social contexts. I bring here some astute observations from scholars who identified some theoretical gaps while at the same time have raised some important questions that, they claim, the discourse of digital networks leaves unanswered. I will briefly discuss these critical perspectives here and will refer to them several times during the course of this book.

While recognizing the evident importance of digital networks for new mobilizations, Nick Couldry, a sociologist of media and culture and communications professor at London School of Economics, points to the surprising lack of attention to "the social" aspect in broader analyses of digital networks and political change. He identified a gap in Castells's network theory, which impedes further analysis of its consequences for understanding the social conditions of political action. Since politics is fundamentally a form of collective action, we must also ask how digital networks have changed the quality of how we come together: indeed, such change has been the main burden of popular narratives of digital democratization. By emphasizing the importance of social practices, local contexts, and other resources needed to sustain political mobilization, he posed a question which, in his perspective, scholars of digital networks leave unanswered: the significance of digital networks for democracy over the long term.

In particular and when addressing some limits to these theoretical accounts, Couldry remains cautious of the neoliberal origins of the overall argument of network theorists about the new types of collectivity that we form when we use social networking platforms such as Facebook. He coined the term "the Myth of 'us'" for the age of digital networks.

> The digital sites from where we draw evidence of new political collectivities— and the language we use to make wider sense of those sites (particularly the language of "networks" and "network society")—are not independent from, but heavily indebted to, that larger framing of social and political change in which the institutions that host digital networks, among others, have a strong vested interest.

I will call that framing "the myth of 'us.'"

Political sociologist Paulo Gerbaudo, a former student to Couldry, has similarly questioned accounts of how digital networks are transforming local and global possibilities for activism. Gerbaudo rejected the notion of "spontaneous" or leaderless movements as emerging characteristics of the contemporary social movements. Among others, in his book *Tweets and the Streets*, he argued that by putting emphasis on spontaneity, multiplicity, and horizontalism, network theorists have neglected the importance of the construction of unity, or a sense of togetherness among participants. This sense of unity, argues Gerbaudo, resides at the core of the process of mobilization and should not be underestimated.

In this regard, this study addresses such concerns and shortcomings in several ways. First, the study builds upon close examination of the evolution and transformation of the Palestinian youth activism seen through three layers of analysis: first, impact of the events of the Arab Spring in the communication practices and emotional motivations for multiple and disparate groups of young Palestinians. Second, the consequences of an ongoing decade-long split between the rival Palestinian Authoritarian rule of the West Bank and Hamas in Gaza for organized, party-affiliated youth activism. Third, the evolution of these new cycles of mobilizations seen against their own particular background of the history of Palestinian youth activism against Israel's occupation of the Palestinian territories—evident in the first and second intifadas.

In addition, the theoretical insights discussed here are closely intersected with scholarship on the impact of social media on authoritarian politics and contexts in the region of the Middle East. In the next chapter, I examine deeply the scholarship of digital networks and state and society in authoritarian contexts, through a critical read of a vast literature about the Arab Spring and scrutinizing them within the particular context of Palestinians of the West Bank and Gaza under Israel's military occupation. This approach allows me to compare some of the conclusions of this book against those of scholars who have used digital networks and NSMs theory to analyze several examples of similar youth activism in the region. While these authors have closely investigated the role of importance of these networks for increased collective actions in authoritarian contexts, this approach alone can't quite explain thoroughly the case of Palestinian activism seen in a context of both authoritarianism and military occupation.

Methodologically, I set the stage for the youth directly involved in these protests to speak for themselves about the difference that digital networks (like blogs, Facebook, and Twitter) made to the ways they mobilized and the ways they organized their protests in each geographic location. This approach also reveals what these SMNs tell us about the activists that adopted them as key means of communication and mobilization. Through the rich voices of the participants themselves I demonstrate how they employed multiple forms of interaction and mediation between online and offline contexts.

Ultimately, my goal in this book is to tell a multifaceted story of the role of the digital networks for Palestinian youth activism. As we will see in the course of this book, uses of social media among Palestinian activists are almost as distinct as their venues and modes of mobilizations in their separate geographic territories in Gaza, the West Bank, East Jerusalem, or Israel. Ultimately, this book claims that they indicate a turning point from collective social movements directed against Israel's occupation to episodes of networked movements against both Palestinian authoritarian rulers and Israel's occupation.

In the next chapter, I position these protests in their own regional context. Considering the effect that the massive Arab Uprisings of 2011 had on these Palestinian protest movements is a good start toward understanding these protests in tandem with the evolution of other youth mobilizations in the Internet age. Taking this into account, I engage with substantial literature on the events of the Arab Spring as a point of reference in the changing mobilizing processes in the region. First, because the Palestinian organizers of similar protest movements in Gaza, the West Bank, and various cities and villages in Israel refer to it unanimously as a foundational moment in their consciousness and in their experience as activists. Second, when the new demands and new forms of activism as present in the Arab Spring made their way into a Palestinian context of a decade of a divided leadership and factional rivalries, we notice an unexpected turn and direction in the Palestinian demands of 2011.

Finally, while no other movement in this digital age has received as much analytical attention as the Arab Spring (Lynch, 2006, 2012; Howard, 2010; Howard and Hussain, 2013; Diamond and Plattner, 2012; Ghonim, 2012, Gelvin, 2012; Cole, 2014; Khatib and Lust, 2014), the Palestinian protests of such a period barely left a mark in the substantial scholarship about these historic events fading instead in the background of the cascade of the popular movements in the region. While other similar movements have received much attention, particularly because of their use of digital networks (most commonly referred to as "social media networks") as mobilizing *means of* collective action and as coordinating tools in the critical task of "getting people on the streets," the mobilizing role of digital networks for Palestinian youth activism—which constitutes the topic of this book—has been ignored or sidelined.

The Rise and Fall of the Arab Spring

From a startling series of unprecedented revolutions to a now well chronicled historical event, the Arab Spring is embodied in the story and the iconic picture of Mohamed Bouazizi, the Tunisian fruit-seller who set himself ablaze in front of a local police station and sparked an unprecedented wave of social movements across the region (Lynch, 2006, 2012; Howard, 2010; Mason, 2012; Howard and Hussain, 2013; Diamond and Plattner, 2012; Ghonim, 2012, Gelvin, 2012; Khatib and Lust, 2014). Underneath this unifying image of a single powerless hero pitted against the power of the authoritarian state, many contradictory narratives emerged, loaded with conflicting views and competing explanations about the origins of these events.

Central to this contradiction was the role of social media for political mobilization and social change in the region of the Middle East. Scholars, Middle East policy experts, and political pundits dissected the role of the existing political structures, versus the role of the new communication technologies in shaping the different political outcomes in the Arab Spring events. Bringing both the advantages and disadvantages of the social media activism in the Arab Uprisings into the analysis of the Palestinian protests helps us recognize some current limitations that the literature offers.

In this chapter, I demonstrate how an overall essentialist approach that characterized an early debate between the "techno-enthusiasts" and "techno-skeptics" seeped into the early analysis of the Arab Spring and social media. In hindsight, it is clear that the first wave of writers and pundits who tackled the value of the new digital technologies was characterized by an simplistic vision of SMNs as being automatically good or bad as a means of social mobilization. Though newsworthy, these episodes led to an imbalance in conclusions about the advantages and pitfalls of digital networks for mobilizations, protests, and activism. Such an imbalance found its way into the first major historical event to tackle both subjects of social media and political mobilization: the Arab Spring.

This influence, I argue, led to a similar positioning in the analysis of the events of the Arab Spring, between the communication scholars in the form of "liberation technology" argument and the social movement scholars through "the Technology Myth" discourse.

The roots of the Arab Uprisings: Between techno-enthusiasts and techno-skeptics

The narrative, which I refer to in this book as techno-enthusiasm, emerged a little bit before the events of the Arab Spring engulfed the region of the Middle East. A broad array of scholars, commentators, and various idealistic inventers and early adopters of the new communication tools held an initial debate on the role of the new technologies of communications in the social and political conditions of societies. Techno-enthusiasts (Shirky, Mason, Bauerlein, Rushkoff, John Palfrey, Urs Gasser, Jay Rosen, Rheingold Deserowitx, Prensky) highlighted the exceptional effects of the new technologies on the social and political practices on societies across different contexts.

These early writers and supporters of the mighty flow of the new digital technologies were the first to create a terminology that attempted to denote the effects and relationship of the new tools and their users. This terminology, as we will see later in this book, endured and made its way in the communication and social movement literature. Rheingold praised the rise of "smart mobs" (Rheingold). O'Reilly cheered the recently discovered "wisdom of crowds." Palfrew and Gasser noted the potentiality of a new group of actors or "wired leaders" and their new "net roots"—as an essential motivating force—referring to the grassroots organizing potential of the Internet. In an enthusiastic era of Internet where techno wizards and web geniuses seemed to be reinventing social norms, Mark Prensky coined the term "digital natives"—celebrating the arrival of a generation born after mid-1980s, who had not known a world without computers, mobile phones, and wireless Internet. The digital natives were unlike the "digital immigrants," the older generation always playing a catch-up game with the new technologies.

Most importantly, this early group of techno-enthusiasts pointed to the benefits of digital networks for citizens of established democracies, countries in transition, and authoritarian regimes alike. In particular, Palfrew and Gasser rated the ability of networked activists to transform politics as the single most important trend in the global Internet culture. They also noted how the traditional hierarchies of control of news and information are crumbling and argued that the instant participation online signified the move away from a broadcast media model and toward a more diverse participatory media model.

It is in this initial analytical trend of techno-enthusiasts where we trace the roots of the early accounts of the social media and the Arab Spring in the Middle East. Following a similar analytical pattern and terminology, the historic events of 2010–11 too were initially simplified in some catch phrases and journalistic hyperboles such as "Facebook Revolutions" and the "Twitter protests." In his gripping memoir "Revolution 2:00," Wael Ghonim hailed as the symbol of the Facebook-fueled revolution in Egypt seemed to embody this techno-enthusiast vision of the influence of social media on contemporary social movements. According to his narrative, masses of youth unaffiliated with formal organizations and political parties, or as he defines them in his memoir "not into politics," were empowered by SMNs and took to the streets to demand political and social change.

Such a narrative was dubbed by Diamond and Plattner as *Liberation Technology*, and it reflected that initial enthusiasm about the new technologies and democratization in the region (Lynch, 2006, 2012; Howard, 2010; Lim, 2012; Diamond and Plattner, 2012; Ghonim, 2012; Howard and Hussain, 2013; Halverson, Ruston, and Trethewey, 2013). It argued that the rapid diffusion of new communication technologies eroded the highly centralized and hierarchical structures of communication and empowered the previously weak civil society in the region. Howard and Hussain wrote their book *Democracy's Fourth Wave*, on the premises of the argument that the Internet, mobile phones, and SMNs transformed politics in the Middle East and North Africa.[1]

In general, the prevalent scholarly conclusions suggested a radical transformation of the Arab political space and a unified Arab public as a result of the rise of the new digital technologies (Lynch, 2012; Howard and Hussain, 2013). For example, Lynch described the Arab Spring as a "a single coherent narrative of regional rage" (Lynch, 2012, p. 13) and "intensely unified political space" (Lynch, 2012, p. 125).

Not everyone agreed with these conclusions. Media and society scholars in the Middle East questioned several aspects of this discourse. Noha Mellor disagreed with the assumption that there is such a thing as a "unified Arab public," stressing the heterogeneity of the national experiences of different Arab peoples (Mellor, 2011). Khaled Rinnawi, far from presenting a unified Arab public, defined the new situation created by the Internet in the Arab World as "schizophrenic"[2] (Mellor, p. 123).

Looking beyond these highly unitary or highly fragmentary aspects of the liberation technology discourse, these accounts remain valid, when they assert the critical importance of the new communication technologies and SMNs in the traditional and authoritarian media systems in the region. While it is relevant to note that this group of authors were right in their argument that digital media—mobile phones, personal computers, and social media—are part of the causal story we must tell about the Arab Spring (Howard and Hussain, 2013, p. 9), it is no less important to point out some problems with this argument and the liberation technology discourse generally.

The first problem lays with its primary emphasis on digital media at the expense of the ways it interacted with the social contexts in which these mobilization processes arose. Too much analysis of the online organizing tactics of these activists led to a disconnect from the offline evolution of their mobilizing dynamics. Second, the initial labels that characterized these social protests, such as "Facebook," "Twitter," or Wikileaks revolutions, risked, in part, in turning somewhat the new SMNs into a "fetish" of collective action (Gerbaudo, 2012).

In conclusion, the liberation technology approach fell short of explaining the complex ways in which the new digital tools and online networks resonated with activists in their particular social contexts. In doing so, this approach may have inadvertently celebrated the neoliberal argument, which underlies the claim that collective action is a result of some sort of technological miracle connecting together dispersed individuals.

In a way, the gaps identified here serve to illustrate how liberation technology made even more important the need to go beyond an online content analysis, as enabled by the new tools and digital networks, to shed light on the offline mobilization and stories of involvement of the activists that used them—a gap that this book seeks to fill in the case of SMNs' role for Palestinian youth activism

In sharp opposition to the "liberation technology" discourse, some leading experts, political scientists, and social movement scholars in Middle Eastern studies brushed off the theories emphasizing the role of the new medias (SMNs) in the events of the Arab Spring as "technology myths" (Ajami, 2012, January 12; Gelvin, 2012, p. 66). Instead, they sought to demystify the Arab Spring by rooting the latest uprisings in local and regional structural factors: economic grievances, diverse social dynamics as legacies of these particular countries' encounters with modern Europe, and the weakness and resilience factors in the various Middle Eastern autocracies (Mellor, 2005, 2011; Gelvin, 2012; Council on Foreign Relations, 2011; Brynen, 2012).

Before I examine some of the views held by these scholars in more depth, it is important to notice here briefly how this analytical trend too has its roots in an early critical assessment of Internet and SMNs. I refer to these early observers here as "techno-skeptics," or those that viewed the new technologies alone as merely technical tools that didn't change anything in the dynamics of historic, social, and political practices and set off another round of far-reaching opinions or analytical commentaries. For example, pointing to some inherent risks of the new technologies, writer Nicholas Carr wondered whether "Google is making us stupid," while commentator Michal Kinsley questioned the overrated value of these new networks, calling them instead as "vast celebrations of solipsism." Malcolm Gladwell, another critical analyst of the impact of social media on activism, argued that significant and meaningful political actions require strong ties as opposed to SMNs which promote weak ties and are therefore unsuitable for revolutionary action. He summed up his position in the now canonical article titled "The Revolution Will Not Be Tweeted." Surely his position has been seriously questioned after the evidence of the role played by social media in contemporary protest movements across the globe.

In particular and when it comes to the effects of Internet and SMNs for activism, researcher Evgeney Morozov is perhaps the most passionate critic of the techno-enthusiasts accounts, particularly with his book *Net Delusion* where he exposed the risks of "slacktivism," or activism for slackers. He also cautioned against political enthusiasm in the age of Internet which also increased possibilities for monitoring by state security apparatuses.

In the forthcoming section I demonstrate how the early conclusion of the techno-skeptics—namely, that SMNs are simply technical means with no fundamental influence in the way people collect together and shape their mobilizations—was surprisingly replicated in the discussion of the Arab Spring, by a wide array of Middle East experts and scholars of social movements in the region, in what I have called here "The Technology Myth" camp.

For example, in his book *The Arab Uprisings: What Everyone Needs to Know*, Gelvin ranked the two most widely shared media beliefs about the Arab Spring: (1) It was a Facebook revolution. (2) It was a youth revolution, as the top two out of ten myths about the Egyptian uprisings (Gelvin, 2012, p. 66). As a techno-skeptic,[3] Gelvin saw the social media as mere tools that facilitated communication among the "real activists" and "would-be participants" (Gelvin, p. 52). Moreover, he differentiated between the protesters as "real activists"—those who belonged to organized movements— and "would-be activists"—those who mobilized primarily through their online social networks.[4]

By simplifying the role of the technologies as merely facilitating communication, techno-skeptics may have underestimated some important characteristics of the new technologies of communication mentioned earlier in the theoretical chapter of this book: horizontal communication instead of a hierarchical flow of information, individuals being both consumers and producers of information, flexible ad hoc networks that scale up and dissolve instantly (Castells, 2009; Howard, 2010). I also believe that by drawing a rather hard line between "real participants" (Gelvin, 2012, p. 66) and "would-be participants" (Gelvin, 2012, p. 66), this approach may have lost sight of new groups of actors, such as Wael Ghonim and his generation, the politically and ideologically unaffiliated youth who choose to initiate and coordinate their actions online, via their digital networks.

In another study, *Taking to the Streets* (2014), Khatib and Lust take a similar approach. While they recognized the importance and the evolution of some newer forms of political activities in the Internet age (Wael Ghonim's Facebook page, the Ultra's club in Egypt, the 20 February movement in Morocco), they problematize the mobilizing structures of these newer movements by emphasizing their lack of roots in the formal existing movements on the ground.

The youth groups that triggered these rebellious episodes have not been able to ripen the dividends of their success. Ironically, the reason for this is their preference for largely loose and networked movements. (Khatib and Lust, 2014, p. 67)

This quote serves as an illustration of a generalized consensus in the conclusions of social movement scholars with regard to the youth mobilizations during the Arab Spring: If they did not find connections between these loose and leaderless networks and the existing social movement organizations, or powerful institutionalized actors, they demonstrated a common tendency to question the relevance of these young activists, as well as their ability to generate sustained mobilization on the ground (Beinin and Vairel, 2011; Khatib and Lust, 2014; Herrera, 2014).

I first want to note here that there is no question about the significance of these scholarly remarks, which weigh these newer forms of protest against long-term structural forces and their relevance in facilitating longer-term political action. Viewed through these lenses, the youth movements that I study have yet to prove their long-term value in affecting longer-term political change, or impacting the larger political field of the Palestinian-Israeli conflict. Further, by highlighting the missing connections of these newly mobilized youth with the existing social movement organizations on the ground, we can understand the durable strength of powerful and resourceful organizational capacity of existing social movements, or social movement organizations. Yet, such focus alone leaves unexamined a myriad of other forms of connections that these youth groups had secured via their digital networks, which ultimately triggered the events of the Arab Spring.

I have summed up here the overall critique to these two dominant discourses regarding the Arab Spring mobilizations: one, the liberation technology discourse, with earlier roots in the techno-enthusiast's approach emphasizing too much the role of the new technologies of communication at the expense of the social and political realities in the region; and the other, however, the technology myth approach with a more techno-skeptic bent, examining the newer forms of protests in the age of the Internet, primarily through their relationship with organized formal activism on the ground, almost insulating them as unique to the region of the Middle East. Taken together, these two approaches contributed to a debate which focused primarily on whether the different communication technologies played a causal or noncausal role in the Arab Spring. Neither of these approaches allowed for a more complex investigation of the effects of the Internet on collective action in the Middle East.

I argue that these accounts missed examining the evolving ways in which activists actually used these digital networks in their unique sociopolitical contexts. In the case of Palestinian youth activism, neither of these approaches can help us understand what difference did social media like blogs, Facebook, and Twitter really make to the ways in which they mobilized and the ways they organize their protests. This approach also does not allow room for a more nuanced understanding of what these SMNs tell us about the activists that adopted them as key means of communication and coordination. Seeking to fill this gap, this book is focused on the concrete and practical ways Palestinians youth activists used these networks to communicate online, get together offline, and shape their mobilizations in the intersection of their online and offline realities.

It is worth mentioning that in his early work on the role of Internet for democratic discourses in Muslim societies, Phillip Howard, professor of Internet Studies at Oxford Internet Institute, had argued that the networked nature of the technologies increasingly threatened authoritarian regimes. This enduring conclusion has recently been reexamined, and further elaborated by a recent wave of publications and authors who, influenced by Howard, argued for a more nuanced approach in the study of digital activism, authoritarianism, and collective action. As such, a group of other scholars of digital activism and political mobilization in this region, post Arab Spring, set the course towards a different approach that allowed the study of social media and contemporary activism to evolve and grow its distinct contextual nature, despite its initial roots in the early contemporary techno-deterministic accounts.

The characterization of these newer movements by their use of social media as a decisive factor that formats and shapes their mobilization became evident in a series of newer publications on the topic of youth activism, social media, and the Arab Spring (Faris, 2008, 2013; Sonay, 2017; Tohamy, 2016). Taken together, these authors argue for both the importance of historic accounts and local contexts, but at the same time examine in depth the ways digital media operates in contemporary social protest movements. This approach goes against the current of a series of books that seek to analyze protest movements of the Middle East as "unique to that region," thus insulating the Middle East from a broader and global political and socioeconomic context, marked by the rise of neoliberal globalization and exacerbated by the global financial crises of 2008.

Of importance here is Faris's study on the impact of digital activism in authoritarian countries through a single case study in Egypt (between 2005 and August 2011). Two of his conclusions resonate with the approaches and conclusions of this book. First, Faris argued that while states have become more adept at surveillance and filtering, SMNs make it impossible for authoritarian countries to control their media environments in the way that such regimes have typically done in the past. He concluded that the more SMNs active in a particular society, the more likely it is that government will be unable to quash stories that it finds threatening.

Second, Faris also claimed that due to reprisals, citizens in authoritarian regimes are unlikely to express their true feelings about their rulers. Particularly in Egypt the use of digital technology is to express that dissent—it violated unspoken red lines about politics. As I demonstrate in this book, the use of digital networks did lead to more action in the West Bank, Gaza, and Israel, though the conditions that shaped Palestinian youth activism are decidedly different from those discussed in the Egyptian case study.

Ahmed Tohamy defines the Egyptian youth activism featured so prominently in the January 2011 revolution and thereafter, as NSMs that represent, or derive from, a rupture in state-society relations that has developed over a more prolonged period of contentious politics, but was invigorated by specific political opportunities that have arisen since 2000. Among others, this author concluded that conventional corporatist youth arrangements were unable to capture or express this mobilization and those consequently new formats for activism organized outside the structures of established youth activism. This conclusion aligns with my results—but Tohamy's study too is primarily focused on Egyptian context and Egyptian historic conditions of state-society relations and youth movements in the region, making it hard to generalize and conclude what these contemporary forms of youth activism—their organizations, mobilizing strategies, and framing—tell us about the wider realm of Palestinian youth activism and Palestinian politics.

In sum, while these newer accounts, grounded in their own respective historic and sociopolitical contexts, are important, as they bring together some of the theoretical insights offered by other disciplines, none treat the phenomenon of Palestinian youth activism with both the historical depth and theoretical sophistication that it deserves. This is why I suggest an approach that combines the theoretical insights of digital networks as NSMs in the digital age with the particular effects that these networks play in the Palestinian context. Such an approach can help us examine the dynamics of Palestinian youth activism in the context of authoritarian rulers, military occupation and territorial segregation. It is worth noting here that a theoretical point of departure for this study is the use of some elements of the SMN theory that I intertwine with the theory of networked social movements in the Internet age, led by Castells.

As mentioned earlier, these authors deserve credit for including these youth protests in the global political discourse, even though their work is solely focused on collective action and youth activism in Egypt. Often Palestinian manifestations of the very same discourse have faded away, either against the backgrounds of such larger movements or by more significant events solely in the context of Israeli-Palestinian conflict. Similar to the work of Faris and Tohamy, this book aims to fill this gap, by situating the Palestinian protests of 2011–13 in the debate of the new networked movements of the twenty-first century. At the time of writing this book, these newer Palestinian mobilizations have been examined primarily through the historic lenses of Palestinian youth activism against Israel's occupation of the Palestinian territory. As such, these newer forms of youth activism that combine digital activism with non-violent grassroots resistance tend to fizzle out against the familiar backdrop of Palestinian collective resistance, such as the First Intifada (1987–93) and the Second Intifada (2000–05). By focusing primarily on the historical context of Palestinian youth activism, scholars may miss the formational dynamics of these newer youth networks, and they tend to underestimate their impact.

The theoretical approach that I suggest in this book allows me to shed light on the emergence of a loose network of Palestinian activists across borders (between Israel, West Bank, and Gaza), whose ties were forged outside of existing party structures through digital networks, and their bonds strengthened through youth-led events on the ground. It also allows the youth activists that were directly involved in these protests to have a voice and to speak for themselves.

My objective, in doing this, is twofold. First, I point out multiple ruptures and hidden tensions occurring amid the newer choices of activism of the Palestinian youth groups and existing patterns of more formally organized movements. These ongoing tensions expose a quiet but ongoing fracture in the current mold of mobilization patterns between these loose and leaderless networks and organized social movement actors and/or powerful institutionalized actors.

Second, I seek to include the Palestinian youth movements of 2011 in the debate on global networked movements and to contribute to the broader understanding of these new movements. One way of doing this is by embedding the actions and protests of the Palestinian activists, in their own particular context of Palestinian authoritarianism and Israeli occupation, while theoretically aligning their actions and protests with similar protest movements across the globe.

Defining concepts of youth and youth activism in the Palestinian context

Considering that the Arab revolutions of 2011 were equated with the unprecedented political mobilization of young people (Bayat, 2010, 2017; Ghonim, 2012; Herrera and Bayat, 2010; Mulderig, 2013; Cole, 2014; Herrera, 2014; Khatib and Lust, 2014), it seems analytically meaningful in this study to define concepts of Palestinian youth and youth movements in this important time period.

It is important to note here that an in-depth theoretical discussion of youth, as a social construct and category of analysis, is not within the scope of this book. Given the existence of a substantial and a well-researched body of work that has already generated important insights on youth, youth activism, and youth movements, (Hamilton, 2003; Wyn and White, 1998; Sherrod Torney, Purta, and Flanagan, 2010), my goal here is to apply these insights while trying to best align the terms of youth and their movements with the objectives of this study. Given the particular context of Palestinian youth, I have adopted here a definition of youth activism that refers to youth engagement in the context of Palestinian politics and more broadly Israeli-Palestinian conflict. In this book, that refers, in particular, to the process of tracing how youth in authoritarian context and patriarchal societies appropriate and navigate between activism as enabled by SMNs on the one side and conventional organizations, authoritarian institutions, and traditional norms and values on the other side. While the dominant terms in the discourses on youth and political activism in the wake of the Arab Uprisings were the "youth bulge" or "youthfulness" of the Arab population (Sayre and Al-Botmeh, 2010; Dhillon and Yousef, 2009; Khalaf and Khalaf, 2011; Mulderig, 2013), the general scholarly consensus is now that these concepts fell short of thoroughly explaining the sudden surge of youth mobilizations in the Arab Spring (Ghonim, 2012; Cole, 2014; Herrera, 2014; Khatib and Lust, 2014). Indeed, in the next section, the outline of the case studies, this book provides demographic data and statistics about the youth bulge, particularly in Gaza and the West Bank but with a primary focus on youth activism and increased social media literary and access for Palestinian youth within the time frame of this study.

Of particular relevance to the aims of this book is the perspective of a group of scholars who looked at the role of the new technologies as a socializing agent for the youth of the Middle East (Herrera and Bayat, 2010; Bayat, 2010, 2017; Ghonim, 2012; Herrera, 2014; Cole, 2014) by engaging with a body of literature on generations, dating to the late 1990s, which affirmed how generational change and technological change are perceived as intrinsically connected in this digital age.

Earlier, it has been argued by influential scholars on youth activism in the Middle East that it is valid to conceptualize youth in the Middle East as a generational cohort that carries features of a wired generation (Herrera, 2014). For Herrera, the term "wired citizenship" captures how communication behavior in this high-tech era leads to a rewiring of users, which changes their relationship to political and social systems, and their notion of themselves as citizens. Members of these cohorts, born between the late 1980s and the early years of the millennium, function in ways that are more horizontal, interactive, participatory, open, collaborative, and mutually influential (Herrera, Wired Citizenship, p. 20).

One example that fits seamlessly with this perspective is the personal background and life of the symbol of the Egyptian revolution, Wael Ghonim. His life, his daily choices, activities and personal interest, and his particular motto "not into politics" before he was catapulted as the unexpected choreographer of the Egyptian uprisings make him the archetype of the "wired generation"[5] (Herrera, 2014) or the "Arab millennials"[6] (Cole, 2014).

"The Internet has been instrumental in shaping my experience as well as my character," begins his narrative (Ghonim, p. 24). In his memoir "Revolution 2.0," Wael doesn't just tell the inside story of what happened in the historic summer of 2010. His narrative, palpable in his first-person account, is a powerful testimony of how the ordinary youth in Egypt and much of the region have been learning culture, forming a generation's consciousness and more actively engaging in politics away from schools and adult authority figures (Bayat, 2010, 2017; Herrera, 2014).

One story in this book exemplifies this conclusion: Ghonim recalls one of his meetings with Captain Refaat, an investigative officer with the State Security Agency, when they called him for interrogation, prior to the Arab Spring. During his interview with Captain Refaat, all the routine questions that had been asked of Ghonim were constructed mainly to discover whether or not he had links with existing religious or political youth movements in the country. Having not proven to have any such links to those groups, he was then sent home and had his file cleared (Ghonim, p. 27).

It is clear from this story that the interrogators were searching for the upcoming revolution's source in the wrong place altogether, in Ghonim's links to the existing social movement organizations on the ground. In a similar way, some social movement scholars mentioned in this book, too, were measuring the values of these social media activists and their new choices and venues for activism through their links with organized social movements or other forms of organized grassroots organizations. All these approaches were considered as theoretical explanations, regardless of the fact that his Facebook page, named "We are all Khaled Said," turned out to be powerful enough to compete not only with those formally organized youth movement but also with official media for readership and followers.

Ghonim has later reevaluated his early enthusiasm about the revolutionary effects of the new SMNs. Yet the above anecdotal quote remains valid when pointing out the risk of missing certain dynamics of movements that are not visible or stay unrecognized by power elites as well as scholars in the region. The insights of Aseef Bayat, especially, may give us important clues about where to look for activists like Ghonim. He incorporates the everyday forms and spaces of political activity as especially important to try and make sense of the growing number of youth whose most shared motto was "I am not into Politics."

Bayat has argued that the mundane practices of the "ordinary," for which he has coined the term "non-movements," both undermine state authority and erode the power of religious institutions in the region of the Middle East. His descriptions of the dynamics of non-movements involve metaphors of cancer, which often does not become visible to the authorities until already past the point of no return (p. 81). Bayat's work and his ideas about "street politics," "youth habitus," "non-movements," and/or the "quiet encroachment of the ordinary" (Bayat, 2010) are relevant concepts to be mindful of, given the tendency of the current scholars to primarily brush off the newer movements of younger activists, for not having a central organizational structure (Herrera, 2014; Khatib and Lust, 2014).

It is important to note here how this group of scholars have recognized the evolution of youth activism in the regional context of the Middle East and have warned against seeing the Arab youth as disconnected or immune to global formats and venues of activism. Bayat and Herrera, for example, have concluded that although far from being homogeneous, Arab youth, with their high susceptibility to intergenerational conflicts, acceptance of human rights, and demands for political inclusion, actually may not be that different from their contemporary youth in other parts of the world (Herrera and Bayat, 2010). I situate the concepts of Palestinian youth in these analytical insights on the critical role of the new technologies as a socializing agent for youth in the Middle East.

The fact that Palestinian youth is part of this wired generation is evident in the annual rate of increase for Facebook and Twitter users in Palestine in 2012–13, the highest rate among all Arab countries, an astonishing 232 percent (Spark, 2013). According to a report published in 2016 by 7amleh—Arab Center for Social Media Advancement—the overall number of Palestinian users (in Gaza, the West Bank, and Israel) on Facebook has reached almost 2,586,400, of which 1,780,000 are Palestinians living in the '67 areas, 170,000 are Palestinians living in East Jerusalem, and 486,000 are Palestinians living in the '48 areas.[7] At the time of writing this book, another public opinion poll of Palestinians, published in August 2018 by the Jerusalem Media and Communications Center. According to this survey, 84 percent of youth polled (aged eighteen to thirty-four) are on social media networks.

The term "'67 areas" is used by Palestinians to refer to the territories of the West Bank and Gaza Strip, captured by Israel in 1967, the year that marks the Arab-Israeli war known as the Six-Day War. Between June 5 and 10, 1967, Israel fought and won against Egypt, Jordan, and Syria and occupied land in these neighboring Arab countries.[8] The term "'48 areas" is used by Palestinians to refer to the territories where Palestinians lived before the creation of the State of Israel in 1948. The year is recognized in the national history of the Palestinians as "Al-Nakba," the catastrophe, referring to the defeat of the Palestinians in the Arab-Israeli wars of 1947–49, and the mass exodus of Palestinians from those areas that now make present-day Israel. In separate chapters, I include more detailed context around these defining events in the broader contexts of the history of the Palestinian-Israeli conflict.[9]

Finally, activists that I interviewed were born between 1987 and 1995. It was the "Oslo" Accords (1993) and the political frameworks which came afterward that informed the historical context in which this generation came of age. For this reason, when referring to the involvement of the young Palestinians, in the movements of 2011–13, I often employ a widely used term "Oslo generation." A good explanation of this term is provided in the study *Jil Oslo: Palestinian Hip-Hop, Youth Culture and Youth Movement* (Maira, 2015).

> Throughout Palestine, this generation has struggled with the political conjunctures of the first and second intifadas, the establishment of a state without real sovereignty, and the formation of separate political regimes governing the West Bank and Gaza after 2007.

Maira's accurate description of this generation intertwined with that of Herrera's notion of changed youth behaviors and activism forms in the digital age and serve as my conceptual basis when talking about Palestinian youth and youth movements in this study.

Gaza's Forgotten Revolution

There is a revolution growing inside of us, an immense dissatisfaction and frustration that will destroy us unless we find a way of channeling this energy into something that can challenge the status quo and give us some kind of hope.

Gaza Youth Manifesto For Change

On a cold morning of November 30, 2009, the Security Forces of Hamas—the ruling authority of the Gaza Strip—stormed in and shut down the offices of an independent Palestinian youth organization,[1] Sharek Youth Forum,[2] which focused on empowerment and capacity building among Palestinian youth in the West Bank and Gaza. Sharek was not the first or last NGO that was closed,[3] nor the only one accused of corrupting the religious sentiment of youth in Gaza with Western values.[4] Yet, for a group of young Palestinians, its forced closure was "the final drop that made our hearts tremble with frustration and hopelessness."[5] In response to that event, they protested in front of the offices of Sharek. Local Palestinian news outlets reported that around twenty protesters were arrested, some tortured, and others threatened.[6]

Later on that day, eight of these protesters, university students, assembled in one of Gaza's coffee shops to express their deep feelings of fear, sorrow, and loss. They talked about the bitter conflict between the two dominant Palestinian parties Fatah and Hamas since 2006, which consumed them on a daily basis. They recalled their experiences of fear during the bloody war between the militias of the two main parties in 2007. They remembered the family members and friends lost during the 2008 war of Israel with Gaza. And here they were, mourning over the closure of an NGO office!

One of them, Imad, remembers vividly the emotions of outrage and powerlessness that overcame him and his friends while debating what action to take. In his interview with me, he conveyed what they discussed in that meeting: "Everyone talks about Gaza; everyone speaks on our behalf! But no one really feels us, hears us or cares about us." Overpowered by a sense of distrust with formal mediums of expression and abandonment from official power authorities, their first instinct was to reject them all outright. First, they created a group, which they called "Gaza Youth Breaks Out."

Deliberately, and beyond government or media control, they chose Facebook as a free online platform to communicate their message of outrage. They were also very well aware of the confrontational language they intended to use to voice their discontent. One of the founders of GYBO, Imad said to me: "We were sick of formal Hamas press releases and tired of the polite talk of sterile NGO reports! We wanted to give it strong to people just like we felt it ourselves! There were going to be no limits to our language—no limits!"

True to their own words and in stark rejection of official narratives, they wrote a message which they called a "Manifesto." They shared it initially with a trusted network of friends who gave their support. The message, written in English, contained a very direct and personalized insult, never ever shared publicly before. But privately and quietly, it was the first word that had slipped from the lips of everyone present in the street on the day they closed Sharek: "Fuck Hamas!" Following that insult, an all-inclusive and unforgiving string of curses poured out from the depths of their troubled young hearts like rolling stones on their Facebook pages:

> Fuck Israel. Fuck Hamas. Fuck Fatah. Fuck UN. Fuck UNWRA. Fuck USA! We, the youth in Gaza, are so fed up with Israel, Hamas, the occupation, the violations of human rights and the indifference of the international community! We want to scream and break this wall of silence, injustice and indifference like the Israeli F16's breaking our wall of sound. We want to scream with all the power in our souls in order to release this immense frustration that consumes us because of this fucking situation we live in. (GYBO, Facebook status update, 2011)[7]

They did not expect what happened next. Their raging manifesto went viral almost instantly—was translated into various foreign languages, shared in global online youth and social activism networks, and covered by major international media outlets.[8] Everyone in Gaza was talking about GYBO, and especially the local police were searching, asking who the anonymous authors were. Initially, word of mouth in Gaza reached the eight friends who in their incendiary document had spared none of the internal or external political actors. Shocked, by both feelings of joy for being heard and fearing for their lives, the GYBO friends called each other and met again secretly. Imad recalls: "We freaked out! We got scared for our families and ourselves. What now? What's next? No one knew us in Gaza. We had no real connections, no strategy, no action plan, nothing." Mahmoud, another founding member of GYBO, whom I interviewed noted the following:

> There was one curse in that statement that was really new and the one that shocked everyone. No one had ever come clean about his or her true feelings about Hamas. Yet, we had no idea how many young people felt and shared our pain and rage! A sense of fulfillment after our emotional outburst was overwhelming. Our voice was finally heard, loud and clear! It seemed like the revolution that we had wished for on Facebook, could actually happen for real, in the street! (Personal Communication, October 3, 2015)

Three months later, in March 2011, after secret meetings and communication on Facebook and Twitter, a handful of such activists from about sixty small leaderless groups became organizers of the March 15 youth-led demonstrations, marching in the streets of Gaza and the West Bank. After endless debates among these groups, they came up with a slogan for their movement: "End the Division." The statement meant the end of the then four-year-long bitter split and division between Hamas and Fatah—the two main parties dominating Palestinian politics: Hamas rules the Gaza Strip and Fatah rules the West Bank. Yet, this formal demand was not at all present in GYBO's ultimatum for change, which had sparked the online rebellion. In this chapter I ask why and how did these groups change their initial position from blaming ALL internal and external actors for their situation (Israel, Fatah, Hamas, the United Nations, the United States) to laying the blame squarely on their parties alone?

GYBO's online manifesto was widely covered as a fragment of the online experiences and offline realities of Gazan youth, while Sharek's closure was referred to as a case in point which revealed the increased political schism between Hamas and Fatah and the increased control of the public sphere from Hamas in Gaza (Sayigh, 2010. pp. 4).

Still, these young and passionate boys and girls and their courageous efforts to speak up and mobilize meaningfully were quickly forgotten. Little was said about what happened afterward to the rebels that wrote the manifesto and how they coped with their loss of that one space that had meant so much to them. How these years of accumulated anger, resentment, and hopelessness influenced or motivated their actions? Or about how, on March 15, 2011, some members of the GYBO group, connected with other youth groups in Gaza, coordinated with their Palestinian peers in the West Bank and became the key organizers of the biggest youth protests in Gaza in years. To start answering these questions, it is critical to go beyond a content analysis of their online manifesto. Bringing the stories of their involvement in these protests, as well as tracing the trajectory of this movement itself in Gaza, helps us understand the conditions that transformed an online manifesto into a call for street protests.

Extensive scholarship, as well as hundreds of Op-Eds and news reports,[9] has largely examined a series of dramatic developments in Gaza between 2006 and 2011, in order to measure their impact on the broader dynamics of the Israeli-Palestinian conflict (Usher, 2006; Hroub, 2006; Shiqaqi, 2006; Zweiri, 2006; Chehab, 2007; Tamimi, 2007). Even in those few cases where some scholarly works mention the GYBO episode that opens this chapter, they primarily do so to examine the broader push and pull factors in the changing relations between the two main Palestinian parties (Hamas and Fatah), Israel, and the rest of world (Sayigh, 2007, 2010, 2011; Brown, 2010; Salem, 2012). This literature does not show how a seemingly irrelevant development on the broader geopolitical reality of the Gaza Strip, such as the closure of Sharek, had a dramatic effect on the daily lives of a small group of university students, regular participants in Sharek's youth programs. The perspective of these youth voices is often missing or covered as an afterthought in these works. Yet their online sentiments of outrage and offline actions of dissent are central to this book. Such focus allows me to shed light on the perspective of the young people who actually endured the month-to-month grind of these dramatic developments, as well as to reveal how such events affected their behavioral relations with their parties.

In addition, when it comes to examining newer forms of activism and protests of Palestinian youth in the wake of the Arab Spring (2011), the latest research primarily focuses on youth activism in the West Bank, while youth protests in

Gaza are often understudied. The 15 March youth mobilizations are an example of this. Although this youth movement took place across different sites in the Palestinian territories and even inside of Israel, it is primarily referred to and analyzed as a case of West Bank youth activism (Christophersen, Høigilt, and Tiltnes, 2012; Hoigilt, 2013, 2015; Salem, 2012, Golan and Salem, 2013; Natil, 2012, Burton, 2017). This is even more puzzling, given the fact that the number of youth who took to the streets in Gaza was reportedly much higher than that in the West Bank (Maira, 2015). In addition, the way that Hamas forces responded to this unexpected youth rebellion was covered in various news reports, but these media outlets were particularly focused on the violent ways by which the protesters were attacked by the police and not on the ways they were mobilized. To my knowledge, at the time of writing this book, the examination and trajectory of this movement in Gaza has not been previously analyzed.

This chapter intends to address these shortcomings in two intertwined ways: on the one hand, it situates the 15 March movement organized in Gaza in the networked 15 March youth movement across the Palestinian territories and more broadly against the backdrop of the regional uprisings of 2010. Such an approach allows more room to identify the impact of the new communication technologies, such as social media networks on their day-to-day communication patterns. It also helps explain how some Egyptian demands of their Arab peers, in the wake of the Arab Spring, resonated with young Palestinians and were spread by the SMNs and winds of hope in their own Palestinian context. On the other hand, I seek to analyze the formational dynamics of these newer protests, in the contextual particularities of the Gaza Strip, in order to explain the different trajectory this movement when compared with its counterpart in the West Bank.

The story of "Gaza Youth Breaks Out"[10] represents a case where small and leaderless youth groups from Gaza Strip, primarily coordinating through social media with youth groups from the West Bank and even inside of Israel, came willingly together to effect change in their world. The activists immediately reacted to a sudden event that disrupted their daily lives, stirring within them a deep emotional well. They used primarily social tools of Facebook and Twitter to communicate and mobilize, willingly bypassing official affiliation with parties or formally organized social movements for change. Next, they turned their online dissent into organized massive street protests, translating their online anger into action on the street.

The chapter argues that despite its ultimate failure to affect the unity of the parties, the 15 March movement revealed instead the permanent strategic rupture between this emerging group of actors and their traditional parties. Through a strategy of shaming their political actors online, a rising network of young activists stripped away their own political affiliations. Such a rupture was an indicator of increased attempts from these activists to be recognized as different from the dominant organizations and their ideological agendas in an evolving Palestinian context.

Youth activism in Gaza

In a context marked by insurmountable constraints such as the complete isolation of Gaza from the rest of the Palestinian territories, frequent wars between Israel and Hamas, and brutal rivalry between the two main Palestinian parties ruling in the West Bank and Gaza, it seemed initially impossible for scattered and small youth groups, led by inexperienced and politically unaffiliated individuals, to overcome their fear and pour in massive numbers into the streets of Gaza to demand change.

Statistics of the last decade, with regard to youth activism in Gaza, reveal similar conclusions. Taken together, they indicate the decline of political activism among youth in Palestine. Sayre and Al-Botmeh (2010) reported that nearly 75 percent of youth were unwilling to be involved in politics, with only 7.6 percent of Palestinian youth claiming that they were members of a political organization. Sharek Youth Forum, an independent Palestinian youth organization, reported in 2011 that a majority (62 percent) of Palestinian youth did not trust any of their political factions. Studies from Fafo (Institute for Applied Social Science) in 2011 and 2013 and AWRAD (Arab World for Research and development) in 2013 published similar results and statistics. At the time of writing this book, the most recent poll concluded by AWRAD reiterated this dismal view, with 73 percent of the Palestinian youth in the West Bank and Gaza projecting "a bleak future outlook." These numbers convey such a doom and gloom picture, implying that nothing is likely to take place in the Palestinian territories

Yet, GYBO and others seemed to defy these low expectations and took to the streets of Gaza, against almost impossible odds. This is why it is important that in this chapter I investigate the formation, member dynamics, and evolution of small Palestinian youth groups into a networked youth movement, in the Gaza Strip, from December 2010 to March 2011. To do so, I delve into the contextual particularities of the Gaza Strip where I trace the evolution and dissolution of four such groups over four months: GYBO, "15 March Youth Group," "15 March Group," and "Palestinian Youth Movement." The timeline for this narrative starts in 2006, with the unexpected electoral victory of the current ruling authority, Hamas. I also factor here the following split between Fatah and Hamas in 2007 and the acute restriction of public space and greater control of NGOs activity afterward. Finally, I interject in my analysis two particular developments that created both a sense of hope (the Arab Spring) and one that exacerbated a sense of despair (Gaza War of 2008/09).

Despite the research questions centering on the 2011 movements, each of the thirty-eight interviewees born between 1986 and 1993 from the Gaza Strip referred to his or her personal experiences during these dramatic developments to explain their motivations. The events are included here as they were experienced through the personal accounts of thirty-eight activists I interviewed via Skype, Facebook and mobile phone and serve to highlight how these particular contextual events shaped the life experiences and their political involvement which culminated with the 15 March movement of 2011.

The activists interviewed shared their experiences from opening their Facebook group pages to the struggle on their social media networks to agree to one common demand, to protesting in the street with thousands of young Palestinians, and then dissolving again. Such detailed accounts of their online and offline activism are helpful in revealing their shared and evolving experiences as young activists: from communicating instantly online about issues that are personal to them to framing their demands as a group and then taking it to the streets of their own communities. Some of the names used in this chapter are pseudonyms in an effort to protect their real identities.

According to these in-depth interviews, each of these events was crucial in fomenting distress and disappointment among a growing number of disillusioned youth vis-à-vis the two major political forces in the Palestinian politics: Hamas and Fatah.[11] Although culminated in the 15 March movement of 2011, these increased sentiments of distrust and outrage were germinated long before that.

There are currently nearly 2 million residents in the Gaza Strip, with three-fourths of Gazans under the age of twenty-nine and nearly half (45 percent) under the age of fifteen.[12] Close to 70 percent of the Gaza Strip population are aged twenty-five years and younger and have known nothing but occupation and factional hegemonies, with Hamas running the main social service network in the Gaza Strip (Roy, 2011). Hamas, the only ruling authority in Gaza since 2006, was initially established in 1987 with the relatively narrow mandate of carrying out armed operations against Israel on behalf of the Gaza branch of the Muslim Brotherhood and establishing an Islamist alternative to the secular Fatah. Yet, the group soon evolved into a complex and multifaceted organization, comprised of an effective political organization, an armed wing, and an extensive network of social service institutions (Chehab, 2007; Tamimi, 2007; Roy, 2011).

The foretold chronicle of a manifesto for change

GYBO's manifesto for change did in fact exceed the group members and their online networks' wildest predictions—as described in the beginning of this chapter. But it was nowhere close to the shock and surprise caused by the results of another manifesto for change in 2006, which captured worldwide attention. It was based on this manifesto that the Islamic Resistance Movement of Palestine (known as Hamas) participated in the historic 2006 Palestinian Parliamentary Elections, which they won against all possible odds (Shiqaqi, 2006). Unlike the lack of political affiliation of the GYBO authors, a remarkable PR group, right at the heart of the Islamic University of Gaza, had quietly put together a manifesto called "Change and Reform List" (Chehab, 2007; Tamimi, 2007). There was a difference in the way this document was formatted: no grand political programs and no ideological frameworks concerned with the Israeli-Palestinian conflict (Zweiri, 2006). Instead, their manifesto focused on the Palestinians' concerns about corruption, unemployment, security, and other daily life issues. The Hamas manifesto "For change and reform" was devised to address the particular popular feeling of revulsion against Fatah[13] (Hroub, 2006). This strategic approach struck a chord with a Palestinian majority in Gaza, particularly the independents and the undecided voters.

"I was very happy when they [Hamas] won. I even got a job as a guard in front of their office," said Adam, an organizer of the 15 March movement (2011) and leader of the "15 March Youth" group in Gaza. Born in 1986 in a refugee camp in Gaza, his parents had taught him that "moral behavior and service is above everything else" and had sent him to learn in the Mosque since he was a child. Soon, Adam grew very sympathetic to Hamas. In his interview with me, he explained his reasons for joining Al Kotla—the Palestinian student-led organization that adopts an Islamic view and supports Hamas in its political stance.

> I liked that they were honest and cared about people. They knew how we felt, what we had and did not have. More than their party goals, they cared about our daily problems and our feelings. I started doing the same. I was always trying to do something good to help my community. (Personal Communication, November 24, 2015)

Like a true political savvy, equipped with this acute street awareness and mindfulness of people's emotional states, Adam became an active member of Al Kotla. He learned how to tap into people's informal networks and heard their complaints. He saw how anger against corruption and lack of law and order was seething everywhere in Gaza.

In fact, for the last five years before the elections of 2006, the Palestinian Center for Survey and Research (PCSR) polls had shown that more than 80 percent of the Palestinian public believed the PA (the official government of both the West Bank and Gaza, from 1993 to 2006) to be corrupt. On Election Day, 75 percent said that they and their families did not feel safe and secure (Shiqaqi, 2006). By contrast, the appreciation that the majority of people felt in Gaza for Hamas's social role as a service provider grew (Roy, 2006, 2011).

In other words, Adam and his friends had felt in person what had shocked most analysts and pollsters at the time: first and foremost with a vote for Hamas, Palestinian voters penalized Fatah in response to its perceived ongoing decay, internal divisions, and record of corrupt and ineffective administration (Zweiri, 2006; Usher, 2006; Shiqaqi, 2006). "But everyone in Gaza already knew that would happen," said Adam, "except of course for Fatah, Israel and the USA."

The Hamas manifesto for change of 2006 and the GYBO's manifesto for change were very different and reached very different audiences, but they did share one similarity: they each captured this dissent and outrage of the Gaza's population against corrupt authorities and thus touched a real nerve, which gave them momentum. This indicates that the anger and other sentiments of humiliation and powerlessness, seething in the GYBO's manifesto for change in 2009, were not something new. It also indicated the growing distrust of these youth groups against party agendas for real social and political change. Yet the platform on which the young GYBO members spread this distrust

(Facebook) was new, and the party against whom they bore most discontent was not Fatah, but this time, Hamas itself.

Hamas's electoral victory in 2006 Palestinian Parliamentary Elections and the international response

Adam was twenty years old when Hamas defeated Fatah in the elections of 2006. His abovementioned quote, in which he explained how everyone in Gaza knew that Hamas would win, but no one else outside Gaza believed, turned out to be true. No one inside or outside the Middle East region expected this twist in a historical moment for Palestinian politics.

"I've asked why nobody saw it coming," Secretary of State Condoleezza Rice said, commenting on Hamas's victory. "It does say something about us not having a good enough pulse."[14] For the first time in the history of the Palestinian Legislative Council (the Parliament of the Palestinian Authority), an Islamist group, designated as a terrorist organization by the United States, Israel and EU, won outright a large majority (72 out of 132 seats in the Palestinian Parliament). Never before, since taking over the reins of the PLO in 1968, had the nationalist Fatah movement been supplanted as the dominant force in Palestinian politics. Regional scholars and analysts concluded that the arrival of Hamas, which emerged in 1987 during the first Palestinian uprising as an offshoot of Egypt's Muslim Brotherhood, would dramatically reshape its relations with Israel and the rest of the world[15](Zweiri, 2006; Usher, 2006; Shiqaqi, 2006). The entry of Hamas into Palestinian politics presented a dilemma for the international actors. Their response to Hamas's victory centered on international sanctions and financial and political boycotts of a Hamas-led PA.[16]

However, this response underestimated the outrage and discontent against Fatah as the primary motivation for the people who voted for Hamas in the first place. Many reports at the time, like the one published by the International Crisis Group (ICG) in 2008,[17] reveal that the impact of these sanctions hurt not the rulers, but the ruled (Sayigh, 2007). By the end of March 2007, a whole year after the imposition of international sanctions, only 13 percent blamed Hamas for the failure to improve economic and security conditions, while 37 percent blamed Israel and 25 percent the United States and the international community.[18] These polls indicate how ordinary Gazans resented primarily Israel for imposing a siege, the West for supporting it, and Fatah for acquiescing to it. Similarly, about 65 percent of my interviewees primarily blamed the same external actors for their economic punishment and Gaza's siege.

The international response toward the new political order in Gaza, centered primarily on sanctions, impacted severely vulnerable parts of an already impoverished Gaza population. This increased the perceptions of Gazans as being punished for their political vote. It aggravated their reality of siege and isolation. As a result, it increased a sense of distrust against the Western political institutions and exacerbated the alienation of those groups of people who had already grown tired of the new authoritarian rulers in their area: Hamas.

The Battle of Gaza, June 10–14, 2007

If it wasn't for a painful personal experience, Adam might have still been a member of Al Kotla today. "I will never forget the moment when I saw Hamas soldiers pointing a gun towards a family member of mine. Something broke in me. It affected me deeply. I thought, 'something is wrong here.'" That personal experience shook his beliefs about both parties, to the core.

What Adam is referring to here is known as "The Battle of Gaza," a four-day war that happened from June 10–14, 2007, between the security forces of the two major parties Fatah and Hamas. A chilling press release from Human Rights Watch indicated the depth of the bloodshed that occurred during those four days.[19] An International Committee of the Red Cross (ICRC) report estimated that at least 118 people were killed and more than 550 wounded during the fighting.

Accounts of killings and frightening executions were haunting everyone's dreams, and they wondered what would happen next.[20] In a 2008 report published by the ICG, a foreign doctor working in Gaza revealed that during the conflict, Gaza's amputee population doubled. On June 14, 2007, after Hamas' fighters soundly defeated his forces, President Mahmoud Abbas dissolved the Palestinian Unity Government. The 2007 war between Fatah and Hamas marked the formal political split between these two parties, with Hamas maintaining control of Gaza and Fatah of the West Bank. Since then, the two rival governments rule in Ramallah and in Gaza City, each claiming constitutional legitimacy and backed by its own forces.

"I resigned my membership in Al Kotla," said Adam to me, and his change of heart was not unique. Similar stories were shared with me by about most of my interviewees, for whom the significance of this event was profound in their personal lives. "It was something terrible, what we experienced here in 2007, which divided brother from brother, and caused a lot of conflict amongst the people," said Yusuf, another future organizer of the March 2011 movement. He resigned from "Al Shabiba," Fatah's youth division, to work with Adam to form a new, independent youth group they named the "End the Palestinian Division."

In addition to these personal experiences, on a broader scale, the Hamas takeover of Gaza in June 2007 and the consequences of that bloody war were devastating. Palestinian public opinion reacted negatively to both the Fatah-Hamas feud and to the subsequent armed takeover. By the fall of 2007, Hamas had indeed lost a significant chunk of support, especially in Gaza. A September 2007 poll by An-Najah National University in the West Bank reported that as many as 57.6 percent of interviewed Palestinians (and 65.4 percent of Gazans) deemed the Hamas takeover as an illegitimate "coup." A 2008 ICG report refers to Hamas support in Gaza falling by at least 10 percent between September 2006 and November 2007 (ICG, "Ruling Palestine I," p. 21). As indicated earlier in this chapter, from my interviewees' perspective, the change in their day-to-day lives was drastic. This change felt more acute with a growing restriction of the public sphere and the political tit-for-tat war between Hamas and Fatah.

Voiceless in Gaza: Restricting the public sphere

For Asmaa al Ghoul, 2007 was one of the hardest year of her life, as well as one that made her a public, yet very controversial figure, in Gaza and outside. She had seen, heard, and felt a lot in that year when Hamas assumed control of all institutional aspects of life in Gaza (Brown, 2010; Berti, 2015).

At this time, Asmaa was blogging passionately, an experience that in retrospect made her "witness some things for the first time in her life, react momentarily and reflect on them years later." One thing that she experienced for the first time was the split between the two parties. Born in 1986 in Rafah in Southern Gaza, Asmaa grew up with a passion for "poetry and freedom." Described by many as a "secularist" or a "feminist," she likes none of these labels. These, according to her, can capture only one glimpse of her reality, at a given time period, but no more than that.

Like that glimpse of her reality in Gaza in 2007 when she wrote a biting piece in Arabic called: "Dear Uncle, Is that the homeland we want?" This was Asmaa's very critical letter addressed publicly to her own uncle, a senior Hamas military leader. Unlike a typical journalistic report, this was a personalized letter where Asmaa unabashedly criticized her uncle for forcing Islamic views on the Gaza population and shamed him for torturing members of their own family in Gaza who were loyal to Fatah.[21] Asmaa's writing has caused very different reactions: in Gaza in 2007, she provoked the ire of her uncle who threatened to disown her. In 2012, the girl who also became famous for defying Hamas with her witty notes such as "Sorry Hamas, I am wearing Jeans today"[22] won the Courage in Journalism Award. In my interview with her, Asmaa recalls that time when she was completely consumed by politics in the streets and her writings in the newspapers and blogs. Most of the experiences that triggered a sense of anger, defiance, and rebellion, as reflected in her writings of that time, had to do with the acute closure of the public space in Gaza.

In their edited volume *Non-State Actors in the Middle East: Factors for Peace and Democracy*, Golan and Salem explain the setback that civil society suffered, which was exacerbated by the top-down approach of authorities in both the West Bank and Gaza (Golan and Salem, 2013). During this period, Palestinian civil society broke into three parts: one supporting Hamas, one supporting the PA in Ramallah, and the third, comprised of liberal, democratic independent organizations, supporting neither (Salem, 2012).

The Hamas government in Gaza, under the leadership of Ismail Haniyeh, closed down or restricted a significant number of NGOs from mid-2008 onward. These were mostly Fatah-affiliated organizations, and the government acted in retaliation for the Palestinian Authority's closure of hundreds of NGOs in the West Bank believed to be affiliated with Hamas. One example is the decision of Hamas to close forty-two local associations in Gaza (Sayigh, 2010). In the meantime, young people working or involved in international NGO activists in Gaza were routinely arrested, threatened, or accused of "immoral behavior." Attacks by Gaza security agencies on peaceful assembly targeted activities organized by Fatah-affiliated associations, while impromptu public displays of political support for Fatah were swiftly, and harshly, suppressed (Brown, 2010).

The media was also brought under complete control. Only two newspapers were allowed free circulation in Gaza after June 2007: *Felesteen*, published by Hamas, and *al-Istiqlal*, published by Palestinian Islamic Jihad. In its first year, the Haniyeh government occasionally prevented the distribution of the West Bank and East Jerusalem dailies *al-Ayyam*, *al-Hayat al-Jadidah*, and *al-Quds* when it objected to specific content, but since mid-2009 it is Israel that prevents Palestinian newspapers from entering Gaza.

Amid growing authoritarianism and closure of the public sphere for participation in Gaza, voiceless young people in Gaza felt even more marginalized and excluded (Brown, 2010, 2012). Asmaa, in danger for her life, and many other critical voices, had to temporarily leave Gaza. My understanding from my interviews confirms my conclusions in preliminary studies of engagement patterns of Palestinian youth online, which I had concluded during my PhD training at the University of Washington. At this time, primarily via blogs, a group of young people, as exemplified in the examples of Asmaa, Yusuf, and Adam, started talking to each other about this invisible, yet massive and fearful wall of silence enveloping them daily. Based on these interviews, the most powerful force for the foundation of that wall starts with the split, or what Sayigh calls "the confidence-destroying behavior of both parties." Less than one year later, the same population endured another devastating war, this time a twenty-two-day long bombing campaign undertaken by Israel with the stated objective of destroying Hamas.

Operation cast lead: December 27–January 21, 2009

Nothing and no one will erase from Mahmoud's memories that morning of December 27, 2008. Eight years later, this GYBO founder and cowriter of their manifesto, in his interview with me, said, "This war was a turning point in my life. I was never the same again. Sometimes I feel so sad, and other times so angry. . . . It is such a difficult situation."

On December 27, 2008, Israel launched a devastating bombing campaign code-named "Operation Cast Lead," a massive, twenty-two-day military assault on the Gaza Strip. This military campaign was aimed at ending rocket attacks from Gaza on Israel by armed groups affiliated with Hamas and other Palestinian factions. Large areas of Gaza had been razed to the ground, leaving many thousands homeless and the already dire economy in ruins. In addition, Israel and Egypt kept Gaza's borders sealed so its 1.5 million inhabitants could neither leave nor find a place in Gaza where their safety could be guaranteed. On January 18, 2009, under enormous international pressure and just two days before Barack Obama was sworn in as President of the United States, Israel declared a unilateral ceasefire and withdrew its forces from Gaza. Several reports issued by Amnesty International, as well as UN fact finding missions, concluded that by January 18, 2009, when unilateral ceasefires were announced by both Israel and Hamas, around 1,400 Palestinians had been killed, including some 300 children, more than 115 women, and some 85 men over the age of fifty.[23] Thirteen Israelis were also killed, including three civilians.[24]

During that fateful campaign, Mahmoud's house was destroyed and his father killed. A young man then, now a father of two young children, the war of 2008 changed Mahmoud's life forever.

> I still remember the day after . . . . I did not know what to do, with myself, with my father, with my house. . . . But then I saw a big crowd of people walking towards me. Many people that I never knew before came to help and organize my father's funeral. I will never forget that moment. That experience of loss and dispossession gave me, for the first time, the true feeling of being a Palestinian. (Personal Communication, October 1, 2015)

Born in a refugee camp in Lebanon in 1986, Mahmoud was ten years old when he arrived in Gaza in 1996, only three years after the Oslo Accords were signed between the Israeli prime minister Yitzhak Rabin and the Palestinian leader Yasser Arafat. At that time, hopes seemed high for Palestinians. In 1994, a self-governing Palestinian Authority was established with an aim to end the conflict. Finally, in 1996, around the time that Mahmoud arrived in Gaza, the first ever-Palestinian parliamentary elections were held to form the first Palestinian Authority government. No further elections took place until 2006.

In my interview with Mahmoud, he told me that he really liked his life in Lebanon and for a brief time of his childhood, in Tunisia as well. But Palestine was the land of his dreams:

> I grew up with a strong sense of belonging and endless heroic stories of the First Intifada. My imagination was bursting with images of proud Palestinian peasants defending their land and the unbeatable Palestinian fighters with *Keffiyeh* fighting for their freedom from Israel. (Personal Communication, October 1, 2015)

Mahmoud discovered an altogether different world in Gaza, yet he shielded himself from this painful reality by immersing himself in his passion for music and his belief that rap could save him and become his daily escape. He found relief in using the new technologies to create sounds from his world of music and share them online with people he knew and many others he didn't know at all. Often his rap lyrics were biting, sarcastic, and angry, revealing most of his feelings about the situation in his strip of land.

In 2009, following Operation Cast Lead, I traveled and worked in Gaza as an aid worker for an international NGO, Mercy Corps. I met with a group of young university students who shared with me their memories of living under such terror: "I will never forget how every night I would text my friends and family from my phone wishing good night and how I hoped to see them alive in the morning. Every morning I would check my phone the first time, trembling with fear that I would hear bad news from some of them." What impressed me most when I spoke with the same group of people, now seven years later, is that to them these events are so vivid—they talk about them as if they took place only a few days ago.

Within the space of a little over a year, these young people had experienced a civil war in 2007, as well as the grueling reality of another war, this time Operation Cast Lead. This double context of authoritarianism and military occupation, evident in the economic and military siege by Israel of Gaza, serves to underscore a bleak reality that shaped the daily lives of these young activists while continuing to limiting their opportunities for normal lives and self-expression.

Heartbroken and traumatized, these young people picked up what was left from their lives and resumed their activities to the degree that was possible. Adam spent most of his time helping families affected by the Israel assault on

Gaza. Imad enjoyed practicing his English-speaking skills in his English Club. Mahmoud used the new technologies to create rap music—his last refuge of peace. Their lack of interest in any form of political activism as represented by their parties and their distrust toward official communication forms and channels, even via social media, is exemplified in the following quote:

> These Parties, NGO-s, International organizations, they still communicate in a top-down way: a Press Release on the Facebook page for example or a report on a certain situation. Yet again they impose and release data, videos, images and information, they don't communicate with us. Plus, they mostly share this information from other parties or formal institutions like them— they don't connect with young people who are not officially affiliated with one or another party. That's the problem. They use the tools, but they reach no new audiences—because theirs are very strict, set and rigid. (Personal Communication, November 2016)

GYBO—The Arab Spring and the Palestinian 15 March movement

Abu Yazan, the founder of GYBO, stated in his interview that their last safe haven where they could conduct fun activities and feel like living a somewhat normal life was Sharek Youth Forum. This was the NGO that Hamas authorities shut down, in the opening story of this chapter on November 30, 2010. The closure of Sharek was described in their manifesto for change as "the last straw that broke the camel's back." Hardwired in their angry manifesto was exactly this accumulation of feelings of despair that this group of young people had been experiencing but were afraid of expressing publicly for a long time.

In addition to the grueling effect of these local developments in the Gaza Strip, some other undercurrents were also evolving. Far from local, these developments were taking place both at a regional and global level. This period coincided with increased access of the digital technologies by Palestinian youth. Official statistics, such as those provided by the PCBS and various providers of social media analytics tools for tracking metrics on Facebook, Twitter, Google+, YouTube, and LinkedIn, and Socialbakers revealed that a solid majority of Palestinian youth was now online.

Roughly 1 million (78 percent of youth as a demographic group) of this youth population was reported by the same source to be active Internet users.

I explain the online engagement patterns of young Palestinians in Chapter 5. But this data is brought here to explain, as indicated by my preliminary analysis, that when the 2011 revolutions took place in Tunisia and Egypt, young Palestinians were online, watching and listening. By that time, the first events of the Arab Spring had started in Tunisia (Dec 2010), followed shortly after by the remarkable events of the Tahrir Square and the Egyptian revolution of January 25, 2011. These were the most profound foundational moments that influenced these young activists in Gaza.

"For the first time, we saw and felt that change was possible. We had a powerful example, right next door," said Adam (featured above as one of the activists who gave up his membership with Al Kotla in refusal to the events of 2007).

> What was true about social media, then, is equally true these days. Facebook, or Twitter, can't measure the pulse of any developing situation only people on the ground can. But once that particular situation ends up on social media an opportunity for the disruption of the status quo will arise on the ground. I want to emphasize because people really make a mistake when they focus on social media alone: What happens on social media really depends on what goes on the ground. (Personal Communication, January 2016)

Adam's and most of the activists whose quotes have been analyzed in this chapter had been in and out of around ten youth groups that would temporarily unite around one specific issue and then dissolve again. During that time, although Adam kept close tabs with a broad network of people, he had noticed a change in his friends' communication habits: "Those days, his friends had found a new outlet to talk about their problems: Facebook." What was amazing to Adam was not where, but what his friends were discussing: "Less and less, they were complaining about politics, and more and more about their daily problems. They were angry. With Hamas!"

> We did not expect people in Gaza to accept our group or our idea—people were afraid to insult Hamas. That was a big red line the majority did not want to cross. Because in Gaza if you start talking against Hamas you get labeled as a collaborator and can get killed for that. If you criticize Israel, you will never be allowed to leave Gaza since they control all the borders and to them you are a terrorist. If you criticize Fatah, you are a Hamas supporter. . . . So yes it was a first time people broke a wall of silence and that was a big deal for us. (Personal Communication, January 22, 2016)

This insightful quote exemplifies the deep awareness of the founding members of GYBO about the internal and external obstacles that youth activists in Gaza faced on a day-to-day basis. It also explains why the founding members decided to remain anonymous, initially, and how from the moment their manifesto went viral, they had to make some fast decisions and look for opportunities to expand their online networks with on-the-ground connections.

> Initially, we decided to stay anonymous at the time. Even when we started doing interviews, we chose not to give our real names, or real identities. Slowly we realized we needed to connect or link with other youth groups, already active on the ground. We started to get stronger and thought of starting a much bigger movement—but did not want to use the Gaza Youth Break Out name—because we wanted to distract Hamas attention from that moment. So we started talking about people who were actually on the ground, more politically involved, and they started talking to other people— and suddenly all these small youth groups around Gaza were talking about the possibility of a movement. (Personal Communication, January 22, 2016)

Perhaps, this is why Adam was not surprised when he heard of GYBO's angry manifesto but did not know who its members were. "GYBO had the manifesto only written in English, but also extensive know-how of the social media platforms and increasing international attention. Our group was already cohesive, had an identity and had a statement, which was 'End the division.' And we had links with all kinds of other groups."

Yet, despite the feelings of despair and seething anger in Gaza, a sense of renewed hope rushed over the youth with the winds of change blowing in their region.

By December 2010, the Tunisian revolts had captured the hearts and minds of enthusiastic young Palestinians as well. The numbers of small groups that participated in the youth movements of March 15, 2011, have been often specified as sixty or less. The final numbers of participants in the streets from various media accounts fluctuate between 30,000 and 100,000 participants. From my direct interviews with key organizers of these events, the reasons for such confusion over the number of the groups, their names, and their communication with the others are the following:

The exact number of these online groups was hard to tell because the strategy of these small groups was such that it prevented a clear understanding of the key organizers and the group members. One of the results of continuous communication between various groups in the West Bank and Gaza was that many small groups (including GYBO) changed their names to be unified under the "15 March" banner. Others changed their names to "Hirak al Shebabi" (Youth Movement). There were so many groups with variations of the "15 March" name, at the time, that it was hard to tell the difference between one and another. One reason for the groups to assume identical names was to avoid surveillance by their own parties and Israeli Authorities and fear of being captured and arrested. When the planned date for the protests grew near, these small groups merged to form larger networks of hundreds of activists. My overall estimation from my 38 interviews in Gaza is that a core group of 200 to 300 activists successfully organized what is now known as the "15 March movement."

People want the end of the division: The 15 March movement

As much as the winds of the Arab Spring stirred the hopes and dreams of young Palestinians for unity and freedom, they also exposed several contradictions in the Palestinian context, marked by territorial division imposed by Israel's occupation and internal political oppression by the PA in the West Bank and Hamas in Gaza. One of these contradictions was that for the first time, impressive mass mobilizations of young Palestinians were protesting not against Israel's occupation but against their own political parties.

As mentioned throughout this chapter, the 15 March movement was not a single episode happening in one location alone. It was coordinated primarily via social media, between youth groups, and living otherwise in geographically separated areas, of Gaza, of the West Bank, and in Israel. For this particular reason, I include in this chapter a few quotes from activists from the West Bank, who were coordinating the 15 March movement with the youth groups in Gaza, via Social media networks. Their insights will serve here to demonstrate how different their situation was in the West Bank and how they actually agreed to protests sharing one common banner and one political vision: the end of the division.

For this reason, prior to focusing on the evolution of the 15 March movement in Gaza alone, it is necessary to explain what the dynamics, goal, and demands of the 15 March networked protests in the West Bank, Gaza, and parts of Israel were.

This massive Palestinian mobilization of Spring 2011 has also been characterized as a "youth movement," a generational description that refers to the young initiators of these protests, coming of age during the historic Oslo period. Despite the different organizing strategies and mobilizing modes and different trajectories of evolution in each of these sites of protests, the young activists generally shared a common political demand: "The people want the division [between Fatah and Hamas], to end."

According to accounts of participants in these mobilizations, both the parties in Gaza and the West Bank employed similar tactics to co-opt the movement: first they tried to manipulate and steal the momentum of these spontaneous youth protests. Initially, they infiltrated the groups of young independent Palestinian activists that organized the movement with members of their own youth wing organization. In Ramallah, the young activists were teased and ridiculed as "NGO kids," locked up in the "Ramallah bubble" and that they naively believed that "Palestine is a Tahrir Square."

The clampdown on activists and the much larger crowds they had managed to bring into the streets of Gaza was reportedly much harsher than that in the West Bank. Local media reports and personal interviews with some activists indicated their arrests, torture, and often even the threat of arresting additional family members. Many of the youth in the protests that began on March 15 had previously been affiliated with various political factions, but particularly after 2007, a general withdrawal from these parties seemed to become a trend. Some were independent and unaffiliated with any party, but others were affiliated but critical of the existing political framework and rigid ideologies of their parties.

The interviews from activists from both the West Bank and Gaza lead to the conclusion that "Hirak Al Shebabi in Ramallah, the West Bank, initially generated the statement 'End the division.'" This was a coalition of politically independent youth, initially conceptualized as an umbrella organization composed of youth affiliated with various political factions and parties, as well as civil society organizations and local groups. They were linked with a network of various small groups spread all over the West Bank and Gaza. Adam's group in Gaza was one of them, but Hirak Al Shebabi's primary center was in the West Bank, and they coordinated their events via online platforms such as Facebook and also over mobile phones.

GYBO members were initially not happy with this "End the division" statement. For that reason, four of the original eight members left their group, and they were not alone. Interviewees indicated that activists between the West Bank and Gaza were initially divided over the "End the division" statement. The youth in Gaza wanted something completely apolitical, free of parties and their agendas. In his interview with me, Abu Yazan also explained how the initial idea was to come up with a simple slogan for which the movement could be recognized, such as the Egyptian example of "Bread and Freedom," despite its political undertone that what people there really wanted was to get rid of Mubarak.

Hirak Al Shebabi, with a longer history of formation and a larger network of participants, managed to bring these smaller groups in line with their statement, which seemed to resonate even more with a large majority of Palestinian youth who at the time were avidly following with great hopes the unbelievable events of the Arab Spring online. My interviews with various activists reveal that from November to March 15, intense discussion, primarily facilitated by phone calls, and exchanges on Twitter and Facebook took place between these activists. Imad, one of the founders of GYBO, left the group after he realized it was getting too political:

> Telling people "Fuck Hamas" and "We want change" is one thing, getting them into the streets is quite another. But telling them what we stand for was much harder than posting a note on Facebook. This much wasn't even clear to us, the people within the group, so how were we supposed to let youth be part of something we still weren't clear about? (Personal Communication, September 22, 2015)

This quote illustrates the internal debates between the members of GYBO, with regard to a long-term political vision or a strategy for these groups to rally after. It reveals their uncertainty about what would happen next and how their lives would be profoundly affected by actions that directly challenged Hamas, the ruling authority of Gaza.

At this time one of the interviewees confided that she herself did not come from an illustrious family in Gaza, with no clear connections with either Hamas or Fatah. She confessed she was sure that if some of her friends would be arrested, they would be looked after in one way or another. But if she got arrested, she was certain no one would vouch for her. So, she left the group as well. About six of the initial members of GYBO told me in their interviews how they scrutinized the real motivations that would enable them to embrace and support this statement. An interesting conclusion deduced from these activists in Gaza is that they expected that Hamas would be much harsher on them than the PA would be on activists in the West Bank. It turned out that they were right.

The start of the preparation of smaller youth groups in Gaza for the 15 March protest meant an increased pressure of the big parties and other Palestinian factions, including Hamas, Fatah, Islamic Jihad, and Popular Front for the Liberation of Palestine (PFLP), to control and direct the scope of the protests. Fear among youth groups that these big organizations were infiltrating the independent initiative via their youth members was obvious in daily discussions about the planned scope of the protests. In Abu Yazan's words,

> Everyone wanted us to do a certain thing—their thing. But we were not them! And we were well enough organized to stick to our own thing. We were just a young group of people who had an idea that resonated really well with other people and who came out onto the street. (Personal Communication, January 22, 2016)

The initial confusion, evident in Abu Yazan's quote, is indicative of the traditional parties' infiltrating strategy in order to co-opt the movement. As a result of such a strategic move from Hamas authorities in Gaza on March 15, 2011, and also Fatah in the West Bank, something quite unpredictable happened. From a protest against the division, the inspiring movement of a group of courageous youth transformed the street into a battleground of loyalties between parties and these small youth groups. The youth wing organizations of Fatah and Hamas, namely Al Shabiba and Al Kotla, joined the demonstration with their party flags, with an aim to decrease the momentum of a movement free of parties. This is what Jihane wrote in her blog, when narrating on the events of that day:[25]

> Right there, we witnessed something unforgettable: Some youth members of Al Kotla revealed that their loyalty was above all to their party, not to Palestine. So did Al Shabiba! Right there in the street, so many of us became

very territorial in our thinking—and it was very difficult to tell who was who within the movement because it suddenly became so chaotic. (Blog Post, March 15, 2011)

Jihane's quote illustrates how the 15 March movement revealed the overlapping loyalties of some youth crowds who had initially joined the movement as independents. But it also demonstrates how the protests helped also those who were distrustful toward these parties to permanently rupture their bond with official parties and organizations. Another interviewee described how he had seen with his own eyes Hamas arresting only those who were carrying the Palestinian flag, as opposed to those who were carrying the Hamas flag. Among interviewees of this study, 70 percent were arrested, jailed, and tortured after the 15 March movement. A few weeks after the 15 March movement, the founder of GYBO and some other key activists left the Gaza Strip in fear of their lives. While some returned, others did not.

"The forgotten revolution"

"How did people so easily forget our revolution?" wonders Asmaa, while talking about the relationship between social media, the Arab Spring, and the abrupt end of the 15 March movement in Gaza.

> How could they? They talk more about the tools than our ideas, our courage. They talk about our failure, but we brought tens of thousands of young people into the street. Yes, we did not unite the parties or bring change, but how could we? We had nothing—just social media to coordinate and our courage and conviction to make it happen in the streets. They had everything: guns, party members and resources. That became clear in the street. This is why, we did not fail that day; we succeeded. But people forget or are too quick to criticize our efforts without knowing much about our situation.

Answers to Asma's questions can be found in the early account of the Arab Spring events, analyzed in Chapter 2 of this book. Too much focus on the power of the new tools to make or break revolution obscured the role of the activists who actually used them. Scholars mostly criticized the heavy reliance of these groups on social media rather than traditional methods of organizing, while public intellectuals criticized their lack of organization and leadership.

Some attributed this movement to the fragmented and depoliticized reality of the Palestinian youth that came of age during the Oslo period. Others questioned the movement's relevance, given that it was not directed against the occupation, but against the Palestinian political institutions. Another perspective maintained that lack of non-violent grassroots movements in Gaza, made it harder for these activists to broaden their mobilizing efforts, beyond their online networks. In interviews with some of these public intellectuals, a certain dismissiveness was noticeable when pressed for answers regarding the youth protests of 2011. One described how irrelevant these youth groups were if they did not truly affect neither the relations between parties nor the broader dynamics of the Israeli-Palestinian conflict.

Still, for these activists, the lessons of the 15 March movement and their take on the political organizing seemed very disconnected from the analysis of their traditional leaders and think tanks. According to them, their lessons from the 15 March movement in Gaza and their perspective as young people who were directly involved have never been discussed. And they learned a lot. Repeatedly, these interviewees conveyed what they learned from that movement.

Abu Yazan stated in his interview that along with the heavy emphasis on the new tools and lack of understanding of what it took for these activists to overcome their fear and take to the streets, there was another important reason why the revolution was so quickly forgotten. In his opinion, it is the strong leaders and corrupt politicians that seemed to want to forget about the event altogether.

> All these professors, leaders, influential people, they look down on us. They are so fixed to their chairs, positions, functions, that they don't care what we say, where we say it and how. This is the problem. They don't see us. They don't recognize us. (Personal Communication, January 22, 2016)

Excerpt from another key leader of the 15 March movement in the West Bank points to a similar conclusion:

> Every one pointed at our mistakes. The political leaders said: "Oh, what is it that they want exactly? And what are these protests and what is their effect on the ground? This is useless!" And the Western media said: "They should do X and follow that path like Martin Luther King." The academics said: "They need to define a goal. They don't have a strategy." Everyone suggested

a recipe! But really, everything new we learned was thanks to our "mistakes." (Personal Communication, November 5, 2015)

Another activist, Maryam, shared more or less the same frustration: "The older generations came and told us 'What you are doing is stupid.'" She shared about how in terms of political activism she and her friends learned it on their own. For most of these activists what they learned by organizing this movement on their own without parties was something quite new for the traditional forms of political organizing in the Gaza. According to Maryam, the simple truth she learned after the failure of the 15 March movement was indeed liberating "We don't need your acceptance."

For this group of activists, the 15 March movement conveyed a strong indicator of the phase in which the Palestinian youth were at the time: emerging attempts to strip themselves of their political past, away from members of parties and transforming into networked individuals. This, in their words, seems to be a process, primarily facilitated by the social media networks and not older structures of parties. This conclusion seems to hold today despite their awareness of increased Internet surveillance.

> Initially, social media was our strength—because it amplified our voices, we were loud enough, that we were being heard. We knew what we wanted to say and had the courage to express it first online. At the time, social media did not prevent us to go in the streets, the Parties did. But today I feel like we are censored by the whole situation. For example, I cannot criticize Hamas—because I have my family there and I now know in what kinds of 1000 problems I would run into—I cannot criticize Fatah because Hamas will use my words against Fatah as proof of support for them. So you feel crushed by this new propaganda machine that's available online, and it's trying to influence and change public opinion as well and for us as individuals it is very hard to move forward under such pressure. (Personal Communication, September 2017)

Finally, the 15 March movement can also be seen as changing the perception of the political behavior of Palestinian youths as people affiliated with existing political bodies. The bitter battle over the narrow partisan affiliations entrenching the internal Palestinian division definitely weakened the mobilizing potential of the PA in the West Bank and Hamas in Gaza and weakened the PLO. Despite its co-optation, the 15 March movement marked the first public rebellion against such narrow affiliations and expressed the need to reinforce national as opposed to partisan attachments.

Concluding remarks

The 15 March movement was the first indicator of an independent and networked youth movement in the Gaza Strip, the West Bank, and inside Israel. Emboldened by the ongoing events of the Arab Spring, a group of networked young Palestinians overcame the fear and took to the streets to protest against their own authoritarian structures: Hamas in Gaza and the PA in the West Bank. Social media acted at the time as the only free space uncontrolled by the government and other institutional actors that these activists relied upon. In addition, a sense of withdrawal from party politics seemed to particularly increase after the 2007 internal war between Hamas and Fatah.

In fear for the "official political," as demonstrated by the loyalty to one or another Palestinian faction, these activists turned to their digital networks every time a daily problem disrupted their troubled lives.

It is there where the sentiments of despair against authorities were initially fermented. GYBO's manifesto resonated so well with Gazan and international audiences, mainly because it was the first overt public rejection of the ruling Authority of Gaza: Hamas. Similarly, the youth groups from the West Bank appeared to be disillusioned from the economic policies of the PA as well as their brutal crush of every pro-Hamas solidarity protest in the West Bank. Still, amid these networks of despair and cynicism, a new emotional sentiment was sparked by the Arab popular movements of 2011.

Inspired by events of the Arab Spring, they were more hopeful and optimistic when they joined the movement. These combined sentiments of hope and sorrow, shared primarily online at a historical political moment for the region, culminated in organized action in the streets. Hardwired into the new demands of the 15 March movement from the start was the major tension that sparked the events of the Arab Uprisings of 2011.

Today, based on interviews with those directly involved in such protests, the youth activists believe that the one demand that brought these groups together—the people want the end of the division—also became one element, which contributed to the quick dissolution of their movement. The parties easily crushed the street protests by infiltrating their own youth crowds into the streets, attacking the activists by targeting their elitist and NGO roots. Similar dominant formal movements criticized these activists for wrongly blaming the Palestinian parties alone without mentioning Israel's occupation. Viewed in this way, the story of the 15 March movement in Gaza and the West Bank may be seen as one of scattered and incohesive youth groups, which failed in achieving the unity of their parties as a result of the lack of leadership, political experience, and long-term strategy.

Yet, further research and interviews as shown in this chapter, seem to suggest that despite its ultimate failure to affect the unity of the parties, this movement also marks the onset of a group of Palestinian youths' search for an alternative path for justice, freedom, and dignity. As a result, instead of achieving the end of the division, this movement signaled instead the permanent strategic rupture between this emerging group of actors and their traditional parties. Through a strategy of shaming their political actors online, a rising network of young activists stripped away their own political affiliations. Such a fracture was an indicator of increased attempts from these activists to be recognized as different from the dominant organizations and their ideological agendas in an evolving Palestinian context.

GYBO's formational dynamics and their relations with other similar leaderless youth groups in Gaza and the West Bank unravel both the limits and potential of social media for activism in the Gaza Strip and the conditions that enabled the sudden evolution of small and leaderless youth groups like GYBO, in Gaza, into a broad-based youth mobilization.

While the 15 March movement in Gaza had its own trajectory of evolution, it also revealed the courage of a few youth groups to amalgamate and challenge their authority, despite Hamas's rule with an iron fist since 2006. Despite their arrest, threats, and, at time, surveillance, these groups managed to pull off the biggest youth mobilization in Gaza, in at least the last decade.

Social Media doesn't prevent us from going in the street. Our own rulers and do. People concluded that our movement was a failure. Some even did not recognize that it actually happened. I personally disagree. This impressive youth mobilization in Gaza was real. It was real to me and those who were directly involved in it. I was inspired, excited and hopeful. I saw it as an opportunity for us to try new ways of mobilizing multiple formats of communication and new free online space to become visible to express our feelings and thoughts. Yes, there were major problems, but significant opportunities for new awareness and new understandings as well. The problem was of course the failing of many small youth groups to remain networked, after the 15 March movement. But the opportunity is that each group however small and however failing does things a bit differently in the next attempt for youth mobilization. So each temporary failure either online or offline mobilization is slightly different. That means that the young people in these groups accumulate an experience of things that go wrong either online or offline, but most importantly, understand why and when things go right. They build on that, then they move to other new groups. (Personal Communication, November 2015)

Finally, a set of mobilizing characteristics present in their movements is worth summarizing here for two reasons: First, they appeared similar to the youth protests ongoing in the wake of the Arab Spring at the time; second, they also appeared to be in alignment with the mobilizing patterns of the youth in the West Bank, despite their geographical segregation and political fragmentation. In addition, the lack of party affiliation and the initiation of such protests, primarily on online digital networks, serve to connect these Palestinian protests of 2011 with an array of newer contemporary youth mobilization in this digital age across the world. Despite its containment and despite the major contextual limitations in the context of the Gaza Strip, the 15 March movement in Gaza demonstrated the vast potential of a network of activists whose ability to connect online and act on the street weakened the abilities of the parties to effectively organize and direct them in support of their formal ideological agendas.

At a Crossroads in the West Bank:
In Search of a Lost Strategy

On November 2011, Mazin Qumsyeh, Associate Professor at Bethlehem University, received a phone call from a student at Bir Zeit University, near Ramallah, West Bank. As the student briefly explained the reason for his phone call, Professor Qumsyeh[1] listened carefully. The student introduced himself as a founding member of the youth group "Palestinians for Dignity." This was a group that had risen out of a complex network of acephalous youth groups. Against the backdrop of the historical events of the Arab Spring (2011), this activist was a member of one of the groups that had organized the 15 March youth movement in the West Bank.

These same activists had now merged into this newly formalized network called "Palestinians for Dignity," moving past their impressive but failed attempts through the 15 March movement (2011) to achieve unity between the two main Palestinian political factions: Fatah and Hamas.

In his interview, Qumsyeh shared how the students' intention was to organize a new and different type of protest from the 15 March movement: "Palestinian Freedom Rides." The student had secured the participation of a close network of friends and activists, including the online support of many Palestinian and international activists. He had also spoken to a group of social media savvy supporters who were prepared to livestream the whole campaign online. No political parties were informed or involved in the planned activity.

Professor Qumsyeh thought that was a great idea and encouraged the student to do it, but the persistent twenty-three-year old had not quite finished his thought and had another request. Qumsyeh was well known both in the Palestinian community and internationally as a tireless and courageous activist in the field of Palestinian human rights. The student proceeded to ask

Qumsyeh if he would personally be willing to participate in the "Freedom Rides" campaign.

At the other end of the line, as he thanked Professor Qumsyeh for lending his support and agreeing to participate in the campaign, the Bir Zeit student[2] smiled and breathed a sigh of relief. He had just received his fifth and final confirmation. Four other renowned Palestinian civil disobedience activists from various cities in the West Bank had also agreed to participate. The sixth participant was going to be Fadi Quran,[3] the originator of the idea for the "Palestinian Freedom Rides" campaign. The idea for the campaign had occurred to this young man while reading the news headlines in the American media. It was the fiftieth anniversary of the Freedom Rides in 1961 when civil rights activists launched a series of bus trips through the American South to protest segregation in bus terminals.

Badia, an activist from Hebron, also loved the idea and agreed to be one of the original six "Palestinian Freedom Riders." During the interview Badia[4] confirmed that he had particularly liked how everything had been planned in such a way and that all the details of this "Palestinian Freedom Riders" campaign were to be kept completely secret until the moment of its launch. The element of surprise captured his imagination. Boarding the bus was also Huwaida Arraf, a well-known Palestinian political activist born in Israel and a previous organizer and participant in the Free Gaza Movement[5] and International Solidarity Movement (ISM).[6]

When asked about this particular campaign,[7] she said that she knew the organizers of the campaign very well, since she had been an active participant in the founding discussions of the PFD network. "Since then something exciting, persistent, youthful and genuine was taking place in Palestine and although I couldn't just yet name it, I wanted to be a part of it." On November 15, 2011, at 10:00 am, this small group of Palestinian activists carried out the "Palestinian Freedom Rides" campaign. In all, six individuals directly participated as bus riders, four of whom were interviewed in person for the purpose of this book. The following is a combined description of their recollections on that event.

That morning, just outside of Psagot, an Israeli settlement southeast of Ramallah in the West Bank, the group boarded a bus bound for Jerusalem, which some of the activists are barred from entering without an Israeli permit. Each of the members of the contingent was dressed in black and white T-shirts with slogans such as "we shall overcome," "dignity," "freedom," and "justice."[8]

Every activist had a small camera attached to their clothing, aiming to record and stream the whole event as it happened. Back in Ramallah, a group of savvy media people were ready to stream what was recorded live, online. The campaign had its own Facebook[9] and Twitter pages,[10] as well as a blog.[11]

After hours of waiting, the six riders finally managed to board a bus. As they were climbing the steps of the bus, one freedom rider from Hebron, attempting to get money out of his pocket for the bus ticket, instead pulled out his Palestinian ID. As soon as the bus driver saw the green Palestinian ID, he told them: "You're not allowed to get on the bus, go back down." Instead, the riders all walked on board and found seats, shocking the bus's driver and the other passengers. Another freedom rider, set quietly and got a book out of his computer bag. As they rode, he began reading the classic novel *Great Expectations* by Charles Dickens.

As the bus drove off toward Jerusalem, four Israeli military vehicles surrounded it. When they reached the Hizma checkpoint, on the northern outskirts of Jerusalem, the bus was stopped. Hours passed, with the freedom riders left alone inside of the bus. Finally, as it grew darker, four soldiers boarded the bus and announced that they were all under arrest. One by one, the soldiers hauled the group off. The freedom riders, refusing to leave their seats, were hit, pushed to the ground, and kicked repeatedly in the stomach. As the soldiers were dragging him out, Professor Qumsyeh couldn't help but draw a broad smile. Although beaten, bruised, and arrested, Professor Qumsyeh was smiling. He was happy! The next day, the freedom riders were hailed as courageous activists who disrupted the settlement process in the West Bank, albeit for just ten hours, by interfering with their transportation system operation.[12] Major international newspapers covered the event, while images of the activists being dragged out of the bus went viral and their Facebook and Twitter campaign attracted enormous traffic.[13]

"The Palestinian Freedom Riders" is an example of a new and successful protest, engaging both online and offline tactics of mobilization that "Palestinians for Dignity" organized as part of a sustained chain of youth protests that took place between 2011 and 2013. In this case, the campaign challenged the occupation and expansion of settlements in the West Bank. While the novelty of the idea to connect the "Palestinian Freedom Riders" with the African American Civil Rights movement gained the support of the core participants, the secrecy surrounding the organizing details of the campaign caught the Israeli military by surprise. The online streaming and broad coverage of the event led to the involvement of the controversial BDS movement, which utilized the campaign to advocate for and succeed in the divestment by "Veolia," a French company that previously ran the bus transportation system for Israeli settlers throughout the West Bank.[14] Over a three-year period, the activists of the PFD network managed to organize roughly 100 campaigns, engaging online and offline audiences, attracting media attention with their new forms of activism, and surprising both Israelis and Palestinian officials with their sites and targets of their protests.[15] In these campaigns, activists marched on Israeli checkpoints to challenge the occupation and expansion of settlements in the West Bank while also occupying the main squares and streets of the West Bank to protest the repressive policies of the governing PA.

Despite the success and frequency of these events, in 2014, just three years after its establishment, the founding activists of the movement formally known as "Palestinians for Dignity" decided to permanently dissolve their group—returning instead to their loose and informal social networks. Why did "Palestinians for Dignity" break up and what caused the abrupt end to a successful series of youth-led protests led by this group?

Substantial literature on the evolving nature of social movements in the region of the Middle East examined new forms of protest and youth activism, particularly evident in the Arab Spring events (Beinin and Vairel, 2011; Khalaf and Khalaf, 2011; Khatib and Lust, 2014; Bayat, 2010; Herrera, 2014). Yet, reviewing the literature on the Palestinian forms of these newer protests, how they are studied as isolated cases of Palestinian youth activism, confined to their geographically separated areas and largely fading in the broader political field of the Palestinian-Israeli conflict (Hilal, 2011; Hoigilt, 2013, 2015; Burton, 2017). In addition, these newer Palestinian forms of movements tend to be examined primarily through the historic lenses of Palestinian youth activism against Israel's occupation of the Palestinian territories. As such, they tend to fizzle out against the familiar backdrop of Palestinian collective resistance, such as the First Intifada (1987–93) and the Second Intifada (2000–05).

For example, some scholars have argued that these newer forms of Palestinian movements should be analyzed in the unique context of the "Palestinian condition" (Hillal, 2011; Hoigilt, 2013). According to them, in order to make sense of today's youth movements and their mobilizing for political protest,[16] it is more apt to compare them with what happened before and during the intifadas of 1987 and 2000. Focusing on the historical context of Palestinian youth activism is essential, but one should not overlook the formational dynamics of these newer youth networks in the contemporary context of networked social movements.

PFD is a case that intends to fill this gap, given the significant number and the success of their protests carried out throughout a continuous period of three years between 2011 and 2014. My analysis in this chapter will demonstrate the sustained mobilizing efforts of a core network of activists behind a seemingly isolated cycle of Palestinian youth protests between 2011 and 2013.

Through several interviews with activists from various cities and villages in the West Bank, as well as their personal stories of their political involvement, this chapter identifies the reasons they abandoned the group and cut any formal ties with its members in 2014. It also demonstrates the online and offline nature of their newly formed ties with existing grassroots movements. Most importantly, it exposes how their sites of protests expanded across the West Bank. This is particularly interesting because most analysis of newer forms of Palestinian activism has primarily referred to the 15 March movement and what came after as primarily isolated cases of Ramallah-based activism (Farsakh, 2011). In reality, though a few interviews for this study took place in the fancy cafés of Ramallah, while most of the individuals interviewed for this chapter come from other towns and villages in the West Bank, near Hebron, Nablus, and Bethlehem.

This chapter argues that behind the static realities of external and internal Palestinian politics lays an informal network of activists, which grows increasingly aware of its power to organize and act outside of their controlling structures. The analysis of the PFD as a case of West Bank youth activism indicates how the limitations posed by current political factors on the ground pushed these activists to innovate and seek novel alternative actions. These include decentralized actions coordinated on the ground with grassroots neighborhood or village committees while facilitating inner communication, as well as exposure to the outside world primarily via SMNs.

The analysis in this chapter also leads to a second argument: as a result of increased oppression by two systems of control—the PA and continuing Israel's military occupation—these activists have abandoned the long-term pursuit of a formalized strategy as set by their official parties. Instead, they calculate the effects of their campaigns to be not so long lasting, but rather quick and shocking to both of the systems of control in place.

To properly understand the formational dynamics of the PFD, a few critical contextual factors that determined the ebbs and flows of Palestinian politics from 2006 to 2011 are examined here. First, excerpts from interviews and personal accounts will serve to illustrate the main reasons that led to the disenchantment of this group of youth with the PA in the West Bank. Second, the effects of the regional development that created a sense of hope (the Arab Spring) are briefly stated here in order to situate a similar youth movement in the West Bank: the 15 March movement. Third, the study examines the implicit ways in which the trajectories of activism of the PFD intertwined with those of grassroots forms of activism known as "Palestinian Popular Resistance." Finally, understanding the history of the Israeli-Palestinian conflict is paramount to understanding and analyzing the current efforts of these networks of action.

As such, an account of three major historic developments leading up to the present is necessary. This will focus on the First Intifada, the Oslo Accords, and the Second Intifada. Although these historical junctures are not the focus of this study, they serve as a historical backdrop and add context to the analysis of the emergence of these newer forms of horizontally networked activism.

I will narrate most of these transformational phases of PFD through personal stories of the many activists interviewed. In what follows, real names are used for those who agreed to be named, while pseudonyms are used for others who preferred to remain anonymous.

"This Kind of Politics": The West Bank youth's disillusion with the PA

When we met, her demeanor was very polite, yet reserved and somewhat suspicious. As soon as she sat down, she said to me thus:

> This is just a chat, not an interview. I've never been a member of any party or any organization affiliated with parties. I no longer belong to this youth group that you want to discuss. I speak only for myself. My individual initiatives have no political motivation. (Personal Communication, October 29, 2015)

Noor, now twenty-six years old, had agreed to speak about her role as a key organizer of the 15 March movement in 2011. She was also a key participant in the founding discussions of the PFD network later that year. Yet, to her mind, as articulated in her quotation above, these activities had nothing to do with parties and were not political. Noor was not alone in this regard. At this point of my interviewing work, a recurrent theme in these unprompted introductory comments from my interviewees was a sort of rush to admit to not being affiliated with any political group and not being active in any form of politically motivated action. Yet, soon after their personal life stories unfolded, they spoke and presented quite a different reality. First, most had been brought up in highly politically active families, loyal to one party, either Fatah or Hamas. That, in addition to their accounts about participation in political demonstrations in Palestinian public universities overflowing with green or yellow flags, massive portraits and banners of one political leader or another, further illustrated an orientation to their political preferences. In short, while insisting in being apolitical, their personal life stories indicated that most had grown up in highly politicized environments.

Noor's quotation captures the paradox of having no interest in political activism, despite being brought up in a highly politicized environment. This paradox is also present in scholarly literature covering the political activism of Palestinian youth. Scholars agree with the characterization of Palestinian youth as highly politicized due to their role as the vanguard of popular uprisings against the Israeli occupation, particularly dominant during the First Intifada (Kuttab, 1988; Barber, 2001, Lockman and Beinin, 1999; Sayigh, 1997; Beitler, 2004; Collins, 2004, 2011; Jensen, 2009; Hart, 2002, 2008). These studies describe Palestinian youth having traditionally been at the forefront of political action and change. Still, the portrayal of the heroism of Palestinian youth in past uprisings somehow faded away, particularly during the Second Intifada (Pressman, 2006). In its place, a quite different narrative unfolds: the portrayal of Palestinian youth as highly fragmentized, depoliticized, and disenchanted with their parties and leaders (Sayre and Al-Botmeh, 2010; Christophersen, Hoigilt, and Tiltnes, 2012; Sharek, 2011, 2013; AWRAD, 2012, 2015, 2016; FAFO, 2012, 2013; Allen, 2013; Casati, 2016).

Against this backdrop, Noor's story starts making sense. She was born in 1990 in Nablus, a city located in the northern West Bank. Through her detailed account, she indicated an acute awareness of her city and colleges' strong political legacy. She told me that Nablus, historically known as Palestine's commercial heart, also carries a reputation of being the center of

Palestinian resistance to Israeli occupation (Doumani, 2004); Leech, 2012). Likewise, An-Najah University, where she studied, also had a long history of demonstrations and resistance. In alignment with Noor's account, the role of the higher educational institutions as forums for propagation of Palestinian youth "political consciousness" is a well-established scholarly conclusion (Taraki, 1990).

But, by the time Noor started college, she had experienced a different political reality. During her high school years, the Second Intifada had turned her city into a strong resistance bed against the Israeli occupation. Nablus at the time was known as a strong base of Hamas supporters. Noor, herself coming from a Fatah-leaning family, had lost a cousin as the militarized Second Intifada grew very violent. By the time she went to college in 2007, Noor had experienced the division between the two main political parties (Fatah and Hamas) and the bloody internal conflict that came afterward in a concrete way at her own campus. This experience shook her faith in political parties dramatically.

On July 24, 2007, violent demonstrations broke out in An-Najah University in Nablus and culminated in the killing of a male student, a supporter of the Islamic Bloc—the youth wing associated with Hamas at Al Najah. The Palestinian Independent Commission for Citizens' Rights published a report on the killing, stressing that "the events must be viewed within the overall struggle between Fatah and Hamas" (PICCR, 2007: 2). This fact had rocked her university years. According to Noor, this incident left a clear mark on An-Najah University students' activities and also on her own political consciousness. She acknowledged that at the center of this consciousness welled up a strong aversion to memberships or association with any political party: in her case, rejection of the PA, the Fatah party, and their youth wing, Al Shabiba. In her words,

> It was this environment that prompted me to stay out of it, out of *this kind of politics*—from the very beginning. I really had no other choice. The one choice I had—Al Shabiba—was being forced on me. So I rejected it. This is the reason why I started to participate in other activities, outside of the sphere of Parties. (Personal Communication, October 29, 2015; emphasis mine)

"This kind of politics!" This expression was common and articulated many times by many interviewees across the West Bank and Gaza. Along with this combination of words, one couldn't help but notice how it triggered an almost acute allergic-like reaction on their facial expressions as well. Here it was again, as Noor spoke about the internal division between Hamas and Fatah: She shook her head slowly, pressed her dense dark curly hair against her scalp, pursed her lips, while rubbing her eyes nervously. Her body language spoke of discomfort and reluctance to speak; it also conveyed a sense of fear and sadness.

"This kind of politics," was a certain resignation signature in their story of disassociation with parties, particularly exacerbated in the Hamas-Fatah split in 2007. It captured the idea that more than "disassociation from politics," Noor and her friend were making a choice. This choice, which involved active withdrawal from the political rivalries between the two main Palestinian parties, Fatah and Hamas, is backed by statistics as well. A 2011 survey by the Palestinian Centre for Policy and Survey Research revealed that over 62 percent of West Bank residents were afraid of criticizing the PA. In a Fafo[17] poll conducted from 2006 to 2011, only 8 percent of Palestinian youth said they had confidence in the political parties, with 12 percent in the PNC (the Palestinian Parliament). It is in this context that I situate Noor's personal story and analyze the expressions of disengagement of the activists from the politics of their parties. Following is a quick account of the political trajectory of the PA in the West Bank, after the unexpected results of the 2006 parliamentary elections and the subsequent civil war in 2007. This West Bank context description serves to show how it defined these activists' mobilization modes, as a result of increased authoritarianism and ruthless suppression of local internal political dissent.

The PA's Rule in the West Bank: 2007–11

On June 15, 2007, after the brief civil war that split the PA in two, Palestinian president Mahmoud Abbas appointed Salam Fayyad as leader of an emergency PA government in the West Bank. In my previous chapter, I focused on what the takeover of the Gaza Strip, by Hamas, meant in terms of political and economic consequences for the Gaza people: their suffering under harsh international sanctions, repeated conflicts with the IDF, and Israeli and Egyptian blockade, leading to Gaza's economic collapse.

In sharp contrast with the desperation and devastation of the population in the Hamas-ruled Gaza Strip, an "economic miracle"[18] known as "Fayyadism"[19] took place in the West Bank. In Ramallah, Prime Minister Fayyad was throwing a celebratory party[20] promising a Palestinian state in the West Bank by 2011. The PA strategy was grand in its ambitions and expensive; it involved building democratic and transparent institutions, fighting corruption, fostering economic growth, and declaring a Palestinian state (Brown, 2010; Khalidi and Sobhi, 2011; Simanovsky, 2011; Leech, 2012; Knutter, 2013).

In December 2007, Fayyad's government proposed the Palestinian Reform and Development Plan (PRDP), a program based on "rebuilding Palestinian national institutions" and "developing the Palestinian public and private sectors."[21] Other reports and proposals with catchy titles such as "Palestine: Ending the Occupation, Establishing the State" (2009) and "Homestretch to Freedom" (2010) kept promoting Fayyad's intention to declare a Palestinian state in 2011. This much desired state would be based on the June 4, 1967, borders.[22] The Fayyad Plan gained tremendous support from Western powers.[23] Congress approved a $200-million deposit into the PA treasury. Meanwhile, donor funding to PA coffers increased to $1.5 billion annually beginning in 2007. Economic growth experienced during 2009 and 2010 in the West Bank was heralded as a sign of the first green shoots of the PA strategy.[24]

But, beneath the fanfare of Fayyadism or the economic effects of the PA strategy, a thick shroud of control and arrests enveloped the West Bank, defined by some scholars as "politics of fear."[25] While some noted the economic growth as a positive aspect of such reform (Knutter, 2013); Simanovsky, 2011), others focused on the increase of authoritarian context in which these reforms were undertaken (Brown, 2010).

In his analysis, "Fayyad Is Not the Problem, but Fayyadism Is Not the Solution to Palestine's Political Crisis," Brown (2010, September) noted how the reform agenda was also built on the intra-Palestinian split, creating disincentives for reconciliation. The new PA security regime has been marked by domestic policing, effective containment of internal political opponents, and an increased authoritarian stance accompanied by increasing incidents of torture, intimidation, and repression of civil rights of the PA's opponents. Human rights violations appeared as another contradiction of the PA's neoliberal agenda and its emphasis on "the rule of law" (Sayigh, 2011; Allen, 2013).

In a report prepared by the Ad Hoc Liaison Committee (AHLC) in April 2010, the Government of Israel reported that in 2009, Israeli and Palestinian military forces coordinated 1,297 operations, amounting to a 72 percent increase compared to 2008. A year later, the same report indicated that in 2010,[26] Israeli and Palestinian military forces coordinated 2,968 operations, amounting to a 118 percent increase compared to 2009.[27] In his study, *Policing the People, Building the State: Authoritarian Transformation in the West Bank and Gaza*, Sayigh described security reforms as being authoritarian in nature that will threaten both long-term Palestinian security and the ability to achieve a recognized Palestinian state. From January through September 2011, the Independent Commission for Human Rights (ICHR) reported 91 complaints of torture and 479 complaints of arbitrary arrests. Further, in 2011 and 2012, PA security forces arbitrarily prevented or violently dispersed nonviolent Palestinian protests and detained and, at times, physically injured journalists covering the events, particularly at events critical of the PA or supportive of Hamas.

These trends and structures, the increased authoritarianism of the PA with the West Bank, and its increased security coordination with the State of Israel shaped most of the experiences and stories of the activists that I interviewed. It is here where the phrase "This kind of politics" originates and where the disengagement from the party politics starts becoming a trend.

This part of the study shows how an increased repression and reduction of political space in the West Bank during 2007–11 influenced young people like Noor to become jaded to existing Palestinian political parties. Noor, her city, and her university exemplify what "being depoliticized" meant to the majority of Palestinian youth born around the 1990s: an increased withdrawal from political rivalries for fear of being caught in between them. Additionally, they felt a feeling of alienation from the PA's increased security coordination with Israel. The combined effect on the mobilizing patterns of these youth was their disenchantment with parties and their search for alternative forms of engagement in more decentralized forms of grassroots activism. In addition to these Palestinian realities on the ground, a historic tide of event, known as the Arab Spring, swept through the region of the Middle East. What follows is an account of how this regional aspect deeply affected mobilization modes and the strategic targets of these activists.

Politics of fear—Networks of hope:
The Arab Spring in the West Bank

It was amid this particular West Bank environment that Noor and her friends witnessed another historic moment, the Arab Spring. Like her peers, Noor views this event as one of the most inspiring moments of her life:

> When I saw with my own eyes how the foundations of systems and people who we thought to be indestructible, crumbled and shattered under popular pressure, I was deeply inspired and hopeful that we, the people, could affect change as well. It changed what I believed about power and politics, forever. I think that the Arab Spring was a window of hope, and inspiration, people saw that change was possible. . . . And yes, it was thanks to social media platforms that made that possible for a majority to see and believe, and then decided to get in the street. (Personal Communication, January 2016)

The same feeling of empowerment and inspiration evident in Noor's quotation was evident in other interviews in different ways. The Arab Spring, the era of "power of the people" (Ghonim, 2012), coupled with the discourse of "liberation technology" (Lynch, 2006, 2012; Howard, 2010; Howard and Hussain, 2013; Diamond and Plattner, 2012), sparked in Noor and her peers a renewed sense of hope for positive change. Increased levels of Internet access and the emergence of new models of organizing, facilitated primarily by social media online, had challenged the concepts and practices of activism in this digital revolutionary age, even under the authoritarian regimes in the Middle East (Khatib and Lust, 2014; Herrera and Mansour, 2015).

Content analysis on Palestinian digital communication patterns, summarized in the methodology section of this book, concludes that as a result of a growing regional information infrastructure and with the large majority of users present online, Palestinian youth skills to consume and produce content online also grew significantly. It also highlighted the particular effect of the blogosphere in the ability of young Palestinians to find and express their own voice through alternative mediums of expression such as blogs.

In short, these broad numbers and statistics indicated that an emerging network of Palestinian youth was connecting with each other online. These results can be better understood when situated in the newer literature that examines the impact of digital activism in authoritarian countries. Howard, in some of his early writings, argued that the networked nature of the technologies increasingly threatens authoritarian regimes. Building on that, David Faris concluded that the use of digital tools leads to more collective action in authoritarian societies. The first and most important outcome in his study of Egyptian activism in the context of the Arab Uprisings was that an increase in the density of SMN usership should lead to an increase in group formation and political mobilization in any given society.

This exposition seems to hold true in the Palestinian context. The decentralized nature of new technologies enabled the formation of multiple new youth groups. Increased use of their SMNs enabled these groups to create and share their own narrative, as well as their original voices, with a local and international audience. And when the torrent of the events of the Arab Spring exploded, the political demands of their Arab peers offered an outlet for these youth groups to stir something deeply missing in the political foundation of Palestinian national bodies: participatory democratic mobilization (Khalil, 2013; Herrera, 2014).

One of these voices was that of Maryam B, aged seventeen years. Until 2011, she had never been to a youth demonstration before. Maryam studies English literature and languages at Bir Zeit University and is a freelance blogger and writer for many online news outlets and an ex-member of PFD.

> Let's be real: social media empowered us. It enabled us to express our thoughts. It enabled us to find people who share our same thoughts. And it connected us in ways that were never possible before. For example: a certain collection of activists from Ramallah would coordinate with a certain collection of activists from Nablus. And all of us were coordinating online with Palestinians from abroad and international activists from all over the world. That was the beginning of a network and community organizing. (Personal Communication, November 6, 2015)

Through her quote, Maryam articulates how she and her Palestinian peers felt about these new tools and the ways they affected their models of action evident in a series of mobilizations during 2011–13 in the West Bank. Through many similar quotes from various interviews, it was not difficult to see that these young Palestinians were likewise shifting formats and venues and using a new political vocabulary that was consequently spreading through the region. As other Arab youth taking part in the ongoing global phenomena brought about by spread of the Internet and improvement in technology infrastructure and communication platforms, so too did Palestinian youth.

At the time, social media helped in different ways—but the main thing was that it connected us across the geographical areas—with Palestinians inside Israel, refugees in Jordan and Lebanon etc. For example, I have never been in Gaza before, but now, I know so many activists from Gaza. This is the one aspect of it that I think that helped us to coordinate. The other aspect that I was personally amazed with was how social media significantly disrupted the previously undisputable power of the traditional media. The fact is, we had been on the ground, much earlier than the Arab Spring events, but no one recognized us as activist. No one came to interview us in the villages where we conducted our activities. But these days, something different happened. We started putting our actions and voices online and the traditional media and journalists suddenly came to interview us. This was a very interesting phenomenon, because before they would go and ask a politician in his office for his opinion, but suddenly they were now interviewing us, who were just in the villages, doing our activities and posting about them on our social media platforms. (Personal Communication, November 6, 2015)

It was through Facebook and Twitter that young Palestinians learned about the framing of the demands of their Arab peers in the region, like Egypt, for example. In other words, they were inspired by not only the new forms of youth mobilizations of the Arab Spring but also the new demands of their Arab peers. Consequently, despite their intentional ongoing withdrawal from party-led "politics of fear," these youth activists would become key organizers of the 15 March movement in 2011. In this movement, Noor and her friends had asked for the unity of the very parties that they were so sick and tired of!

The 15 March movement: People want the end of the division

As much as the winds of the Arab Spring stirred the hopes and dreams of young Palestinians for unity and freedom, they also exposed several contradictions in the Palestinian context. One of these contradictions was that for the first time an impressive mass mobilization of young Palestinians were protesting not against Israel's occupation but against their own political parties. Before delving into the verbal interview accounts, it is important to briefly summarize here the 15 March movement in the West Bank in order to better understand the stories of the involvement of the activits from the West Bank. Despite the different trajectories that the movement followed in Gaza and the West Bank, there was strong agreement between the majority of activists as originally proposed by members of PFD, about their main political demand: "The people want the division (between Fatah and Hamas) to end."

While there was no clarity about what the alternative vision exactly was, or what the strategy for a longer-term political change would be, it was apparent that these youth groups were moved to engage in protests, to publicly confront the PA in the West Bank and Hamas in Gaza.

In verbal accounts from at least ten of twenty-two interviewed Palestinian activists from various cities and villages of the West Bank, they mentioned the events that were leading up to the 15 March movement.

The first was a support event for the Tunisian demonstrations on January 20, 2011.[28] The second was a gathering in the Al-Manara Square to support the inspiring events underway at the time in Egypt.[29] In each case, the PA responded by first banning any form of protest in solidarity with the Tunisian or Egyptian Uprisings.[30] In addition, the presence of many *Mukhabarat* (secret police) was reported later to have infiltrated the crowd in order to break up the protests.

One activist[31] recalls how the PA police did not allow the youth to carry the Tunisian flag in support of the Tunisian people, nor the Egyptian flag in support of the Egyptian people. He told me that one particular PA tactic angered them the most. Whenever they organized a solidarity rally in support of the Arab Uprisings, the PA would outnumber them by sending large groups of supporters of the ruling Fatah party, at the same time and place, to stage a demonstration in support of Palestinians held in Israeli jails. It was during these events that the core group of organizers faced, in full force, the brutality of the PA security forces.

> For the first time in my life, I saw our own people turning against us. I will never forget seeing my friend being beaten in front of me—by our own people! It was very humiliating, disempowering and frightening. You are used to seeing an Israeli soldier putting his knee on your chest, beating you with cruelty—but you take it—because you know he is your enemy. But this time this was devastating and very personal. (Personal Communication, November 16, 2015)

This quotation articulates a sense of desperation and alienation, echoing Noor's experience in Nablus. The same activist expressed that the sentiment of anger against the PA drove the core organizers to plan an even bigger demonstration. So right then and there, the angry activists posted another Facebook event, this time their own Palestinian Spring event. About five core youth groups, active since 2007–09, invited all their followers to attend the protest. This sentiment resonated with a much wider audience of Palestinian youth in the West Bank, who responded to the group's Facebook call for another, much bigger, protest in Al-Manara Square.

This is how, partly as a reaction to the police brutality and partly inspired by the Arab Spring, about 7,000 Palestinian Youth packed the main squares and jammed the streets of cities throughout the West Bank on March 15, 2011. A report[32] indicated that 3,000 staged their protests in Ramallah, 2,000 in the northern part of Nablus, and similar numbers in Hebron and Bethlehem. These reports are particularly important, given that most analyses on this movement focus only on the protests that took place in Ramallah. The event was quickly co-opted by the PA despite the passion and the enthusiasm of the activists. Four of the interviewees who were key organizers and participants in the street protests in Bethlehem, Nablus and Ramallah shared their experiences for this book.

They explained how it all started as planned with the youth singing patriotic songs and waving Palestinian flags. But soon the protest was also plagued with confrontations between supporters of different political groups, spoiling the organizers' attempts to keep the movement apolitical. Noor, who was a participant of this protest in Nablus, recalls how shocked she and her friends were when confronted with these large groups of people who were there to break up their protest.

> We rushed, we assumed too many things. We assumed first of all that we were like every other case in the Arab world. Right there in the street we were confronted by the bitter truth: We were wrong. Thousands of People showed up for this protest, but they were not with us, not the majority at least. They were screaming at us, directly in our faces: "Palestine is no Arab Spring—we are not like other countries in the region. We are occupied." They teased us about our slogan: "Unity?! Freedom of Expression?! What about Hamas? What about the occupation? Who is causing the division?" . . . So, because we approached our own political parties as the only enemy (target of our protests), it made it easy for the PA to hijack our movement. And so they did! (Personal Communication, November 6, 2016)

Noor's quote illustrates the main contradiction that engulfed these and other youth groups at the epicenter of the protest in Ramallah's Al-Manara Square: the demands of their youth movement, which could make it successful in the context of the Arab Spring, were the very same ones which caused its implosion in their own West Bank context. Al-Manara was no Tahrir Square! It is important to focus here on this controversial aspect of this movement, because it indicated the larger effect that the Arab Spring uprising had on Palestinian movements and Palestinian politics. Through the 15 March movement and its demands these youth groups demonstrated that the struggle against the repressive authorities was indeed a Palestinian struggle as well.

The controversy embedded in this unexpectedly popular youth-led movement prompted a scholarly analysis and debate among Palestinian academics. An independent group of Palestinian scholars called "al-Shabaka," which means "the Network," organized a round table discussion titled "The Palestinian Answers to the Arab Spring."[33] A group of Palestinian scholars dealt with the effects that the Arab Uprisings had on the Palestinian movements and Palestinian politics (al-Shabaka, August 1, 2011). In this brief, Hilal concluded that the answers to the Palestinian Spring should not be found in the context of the Arab Spring, but in the uniqueness of "The Palestinian condition." Hilal's analysis hinged on an understanding of the nature and history of the fragmentation of the Palestinian body politic, starting primarily with the signing of the Oslo Accords.

While the 15 March movement demands against their divided Palestinian leadership should have been examined against the backdrop of the Arab Spring events, internally, it was primarily analyzed through the lenses of a mass-based Palestinian mobilization against the Israeli occupation, evident in the first and second intifadas. When asked about this overall conclusion, Maryam seemed very aware and particularly cynical about this issue. To Maryam, this was an indicator of another narrative that hijacked their 15 March movement.

This is the narrative that the "older generation" created to make us feel stupid. They never helped—they only told us what we did wrong. We learned everything on our own way. We learned how to give advice without dictating. We learned that we should empower, whoever is taking a lead role on the ground. This is our strategy—they just don't like it, because it doesn't empower them, because they can't control it. The most important point in this moment right now is a shift in consciousness—not the effort on the ground. It's creating a dramatic shift. We should go now inside this vacuum and add our narratives one by one—while simultaneously trying to create alternative ways—where social media plays a role in it. (Personal Communication, November 6, 2015)

Among others, Maryam's quote here articulates a generation gap triggered primarily by the Arab Spring, but in a Palestinian context. In this case, it was an Oslo generation, being portrayed as depoliticized and fragmentized—set against an intifada generation, presented as unified and patriotic. Yet some of the Oslo generation characteristics were remarkably similar to global networks of action. They seemingly share determination to remain unaffiliated with any political party; their commitment to civil, nonviolent forms of action; their decentralized and leaderless networks of action; their reliance on social media platforms as their primary coordinating and communicating tools; and the "occupation" of the public streets and main squares as their protest sites.

This section has demonstrated how two overlapping aspects of the Arab Spring became visible in the 15 March Palestinian youth movement: first, the public youth revolts against the Palestinian authoritarian regime, and second, their increasing reliance on social media platforms for coordination and mobilization. Through this set of emerging elements, they can also be seen as part of a global trend of contemporary mobilization (Bimber, B., Flanagan, A. J., and Stohl, C. 2005; Langman 2005; Earl and Kimport 2011; Bennet and Segerberg 2013). So far, some of these elements have been demonstrated in this study. Yet, these forms of protests must also be seen as deeply conditioned and affected by the West Bank context: Israel's occupation of the West Bank. Following is an account that aims to explain the distinct modes of mobilization that came after the 15 March movement and that brought about creation of the PFD network.

The Birth of the Palestinians for Dignity (PFD) network

The "Palestinian Freedom Rides" campaign[34] discussed at the opening of this chapter was an example of a systematic wave of protests and campaigns organized by the PFD network. This strategic pattern of switching targets of protests, alternating between the PA and the Israeli government, was partly a lesson learnt from the criticism addressed to their 15 March movement, as explained earlier. Yet my interviews with its key founders, as well as the circulation of this name in the online media, indicate that PFD emerged out of the same core groups of urban Palestinians that organized the 15 March movement in the wake of the Egyptian and Tunisian Uprisings. Several online youth groups, such as the 15 March group, the Al-Manara youth group, Al Hirak al Shababi, and Benhib il Balad ("We Love Our Country"), merged under one umbrella now called "Palestinians for Dignity."

A close look at the protests, campaigns, and activities organized by these groups in the period of time between 2011 and 2013 reveals a window into the significant obstacles that these youth faced while operating on the ground. When these young activists were kicked out of their public streets and squares of the main cities by the PA, they quickly directed the target of their protests to the occupation. They did this by marching at checkpoints and driving through Israeli settlements surrounding Palestinian villages inside of the West Bank. When arrested by IDF forces, they again shifted their targets back to their own authorities. By looking closely at some of their campaigns, we can start seeing the genesis of a strategy of resistance characterized by defiance against the Israeli occupation, the PA, and the two main Palestinian political parties Fatah and Hamas.

PFD in 2011–13: Targeting both the Palestinian Authority and Israeli occupation

On June 30, 2012, July 1, 2012, and July 3, 2012, the PFD held broad-based protests in Ramallah over a three-day period, primarily targeting the PA's policies of negotiation with Israel.[35] The PFD had called a similar demonstration on January 2012,[36] protesting the PA's return to negotiations with the State of Israel.[37] This time around, the activists organized these particular demonstrations to protest the decision of the PA President Mahmoud Abbas to invite the ex-Israeli defense minister and Chief of Staff of the Israeli Occupation Forces, Shaul Mofaz, to Ramallah.[38]

The protests were attended by 500 to 1,000 youth and met with violent repression.[39] Pictures of the PA's police using batons and tear gas to attack the protesters went viral.[40] Stories of cracked bones and skulls crushed by the

Palestinian police were widely shared in news networks such as *Electronic Intifada*.[41] Lina Al Safeein wrote in her personal Facebook page:

> I saw a friend being dragged away by four thugs, and immediately went after them, trying to get my body between my friend and the thugs so that they wouldn't take him. The same thug drew back his arm and slapped me hard across the face, in broad daylight on one of Ramallah's busiest streets, shouting "WHORE! PROSTITUTE!" Getting slapped like that can break your spirit. I would have preferred being beaten on the ground by a mob of police. I can't describe the humiliation I felt at that moment, the rage that swept through me as I tried to go after the thug, screaming at him that his day will come at my hands one way or another. People were pushing me back, telling me to calm down. I turned on them, shouting at them for just standing there and not doing anything, not going after the thugs themselves. (Facebook status update, March 15, 2011)

Another female activist described how she experienced that moment in the square:

> When we protested against Israeli brutality and the occupation, they called us Heroes! When we went after the brutality of PA, they called us Whores! I wanted to scream at the top of my lungs: People, decide! Are you against ALL forms of oppressions or are you being selective?

These two quotes exemplify how the extreme use of force of the PSF sparked strong emotional sentiments such as anger, rage, and humiliation. It solidified the conviction of these youth groups to continue to confront and rebel against the PA. The extreme use of force and PA's subversive tactics to infiltrate and manipulate these youth groups shifted the attention of the PFD to now organize a new rally against the political arrests and police brutality of the PA.[42] In a press release that they posted on their website,[43] they wrote the following:

> "Palestinians for Dignity," call on all Palestinians in Palestinian cities and villages, from Haifa and Jenin to Hebron and Ramallah to participate in a protest and march planned for Tuesday July 3rd at 17:00, moving from Al-Manara to the presidential quarters at Al-Muqata'a. We state clearly and decisively that the pain of beatings disappears with time, but shame does not; with each blow their clubs become weaker and our determination stronger. (Facebook status update, July 3, 2012)

After the public backlash at its actions, the PA did not confront the planned demonstration and let the 500 protesters march to the presidential compound of Mahmoud Abbas to vent their frustration. On September 11, 2012, the PFD organized protests[44] targeting Salam Fayyad's government decision to raise prices on many consumer products, including fuel.[45] "Palestinians for Dignity" worked with other Ramallah-based groups to organize a rally that would head toward the Muqataa, the seat of presidential power for the Palestinian National Authority.[46] Only hours before the march was set to commence, Emergency Cabinet Prime Minister Salam Fayyad announced that the decision to raise consumer prices would be reversed for everything except car fuel.

PFD campaigns also challenged the political status quo by the international powers, including the United States[47] and the United Nations.[48] For example, in March 2012, protesters gathered to reject US President Obama's visit to the occupied Palestinian territory.[49] In May 2012, they surrounded the headquarters of the United Nations in Ramallah, demanding the closure of their offices in an effort to pressure the United Nations to publicly criticize administrative detention. The PA repeatedly cracked down on such protests, arresting and intimidating the key organizers and participants. The way the PA responded to such nonviolent protests is a persistent indicator of a structural limitation which the PFD faced due to the increasingly authoritarian context in which they operated. In an effort to overcome this limitation, the PFD would shift the attention of their protests for some time to focus on the Israeli occupation.

The PFD had started a cycle of unarmed confrontational campaigns through their "Freedom Rides" campaigns in 2011, drawing attention to the Israeli occupation, the military checkpoints, and Israeli expansion of settlements in the West Bank. By 2013, this campaign had taken on a different form. On January 11, 2013, a group of about 200 Palestinian activists, among whom members of the PFD group were also present, had another idea. They decided to improvise a Palestinian settlement in Israeli-occupied land, between Jerusalem and the West Bank.[50] Young activists erected tents on the same piece of land where the government had recently approved plans for construction of a major Jewish settlement. As soon as the first tent was erected, Palestinian and international media reported that the activists had announced the establishment of a Palestinian village called "Bab al-Shams" (Gate of the Sun) in the area and that the Palestinian owners of the land had agreed to this move.

This quickly drew the attention the activists had sought and was covered by major international news outlets, like the *BBC*, *The Guardian*, and *The New York Times*. By the time the Israeli authorities had the necessary court rulings to dismantle the tents and arrest the activists,[51] around 2,000 Palestinians had visited or tried to visit the site.[52] After Bab al-Shams, four more villages were established along the same pattern in the course of less than a year.[53] These are examples of some protests that directly challenged the occupation and other initiatives that shared the same concern of losing land and the tactic of directly confronting the occupying force.

These campaigns indicate another notable moment in the evolution of the PFD. First these protests were conducted away from PSF-controlled regions of the West Bank in Areas C and B—Palestinian territories designated under the Oslo Accords to be fully or partially administered by the Israeli authorities. Second, the novelty of their ideas amplified via social media raised the public profile of PFD in the eyes of rural Palestinian community. Third, the shift in the venue of the protests exposed new major obstacles within Israel's occupation of the West Bank

These new forms of activism did not cause difficulties for the PA, which committed itself to support the security interests of Israel in the West Bank but not in areas that were already under Israel's security responsibilities, as per the Oslo Accords. Consequently, the Palestinian authorities felt no need to crack down on groups like PFD and this kind of online activism and offline grassroots movements. Instead, Israeli authorities cracked down on these activists quickly.[54] They arrested some, threatened others, and jailed most of these activists for short periods of time. Every time these activists would be arrested,[55] social media campaigns would be organized to demand their immediate release.[56]

While the stories of Palestinian Freedom Rides, Bab al-Shams, and others were an international success and an inspirational success story for many Palestinian activists, it also highlighted another quiet yet important development: these networks of activists were creatively connecting with some non-violent grassroots movements in Palestinian society. The quiet alteration of the format and venues of protests away from the PA-controlled urban streets and toward social and community work in villages marked a new phase of networking between these isolated city-based movements led by the younger activists and grassroots rural protests led by popular committees.

It is here, resulting from this continuous variation in their strategic targets and continuous efforts to evade these two major limitations, that we start noticing the beginnings of a more complex and broad-based network. These events made an explicit connection between the PFD and other kinds of non-violent grassroots activism that had remained largely implicit in years prior.

For example, by 2013, we notice fewer events posted on the PFD's Facebook page and their alternative social media networks, but more on the website of the Palestinian Grassroots Anti-Apartheid Wall Campaign.[57] This online and offline shift indicated personal and networked integration on the grassroots level. The events analyzed so far reveal how the twofold strategy executed by the PFD brought about their integration in the networks of Palestinian popular resistance committees.

Strengthening ties with the Palestinian popular committees

Bassem Tamimi, leader of the popular committee of Nabi Saleh village in the West Bank, heard about the Bab al-Shams village while awaiting his trial in an Israeli jail. Nonetheless, he became very excited about the news. He spoke with wonder and excitement about their novel ideas and the creativity these young activists applied in their thinking about new forms of protests. Arrested nine times throughout the course of his lifetime (so far), Tamimi has been declared not guilty and was released each time. Amnesty International has declared him a "prisoner of conscience."[58] In his interview with me, Tamimi credited the young PFD activists and other youth groups with rekindling the spirit of popular protest and bringing it back to life in both cities and villages of the West Bank.

Tamimi's story and that of the popular resistance protests of Nabi Saleh intertwine with the trajectories of the activism of these youth groups in quite unforeseen ways and in a multitude of different forms. In their search to avoid institutional repression and top-down ways of political organizing, these activists had started engaging individually in grassroots activism, becoming more aware of the daily needs and wishes of local communities. They did all this at a much earlier phase and prior to being bound together as the formal PFD network.

The first village to welcome groups of young activists from the city with their new ideas and new technologies was Nabi Saleh. Eager to experience a sense of renewal in his own village protests, Bassem welcomed them into his village together with their ideas and online networks of activism. In return, the activists started integrating their efforts more and more with the village protests of Nabi Saleh. In my interviews with key members of the PFD, I learned that several of their previous youth groups had at some point or another all been part of the Nabi Saleh protests.

The Nabi Saleh strategy

Every Friday, after the midday prayer, the people of Nabi Saleh village march in protest against the Israeli occupation. Together as a group, men, women, and children walk from the center of the village toward a natural water spring, which has been seized by Israeli settlers living nearby. In the process of demanding access to the spring every Friday, the villagers clash with the settlers who are protected by Israeli soldiers. Maryam, the social media savvy and eager participant in the 15 March movement, told me that when she first went to Nabi Saleh, her primary goal was to document the weekly nonviolent demonstrations of the people of Nabi Saleh and expose their actions to a wider international audience online. It was in these popular protests that Maryam saw young Palestinians hurling rocks at the Israeli soldiers and their military jeeps for the first time in person. It was also her first time experiencing the sight and smell of blasts of a noxious liquid known as "skunk," as well as tear-gas canisters, which Israeli soldiers use to disperse the crowds of people and prevent the villagers advance toward the spring.

Thanks to the efforts of Maryam and her friends' networks, email lists, and journalistic contacts, Nabi Saleh was fully online by 2011. The village had a blog,[59] a Facebook page,[60] its own YouTube channel,[61] and a steady outpouring of tweets called #screamingtamimi.[62] By 2013, the international press was actively covering the non-violent popular struggle in Nabi Saleh, including broadcasts by *Al Arabiyya* and *Al Jazeera*.[63] Journalists from *The New York Times*, *The Economist*, and *The Guardian* covered Tamimi and Nabi Saleh in depth.[64] Most of these articles focus on Tamimi's personal life[65] and his life goal: that one day his village protests would transform into a massive popular uprising against the Israeli occupation.

Bassem Tamimi explains in this book his personal quest for that model and strategy. The reason for including him in many interviews that revolved around the youth mobilizations of 2011–13 were multiple. From the beginning he saw a role for these younger networks of activists that had helped transform his village protests into an international success story of nonviolent activism. But did he see in them any political potential, given the current Palestinian context? Some of these answers may be found in his story of a lifetime of activism. He described his own life as defined both by a strong sense of belonging and awareness of his roots and an acute experience of defeat. Tamimi's own quest for a strategy started in his very village. In his twenties his quest for a purpose and a life strategy was defined by his experience as a youth organizer during the First Intifada. He witnessed and felt the consequences of that Palestinian Uprising and the Oslo Accords very personally. It is in his village where he started his first protest and where he, now in his fifties, still leads the protests. While the strategy and means of organizing these protests have evolved, the goal remains the same.

Tamimi's first protest

Bassem was born in Nabi Saleh in 1967, the year of the Israeli occupation of Palestinian territory, which prior to the Six-Day War had been controlled by Jordan and Egypt. He participated in his first demonstration in 1976, at the age of nine, when villagers organized to oppose the stealing of their land for the construction of the Israeli colony of Halamish. The demonstration did not ultimately prevent the settlers of Halamish from establishing and expanding onto his village's land, but it was a pivotal moment for Tamimi. From that time Bassem never stopped demonstrating. What kept him going, he told me, was a sense of purpose. Today, forty years after that first protest, he now leads and organizes the similar sort of protests he participated in as a child. If there was one basic lesson that his whole life as an activist had taught him, it is to never give up, especially when surrounded by the reality of defeat. "It is in these protests," he told me, "where you renew your sense of purpose and solidarity and you stay connected to your roots."

Bassem's story, as leader of the Nabi Saleh's popular committee, led me to research more literature about the Palestinian Popular Resistance.[66] At the same time, his active role as a youth organizer during the First Intifada pulled me back to the modern history of the Palestinian youth activism, which is primarily analyzed through the lenses of the First Intifada and youth's highly active role in political mobilization associated with political parties (Lockman and Beinin, 1999; Sayigh, 1997; Beitler, 2004). No matter what period you analyze, in terms of Palestinian political activism, all roads lead back to the First Intifada. In an effort to navigate the historical undercurrents of the intifadas, the intersection between these newer forms of activism and more broad-based popular movements in the Palestinian context steered the focus of this research. This led to digging deeper into the history of popular resistance committees, generated in the historic period, now known as the "First Intifada."

First Intifada (1987–93)

"I am not your typical First Intifada generation person." In this first statement during an interview, Bassem articulated his discontent with the way that the traditional narrative on the First Intifada has come to sink into the political imagination of the younger activist: as a top-down party lead movement. The First Intifada[67] was a revolutionary, mass, popular uprising. It is considered by an overwhelming majority of scholarly literature as an opportune historic juncture in the Israeli-Palestinian conflict (Lockman and Beinin, 1999; Sayigh, 1997; Beitler, 2004). Politically, it is often referred to as the one bright moment that dramatically altered the way the world saw the Palestinian struggle. It transformed the dynamics between the Palestine Liberation Organization and Israel. It put the Palestinian struggle at the center of the international agenda and generated support from world powers. From a social movement perspective, it represents the most diverse forms of resistance constituted by labor strikes, general strikes, tax revolts, consumer boycotts, flying illegal flags, political graffiti, hunger fasts, defying school closures and education bans, reclaiming land through agricultural projects, and so on. Such an unplanned outburst caught everyone by surprise, including the PLO. Despite the forceful response of the IDF, the intifada could not be stopped, continuing for years, finally waning in 1991 with the beginning of formal negotiations between Palestinian and Israeli leaders.

"It really doesn't matter much what these activists know or have been told about the First Intifada," Bassem said, "what matters most is what they don't know." His problem with the traditionally accepted narrative is that it stops short of explaining what the intifada was about and how it was sustained. Bassem insists that while the spark for the uprising was spontaneous, the popular committees were anything but spontaneous. To him, the connective tissue of this movement, now called an "intifada," were the popular committees, community self-governing networks that were the true initiators, and the organizing bodies that sustained the First Intifada over a period of five years. Scholars of popular resistance highlight the First Intifada as predominantly and deliberately an unarmed uprising (Awad, 1984; Qumsiyeh, 2011; King, 2007; Zaru, 2008; Kaufman-Lacusta, 2011).

"*Muqawama sha'biya*," the term commonly used in Palestine, is roughly translated in English as "popular resistance." An Internet search of "Palestinian popular resistance" now gives over 8.5 million hits (Qumsiyeh, 2011). In his book, *Popular Resistance in Palestine: A History of Hope and Empowerment*, Qumsyeh explains that those who engage in acts of popular resistance believe that it is possible to change the behavior of their (violent) opponent by peaceful means. The basic assumption of this kind of non-violent grassroots activism is that it is possible for individuals to effect social change (Qumsiyeh, 2011, pp. 22–23). These scholars approach the First Intifada as a powerful example of organized civil resistance, obeying the logic of direct nonviolent action and alternative institution building. In his book, Qumsyeh explains how the institutional vacuum in the West Bank and Gaza led to the creation of a "bottom-up infrastructure." This infrastructure consisted of decentralized community-based organizations and neighborhood committees, which encompassed Palestinian society. These new networks were characterized by direct democratic decision-making, the absence of ideological squabbles, and a high capacity for adaptation, all of which made it very difficult for the Israeli-occupying power to effectively stop the uprising.

From this short account of the First Intifada, one can draw similarities to today's political environment, marked by authoritarianism and political repression. This environment has alienated youth from their current leaders and institutions while seeking alternative ways to resist. The conditions today, though very different, have fostered similar kinds of decentralized and horizontal networks of activism that characterized the First Intifada. Amplified by the decentralized nature of the new technologies, these new groups represent another quiet, circumstantial development of renewed forms of more traditional decentralized grassroots activism.

From Intifada to Oslo and the generation gap in between

The Oslo Accords have shaped the political environment in which these youth operate, as well as their forms of activism. The PA is part of the present-day framework established by the Oslo Accords, and was outlined above as being part of what these youth movements oppose. In the midst of the ongoing conflict during the First Intifada from 1987 to 1993, Palestinian and Israeli representatives initiated diplomatic negotiations aimed at ending the conflict and establishing a recognized Palestinian state with agreed upon borders. The parties' commitment put into effect the Declaration of Principles on Interim

Self-Government Arrangements on September 13, 1993.[68] The signing of these accords, now referred to as the Oslo Accords, brought the First Intifada to an official end.

The accords resulted in the creation of an interim Palestinian governing body known as the Palestinian National Authority (PA). Based on these accords, the parties agreed to a temporary framework for their relations during an interim period lasting five years.[69] During that time, the two sides would agree on important issues such as borders, refugees, Jerusalem, and settlements through bilateral negotiations.[70]The agreement increased the PA's responsibilities and territorial control through the categorization of land in the Palestinian territories into three types of areas: Area A, Area B, and Area C. Area A included the Gaza Strip and 17.2 percent of the West Bank containing the most densely populated cities and communities. The framework of the Oslo Accords laid out that the newly formed PSF would assume full responsibility for internal security, public order, and civil affairs in Area A.

Area B included 23.8 percent of the West Bank and included mainly urban and rural areas directly surrounding Area A lands. In Area B lands, the PA assumed full responsibility for civil affairs and public order, while Israel maintained responsibility for security. Lands categorized as Area C made up 59 percent of the West Bank and include all "connective" lands between Palestinian population centers. In Area C the Government of Israel maintained full control over security, public order, and civil affairs. Area C lands contained Palestinian agricultural land, nature reserves, Israeli settlements, designated military reserves, the Jordan Valley, and large tracts of land where Bedouins roamed. Israel retained responsibility for security in and surrounding Israeli settlements, as well as overarching security control over the West Bank and Gaza.

The Oslo Accords

"You know . . . when Oslo came it was supposed to give our generation so much hope. If you looked at it from outside, it was like a dream come true . . . but in a lot of ways, it turned into a nightmare" (Personal Communication with Bassem Tamimi, October 2016).

Bassem ended up feeling the "nightmare" personally in the form of the division of Nabi Saleh village into two administrative areas as a direct consequence of the Oslo Accords. After Oslo, Bassem's village was split between

Area B and Area C. This arrangement left all residents of the Israeli-controlled portion (Area C) with significant difficulties in establishing normal lives. For example, they were unable to build or develop their land without securing rarely granted Israeli permission. And when they built without permission they became targets of potential home demolitions, in addition to already being vulnerable to land confiscations and arbitrary arrests. When Israeli bulldozers came close to Nabi Saleh to construct the Halamish settlement, now under the administration of Israelis in area C, it became clear to Bassem that the Oslo Accords and all of its mechanisms would never lead to a two-state solution.

By 1987, "52 per cent of the area of the West Bank and 42 per cent of Gaza had come under direct Israeli control, while the number of Jewish settlers had reached 67,000."[71] By mid-2012, just over 650,000 Israelis were settled in Palestinian lands, with over 350,000 Israelis living in the West Bank and 300,000 Israelis living in East Jerusalem in 124 settlement communities in the West Bank and 12 settlements in East Jerusalem.[72] In 2010, the settler population growth rate in the West Bank was 4.9 percent, while the growth rate of the general population in Israel was 1.9 percent. Israeli settlement construction in the West Bank grew by 20 percent during 2010 to 2011, which contributed to a doubling of the number of Palestinians displaced by demolitions of Palestinian property near the settlements. In the summer of 2008, Israeli settlers from Halamish seized control of a number of natural springs, all of which were located on private Palestinian land belonging to residents of Nabi Saleh. The villagers resumed their protests.

Oslo: What went wrong?

Oslo Accords have been controversial since the moment they were signed.[73] Critics have targeted both its contents and the degree to which the Israeli and Palestinian official governments followed through on the commitments they made in the Accords.[74] Some called it an excellent achievement of diplomacy, which created extraordinary and cooperative order between Israelis and Palestinians. At the same time, others describe it as the capitulation of Palestine and the signing of the "Treaty of Versailles,"[75] or a nail in the coffin of Palestinian nationalist politics (Allen, 2013).

Substantial literature deals with the consequences of the Oslo Accords on political mobilization. The fragmentation of the national territory, the deterioration of the economy (Roy, 2006), the formation of the PA (Parker,

1999: xii), and the professionalization of NGOs (Hammami, 2000; Dana, 2009) have all been analyzed as causes for the increased distance of Palestinians from the political process. NGOs mushroomed after the signing of the Oslo Accords. Rema Hammami argues that the depoliticization is rooted in an ongoing process of NGO retrenchment from a popular constituency that predated Oslo, but which has sharpened with continuing depoliticization of the society that has marked the formation of PA rule.[76] Tariq Dana identified four dimensions of "what went wrong" since Oslo. He focused on the shift in organizations' agendas, the role of the grassroots, the status of politics, and the production of knowledge, concluding with recommendations to revive civil society as a fertile terrain for profound social transformation.[77]

NGO-ization and popular committees

When Huwaida Arraf[78] arrived from the US in Palestine she was working as a youth coordinator for an international youth organization. She told me how she initially believed that this NGO was working toward peace and was there to bring people to dialogue, so Huwaida wanted to be part of that process. She imagined being able to participate through her work and her individual protest efforts. That said, striking a balance between the two was easier said than done.

> I was told: you can protest, but you have to stay out of the jail and also keep your face out of the media, because as an NGO we can't be affiliated with such protests. So that in a way became a limitation for me, because as a youth program coordinator I wanted to get the workshop discussions that these kids were having in the street. The students hadn't seen before a home demolition let alone participate in protest against it. For example once we decided we would raise tents in the homes that were set up for demolition and we would stay there. This was actually against what the leadership of the organization told us, but I continued to do it anyway. So I kept going out in the street and then my face was suddenly everywhere in the media. (Personal Communication, October 21, 2015)

That was the day that Huwaida resigned from her position with this youth organization, since it was clear that she could not be an activist while also abiding by the organization's policies. Huwaida's story of disillusion with NGOs is not a unique one. It is a succinct illustration of a scholarly discourse which argues that advocacy organizations in today's world are prone to prioritizing institutional over public venues in order to influence their environment (Lang, 2013). In her book *NGOs, Civil Society and the Public Sphere*, Sabine Lang refers to this process as NGOization, defining it as a process by which social movements.

Some scholars describe a process of NGO-ization of Palestinian youth activism as a direct result of the Oslo Accords. Just over a third of Palestinian organizations were established during a mushrooming of NGOs in the first half of the 1990s when the Oslo process was underway. International funding patterns in conjunction with the establishment of the PA guided the way these NGOs functioned and how they set their priorities in accordance with funders' agendas. Many view this financial and institutional growth of NGOs to be the cause of a kind of desocialization and depoliticization of some Palestinian youth. The NGO that Huwaida was working for, represents yet another aspect of the NGO-ization of youth activism in the Palestinian context: the corralling of NGOs and program participants toward a particular vision of peace, which many Palestinians felt was skewed away from actual potential to achieve freedom (Allen, 2013).

This partiality contributed to these organizations' declining credibility in Palestinian society, distancing them from the Palestinian grassroots while at the same time expanding career paths for young Palestinians into NGO work. Noor, the 15 March activist from Nablus, for example, told me how during the years of the Second Intifada, when she was still in high school, she participated in many NGO workshops, primarily focused on human rights:

> I remember, one of the workshops was about the environment—The examples that they brought to us to explain this concept were things like "burning tires during protests hurts the environment." These peace lovers were talking to kids like us, whose houses were bombed or destroyed in one way or another during the second intifada. When I think about it now, I just laugh because I find it hilarious. But if someone told me these stupid examples now—I would probably punch them in their face! (Personal Communication, October 29, 2015)

Just like Noor, Huwaida had quickly come to realize that these activities for peace primarily took place in workshops and indoors. Huwaida herself had started to firmly believe that they needed to "take it to the streets." So in many ways the work with this international youth organization work no longer felt relevant to her anyway. Freed of her NGOs' limitations, Huwaida continued participating in local demonstrations. Over time she recognized how disastrous these demonstrations were simply in terms of numbers of injuries and lives lost when Palestinians were protesting on their own. She began to think about connecting with international activists to participate and be present with the Palestinians during their protest. Huwaida believed that such a presence of international activists could potentially help prevent some of this damage and also help change the way the media was covering such protests. "Someone suggested that we bring a large number of international activists," she said, "to elevate the profile of our protests and we thought that was a great idea." This idea defined the next four years of Huwaida's activism. She organized, participated in, and was the spokesperson for three international movements: the International Solidarity Movement (ISM), the Flotilla Movement, and the Free Gaza Movement.

"When I started I had hoped that ISM would become the organization that would actually define the strategy that would become a renewed national strategy," Huwaida told me. "This is not what it ultimately became." Huwaida had also initially hoped that such organizations, particularly ISM, would bring more international activists to the ground and reinvigorate Palestinian popular resistance. But the focus of the ISM remained primarily international and virtual. For Huwaida Arraf, the internationalized focus of such organizations was a good thing that needed to happen, but was simply not *her* intention. For Huwaida, the *real* struggle was to address the issues in the streets and to discover ways to empower people protesting on the ground. Huwaida, one of the original "Palestinian Freedom Riders," was also invited to contribute regularly to the PFD protests. In addition, she went back to local popular protests, demonstrating side by side with Bassem Tamimi in Nabi Saleh.

Within Huwaida's story and her involvement with ISM and the Flotilla Movement, unfolds another stage of Palestinian activism, namely its internationalization and establishment of international support networks. Taken together, the narratives of Huwaida and Bassem as activists seeking to connect old and new networks of popular resistance during two periods of the Palestinian mobilization have a central place in this part of my analysis. I discovered that there were many areas of overlap between the forms of activism pursued by the online networks of youth groups, international online activism, and popular committees on the ground pursued by people like Bassem Tamimi.

Second Intifada (2000–05)

Just as the Second Intifada was progressing at full speed, a quiet, different form of popular resistance was also underway. Bassem and others from Nabi Saleh had begun attending demonstrations in Budrus, a village just twenty minutes from Nabi Saleh by car. This village was in danger of being cut off from the rest of the West Bank by Israel's planned separation barrier. This is the concrete wall and electrified chain-link fence that snakes along the border, and in many places juts deeply into Palestinian territory to carve out sections of land for Israeli settlements. Residents in Budrus began demonstrating. Palestinians elsewhere were fighting with Kalashnikovs, but the people of Budrus decided, according to Ayed M, an old friend of Bassem's who organized the movement there, that unarmed resistance "would stress the occupation more." Their strategy appeared to work. After fifty-five demonstrations, the Israeli government agreed to shift the route of the barrier to the so-called 1967 Green Line. The tactic spread to other villages including Biddu, Nil'in, and Al Ma'asara and, in 2009, to Nabi Saleh. Together they formed what is known as the "Popular Resistance," a loosely coordinated effort that has maintained what has arguably been the only continuing form of active and organized nonviolent resistance to the Israeli occupation in the West Bank since 2003.

> Our main quest is to convince our society about the value of these unarmed popular protests. To do that we had two ways: First, the academic way—spreading formal knowledge through workshops, seminars, meetings, etc. but for our culture and the way we really absorb active learning, these methods were not suitable. The second is creating a model on the ground as a demonstration, so we can convince society through more of a "seeing is believing" approach. (Personal Communication, January 22, 2016)

Bassem's goal, as articulated in this quotation, was to demonstrate that it was still possible to struggle and to do so without taking up arms. His thinking was that when the spark came, resistance might spread as it had during the First Intifada. In Bassem's mind, the spark would likely come as a direct effect of the ways social media has influenced the mobilizing forms of the "Oslo generation." Together, they are trying to find a model, a recipe that could spread the unarmed revolt across occupied Palestine.

"Every young Palestinian is an Ahed Tamimi"

Just a year after this interview with Bassem Tamimi, the situation on the ground has significantly shifted. Interestingly, the timing of a new video and its authentic content propelled, once more, the Nabi Saleh popular resistance into the spotlight of global attention. The image of Ahed Tamimi, a new, hopeful, and youthful face of Palestinian activism in the Internet age, continues to be widely circulated and shared in a variety of SMNs. The US President Donald Trump's dramatic declaration from the White House, officially recognizing Jerusalem as the capital of Israel, has caused a new political whirlwind in Israel and Palestine. Along with this dramatic event, a compelling new online story in the form of a YouTube video from Bassem's village spread virally across the web. Though seemingly unconnected, these two events—Trump's declaration on Jerusalem and the YouTube video streamed online—have converged once again in Nabi Saleh, fueling an instant tide of sentiments and responses via SMNs.

Though I was unable to meet or interview Ahed, on January 13, 2018, Bassem agreed to meet me at his home in Nabi Saleh to talk again about the evolving role of social media for youth mobilizations in light of this most recent event. The video of Ahed, which triggered her arrest and subsequent revived attention to Nabi Saleh, Bassem argues, should be understood in the general context of despair and resentment that the most recent US declaration has caused among ordinary Palestinians. In his words, the sight of a fearless unarmed girl slapping the occupation in the face has resonated emotionally with young Palestinians across the West Bank and Gaza.

To be clear and as demonstrated so far in the second part of this chapter, this is not the first video that originates from Nabi Saleh. Like other videos before it, this one too offers a glimpse of the daily realities of ordinary Palestinians, revealing the asymmetric balance of power in the conflict, as witnessed regularly on the ground through the weekly protests of villagers from Nabi Saleh. In this latest video, Ahed Tamimi, Bassem's sixteen-year-old daughter, is seen confronting a heavily armed Israeli soldier in the courtyard of her home in Nabi Saleh, slapping and screaming at him to leave. Along with agitation and anger that Trump's declaration has caused in the Palestinian online space, the fearless image of this young girl refusing to stay silent in the face of the occupation touched a real nerve. The mere sight of an unarmed sixteen-year-old

Palestinian girl confronting a soldier of the occupation in that way caused an unusually strong wave of support online for this Palestinian teenager.

"The people understand and feel my daughter's rage against the occupation in that video—they connect with her immediately. Ahed did what every Palestinian wants to do. Everyone young Palestinian is an Ahed Tamimi" (Interview with Bassem Tamimi).

While experiencing a roller coaster of emotions and expectations, ranging from anger and pride, to fear and hope, Bassem appeared mostly hopeful and optimistic about the role of social media in exposing the efforts of grassroots popular movements such as those in his village of Nabi Saleh. "Videos like this"—he said—show to the world new and mostly unseen sights of this conflict, and to the Palestinians they show another way of resisting, the Nabi Saleh way.

The stories of Noor, Maryam, Huwaida, Bassem, and most recently, Ahed exemplify how deeply intertwined are these forms of activism and their initiatives. While they all intersect in one protest or another, organized at recent times by the PFD, each story of activism diverges again in different times and phases of Palestinian activism all across the West Bank. Despite major episodes of war and violence, party authoritarianism and police brutality, Israeli military checkpoints, occupation and geographical segregation, the stories of these networked individuals also demonstrate continuous willpower to go beyond such limitations.

The presence of these multiple networks of actions, which bridge generations and different forms of activism, can be viewed as elements of a bottom-up infrastructure where many factors can be set into motion at the right moment. This may also be seen as glimpses of a still-developing strategy, grounded in networked social movements and decentralized mobilization, growing outside of the organizational structures of main parties and formal social movements.

Concluding remarks

The story of PFD, as brought here, is not only the story of a group of activists who, inspired by the Arab Spring, organized the 15 March movement and a series of other protests afterward. It is also a story of evolving networked movements in a Palestinian context. The inclusion of the original six freedom riders of the "Freedom Rides" campaign, that opened this chapter, was part of a strategic effort from the activists of the PFD to connect their actions with those of ongoing grassroots movement in the occupied West Bank. The different strands of narratives of activists from different backgrounds, locations, and even generations are tied together here through their common quest for a networked grassroots movement, outside of the organizing structures of the Palestinian parties.

While the PFD was created by building upon the existing social and online networks of the 15 March movement, the span of activism and activists of these groups spread way beyond Ramallah. Although deeply affected by the ebbs and flows of Palestinian political realities, PFD expanded their online-decentralized networks of action and increased their impact by linking their campaigns and protests with ongoing revolts of existing popular village committees.

The ideas, protests, and stories of the activists in this chapter reveal that underneath a seemingly isolated cycle of protests and small leaderless groups lies an impressive ecosystem of creative ideas, organizational capacity, and passionate resistance. PFD activiti and activists are a case in point in demonstrating that through creative use of social media, they expanded not only their networks of action and sites of protests. They also brought a noticeable change in the repertoire of the existing nonviolent grassroots resistance in the Palestinian context.

By studying evolving dynamics of the PFD network from the inside, it's possible to trace an emerging pattern in their mobilizing tactics and structure of their campaigns. This pattern consists of an authentic idea for a protest—symbolic in its message and the degree to which the idea resonates emotionally with the immediate participants. Having a tight supportive network for an original idea and an element of secrecy in the way it is organized, both appear crucial in order to catch both the Israeli and Palestinian authorities by surprise. Finally, choosing the right social tools and networks to spread the event makes the protest highly effective instantaneously. Almost all of PFD's protests have followed this same pattern.

While these emerging tactics and formats of their protests are extremely vulnerable to the political constraints as mentioned earlier, they do allow for the growth of a network of highly effective activists outside of the established structures of Palestinian political parties. These networked activists are slowly working toward building a networked movement with multiple strategic goals. Through these creative protests and campaigns they managed to establish a block of successful examples, serving as inspirational moments for a broader mass of activists, working informally on the ground to build inter-community trust. Another outcome of such online and offline protests, is an experienced pool of leaders able to transfer their successes from an informal community of sustained interest to a larger and more visible network of actions, evident in the case of non-violent popular committees. Despite the obstacles represented by these realities, PFD moved beyond fragmented efforts into a continuous and disruptive cycle of nonviolent protests, which lasted for more than three years. This, in itself, is a remarkable achievement of these young activists who repeatedly engaged in confrontational resistance against the ongoing Israeli occupation while at the same time remaining highly defiant of the Palestinian leadership and its political parties. It is a further demonstration of my overall argument in this book that a networked movement, taking place outside the structures of official parties and hierarchical organizations, where these small networks of youth regularly and meaningfully contribute, is quietly growing.

Between Old Demands and New Protests: Stop the Prawer Plan Movement—a Case Study of Palestinian Youth Activism in Israel, 2011–13

In September 2011, a new bill on the Arrangement of Bedouin Settlements in the Negev Desert was announced to the Israeli public.[1] The bill, commonly known as "the Prawer Plan,"[2] aimed to relocate approximately 40,000 Bedouins[3] from the Southern arid region of Israel, known as Negev in Hebrew or Naqab in Arabic, into state designated locations for the Bedouin population of Israel.

While the Prawer Plan was new, the battle between Bedouin land right activists and state policies in Israel was not. Between 2011 and 2012, various UN and EU committees, as well as Arab civil society organizations within Israel, made calls for the Israeli government to withdraw the legislation.[4] These critics viewed the plan as further proof of the state's policy of marginalization of the Bedouins of the Negev, who consider this desert area as their historical land.[5] Undeterred by such criticism, the Prawer Plan passed its first reading at the Knesset (Israeli Parliament), by forty-three to forty votes on June 24, 2013.[6]

The news caused Amal, aged twenty-two, whose family lives in the Negev/ Naqab desert, to relive painful flashbacks from 2010, when hundreds of Israeli police officers and heavy machinery had rolled into the Bedouin village of Al Araqib to evict all of the families and demolish their houses. Before it was shattered into unrecognizable pieces,[7] Amal had quickly collected some cherished objects from her room. Then, on her mobile, she recorded her own home being demolished and shared it on her Facebook page. For Amal, this was not merely a legal or political issue, but a deeply personal one. For her and her family, the Prawer Plan represented their severance from their land.

In the meantime, Maysan, aged twenty-two, from a Druze village in Northern Israel, and Majd, aged twenty, from Haifa city in Israel, received the news through their connections with a network of about fifty activists and spread it across four youth groups, under the name "Naqab for Human Rights." Inspired and encouraged by the popular movements of 2011 starting in Tunisia and Egypt, these individuals were part of a group of young Palestinians within Israel who had organized and participated in a series of protests across the north and south of Israel in the period of 2011–12. Neither Maysan nor Majd were Bedouins, but they decided to protest nevertheless.

In line with their involvement in previous protests, these young activists turned first to their digital networks, relying on hashtags such as #StopPrawerPlan and #AngerStrike on Twitter to raise awareness about the bill. Next, they created a Facebook page called "Prawershallnotpass,"[8] in which they urged young people to join them in their call to action. Thanks to these actions, initiated primarily via social media platforms, massive youth protests took place initially on July 15 and August 1, 2013, in Northern and Southern Israel,[9] culminating on November 30, 2013. Palestinians of Israel,[10] together with Palestinians of the West Bank,[11] Gaza,[12] and East Jerusalem, organized separate demonstrations on the same day within their geographic areas.[13] Two weeks later, the Government of Israel dropped the Prawer Plan bill.

Several elements stood out most in these protests. First, large youth crowds composed of different religious and minority groups in Israel—Muslims, Christians, Druze, and Bedouins of Israel—collectively took to the streets.[14] Second, like rarely seen before inside Israel, these protesters waved hundreds of Palestinian flags while wearing black and white *keffiyeh*. Daring young Palestinians of Israel, usually referred to as "48ers," held banners likening the Prawer Plan with a "Second Nakba," referring to it as "the biggest Israeli land-grab since 1948."[15] Why and how did a protest demanding Bedouin rights within Israel turn into a cross-border Palestinian youth movement, demanding Palestinian rights? What motivated this visible shift in the framing of these youth protests from one of social struggle for minority rights within Israel, to one of a Palestinian national struggle? What conditions enabled the coordination of a networked Palestinian youth movement across the Green Line?

Substantial scholarship has analyzed such protests primarily in the context of Bedouin land rights activism, set against their systemic marginalization within Israel (Abu-Saad, 2008; Cole, 2003; Kedar, 2004; Shamir, 1996; Abu-Rabia, 2001; Hall, 2014; Yiftachel, Roded, and Kedar, 2016; McKee, 2015; Swirski, 2016; Kark and Frantzman, 2012). However, studies that examine the dynamics of the Prawer Movement in the context of new forms of youth activism in the age of social media are missing. When reviewing scholarly literature on this subject, I found that much of it is focused either on Palestinian youth of the Palestinian territories or on Israeli Youth of Israel. This narrow framework of analysis has resulted in less attention to efforts by young Palestinians of Israel in a post–Arab Spring context.

For example, when studying NSMs and forms of youth activism in the Internet age, there is substantial focus on the Jewish Israeli youth protests movements during the summer of 2011 (Alimi, 2012; Grinberg, 2013; Shechter, 2013; Amram, 2013; Marom, 2013; Schipper, 2015). These protests, directed against house pricing in Tel Aviv, started with a small encampment on the Rothschild Boulevard in Tel Aviv and evolved within two weeks into large youth mobilizations. Overall, such protests were seen as part of the newer global protests in an increasingly neoliberal world.

Similarly, in the context of Palestinian youth movements, much of the media and scholarly attention at the time focused on youth of the West Bank and Gaza and their demand for an end to political division between their two main political factions, Fatah and Hamas, or an end to Israeli Occupation of the West Bank and Gaza (al-Shabaka, 2011; Casati, 2016; Christophersen, Høigilt, and Tiltnes, 2012; ACRPS, 2012; Farsakh, 2012; Hilal, 2011; Hoigilt, 2013, 2015; Maira, 2013; Sayre and Al-Botmeh, 2010). Taken together, these scholars overlooked the study of other Palestinian youth actors, outside of the Palestinian territories, and particularly those in Israel.

The following chapter addresses these shortcomings in the literature by analyzing the Prawer Movement in the larger context of emerging Palestinian networked youth movements at the wake of the Arab Uprisings of 2011. Besides the mobilizations against the Prawer Plan, the inclusion of a series of protests organized by young Palestinians of Israel during 2011 is relevant in this chapter, because the key organizers of the massive youth mobilizations of the Prawer protests were the same core networks of activists directly involved in the protests of 2011–12. Such a sustained cycle of protests speaks further to the main argument of this overall study: the emergence of a loose network of Palestinian activists across borders, whose ties were forged outside of existing party structures through their digital networks and whose bond was strengthened through such events.

This chapter demonstrates that the shift in the framing of these protests from the Bedouin of Israel to the Palestinians within Israel marked a turning point in the political awareness of young Palestinians of Israel. The use of social media networks to coordinate these protests also exposed the political potential of a network of Palestinians who were able to unite efforts across the fragmented segments of Palestinian society into one broad-based movement within Israel. Finally, the Stop the Prawer Movement demonstrated that despite geographical and political fragmentations, a growing network of Palestinian activists across borders forged new connections and strategies for resistance.

It is important to briefly explain the historical context and current composition of the various Palestinian-Arab minorities that live in Israel. Within this account, personal stories of some activists from Israel are interjected to account for the particular evolution of the movement rooted in the complexities of their own communities. Situating their protests against the backdrop of the contemporary events going on at a regional level—such as the Arab Spring—this chapter will also indicate the ways that SMNs affected their movements and translated their personal experiences from participating in online and offline protests, into the organizing strengths of the Prawer Movement.

Palestinians of Israel

The primary focus of this book, up to now, has been on the evolving dynamics of networked Palestinian protest movements between 2011 and 2013. Concurrently, in separate chapters, sociopolitical conditions have also been included in order to weave this narrative into a broader socio-historical account for each group of Palestinians living in their segregated geographic area, such as the Gaza Strip and the West Bank. This chapter follows the same logic by outlining a comprehensive background of the Palestinian citizens of Israel while maintaining the same focal narrative on protest movements by Palestinians of Israel in the post–Arab Spring context. This approach enables the interjection of these seemingly isolated movements and the stories of the activists involved, in the broader narrative of Palestinians of Israel and their constant search for empowerment and political expression.

The multiple and ever-changing terms defining the Arab community of Israel reveal, at least symbolically, the uneasiness over referencing the troubled history of this particular community, at times dubbed as "Israel's Achilles's heel."[16] For over half a century, scholars writing on Israeli/Palestinian affairs have used the definition "Israeli Arabs," as those living "on the inside," meaning inside the 1949 armistice line, otherwise known as the "Green Line" (Zureik, 1979; Lustick, 1980; Peled, 2013; Rabinowitz and Abu-Baker, 2005).

Yet, among the activists interviewed and in various reports and studies produced by Palestinian NGOs, observers of Palestinian-Israeli affairs, and so on, another term, that is "48ers," seems prevalent. These multiple definitions demonstrate the extent to which the legal standing and political future for various groups of Palestinians differ. The term "48ers" is a symbolic marker of the year 1948, where the foundation for two sharply contrasted narratives lays: For the Israeli people, the historic year marks the creation and declaration of independence by the State of Israel. For the Palestinian people, it is the catastrophic year when they fled in terror from their homes, when the tragedy of their great exodus occurred which they refer to as al-Nakba (the "catastrophe" in Arabic).

In 1948, 85 percent of the Palestinians living within Israeli-controlled territory delimited by the Green Line, determined in 1949, were uprooted and became refugees (Morris, 1987; Kimmerling and Migdal, 1993; Khalidi, 1997; Shlaim, 2000). The Palestinian refugees of 1948 fled to the West Bank and Gaza, as well as to adjacent Arab states, such as Jordan, Lebanon, and Syria. The particular predicament of the Palestinians of Israel is that in that fateful year, 1948, when the rest of their fellowmen became either stateless or refugees, they remained in their homes and lands and emerged as citizens within the borders of the newly created State of Israel.

In Chapter 1 of this book, I have provided detailed and specific data about the religious and ethnic composition of Israel's Palestinian-Arab population which totals roughly 1.6 million. In addition, around 200,000 of this population are Arab Bedouin citizens, members of the indigenous Palestinian community who remained on their lands in the Negev (Naqab) region. Furthermore, Palestinian youth constitute more than half of the Palestinian society in Israel, with the age group ranging between zero and twenty-nine years old constituting 62 percent of the Palestinian population in Israel.[17] About 36.0 percent of the population are aged fourteen, and the median age of Palestinians in Israel is twenty-two in the north and just fifteen years in the south.[18] In addition, 96.1 percent of Palestinians in Israel (fifteen years and above) are literate.

In this study, the term "Palestinian Citizens of Israel" refers to the different segments of the Palestinian minorities living in Israel. The term "48ers" refers to the activists involved in the Prawer protests, born around 1990, and spread across Southern and Northern Israel. The reason for this is because that is what these activists called themselves in their interviews. Also for the sake of clarity, the book uses both terms as interchangeable, to refer to the segment of the Palestinian nation which lives inside Israel, holds Israeli citizenship, and maintains civic relations with the state, along with some rights.

A substantial body of research that focuses on the Palestinian Citizens of Israel characterizes them as collective, fraught with external pressures, and charged with inner tensions (Zureik, 1979; Lustick, 1980; Peled, 2013). The general consensus between these scholars is that such internal and external dynamics have created a paradoxical situation by placing the Palestinians of Israel at once on the periphery of both Israeli and Palestinian societies.[19] In addition, Palestinian Citizens of Israel as a particular group within Israel has a significantly lower socioeconomic status and fewer social resources than the Jewish majority (Hammack, 2010; Gharrah, 2015).

External pressures, usually felt in the form of larger events defining Israeli-Palestinian relations, such as the First Intifada in 1987–92, Oslo Accords of 1993, or the Second Intifada in 2000–05, were described in more detail in the chapter on West Bank. As a result of such events, Palestinian Citizens of Israel were further distanced from the rest of the Palestinian population. Furthermore, the message from the Palestinian Leadership to the Palestinian population of Israel has been that they are not on the agenda of the Palestinian national movement; their problems are their own and should be solved within the Israeli context (Al-Haj, 2005).

Internal tensions, consisting of the relations of various Palestinian minority groups with each other, and vis-à-vis with the State of Israel, are also a defining feature of the Palestinians of Israel (Rabinowitz, 1997; Shafir and Peled, 2002). These tensions, rooted in socioeconomic differences, as well as different rights and privileges for different groups as controlled by the State of Israel, have also pushed them to the margins of the Israeli society (Al-Haj, 2004, 2005). In short, while in theory the rights of the Palestinians of Israel are guaranteed by Knesset legislation, as well as the Declaration of Independence and court decisions, these minority groups of Israel are discriminated against, whether overtly or covertly, and a wide gap exists between them and the Jewish majority (in favor of the latter) in every conceivable field (Rouhana and Ghanem, 1998; Mazawi, 1994; Dowty, 2004).

This broader social context of the various segments that compose the Arab Palestinian community in Israel is important, because as I demonstrate later in this chapter, the mobilization modes and the issues that generated the series of the Prawer Plan protests were directly tied to the complex realities of those communities. By rooting these activists and their movements within their own communities and by situating them in their broader sociopolitical context in Israel, we can better comprehend the particular challenges they face, as well as their evolving modes of mobilization within and outside of their communities. As a result, some particular features defining the identity struggle of the Palestinians of Israel: both citizenship and Palestinian national components were also present in the issues that drove them into the streets and the ways they framed their protests.

As the opening episode of this chapter indicated, the issue that sparked the youth mobilizations of the "48ers" in Israel was the relocation of large numbers of Bedouins from the Negev desert in state designated locations within Israel. For this reason, it is analytically meaningful in this section to situate the dynamics of the youth mobilizations of the "48ers" of Israel against the backdrop of the Bedouins' history in Israel, and their relationship vis-à-vis with the Israeli State Authorities. I would like to specify that while a lengthy discussion on Bedouin land ownership in the Negev desert goes beyond the scope of my study, a short account is necessary of how the Law for the Arrangements of Bedouin Settlement in the Negev, commonly referred to as the Prawer Plan, came to exist.

"Bedouin" is derived from the Arabic *badowi,* which can be best translated as "desert-dweller." In his article "The Bedouin Refugees in the Negev," Rabia explains how the term not only denotes a way of life that was specialized and evolved around steppe-based herding but also refers to a "group identity." Considered integral to the fabric of the societies in the Middle East, the Bedouin make up 30 percent of the overall population in the region with their contemporary presence spread throughout Syria, Iraq, Egypt, Jordan, Israel, and Saudi Arabia (Abu-Saad, 2008; Kedar, 2004; Shamir, 1996; Abu-Rabia, 2001; Kark and Frantzman, 2012). Out of a population of around 7.5 million in Israel, in 2010, there were 193,000 Bedouin, or about 2.5 percent of the Israeli population.[20]

Over the past 150 years, a series of laws were introduced by various administrations that substantially changed the Bedouin's state of affairs in the region. Of special relevance for the purpose of this study is the introduction of a particular law issued by the British administration and called the Mawat[21] Ordinance of 1921. This law (in turn, an interpretation of a previous Ottoman law) is particularly relevant here because it directly affected the Bedouin in Mandatory Palestine, and it also shaped the contemporary Israeli State's policy toward the Bedouin. In a nutshell, a controversial interpretation of this law does not allow registration of unregistered land after this date (1921). Furthermore, most of the Bedouin did not officially lay claim or register their land claims before that date (Falah, 1989; Kark and Frantzman, 2012).

On the basis of this law, the State of Israel denied the status of "village" to all Bedouin communities in the pre-1948 Negev, thereby practically classifying all Negev lands as "dead" (Mawat in legal Ottoman) and then declaring them as state owned. These state claims are strongly contested by other legal analyses (Yiftachel, 2012; Yiftachel et al., 2016).

According to Rabia (2001), today the Negev Bedouin can be divided into two groups. The Bedouins of the first group, about 86,000 people, reside in towns planned by the authorities: Rahat, Tel al-Saba' (Tel-Sheva), Ku 'Ar 'ara, Shqeb al-Salam (Segev Shalom), Hura and Laqiya and are considered as recognized villages. The Bedouins of the second group, about 70,000 people, is comprised of those who live outside the seven government-built townships in unauthorized locations (known as unrecognized villages).

According to the Association for Civil Rights in Israel (ACRI), the state refuses to provide the Bedouins that live in the unrecognized villages with a planning structure and place under municipal jurisdiction. It also denies basic services such as electricity, water, health clinics, sanitation, roads, public transportation, and education. Such nonrecognition by the State of Israel of the status of the Bedouins living outside designated locations means that their housing is also considered illegal. For this reason, unrecognized localities and the populations living in them suffer recurring waves of state violence, amounting to about 800 to 1,000 house demolitions each year of the period (2010–13).[22]

This complex history of land laws, state policies, and Bedouin land rights, as enacted and interpreted differently by different administrations over a span of almost two centuries, forms the backdrop for the scope and reach of the Prawer

Plan in 2010. Prawer was the latest attempt by the Israeli government to address this situation and permanently solve the problem of the unrecognized Negev Bedouin communities. For its critics, the plan ignored many Bedouin villages' historic ties to their lands. It deprived Palestinian citizens of Israel from their lands, homes, and livelihoods, as well as their basic right to determine where to live.

Still, up to this point, substantial literature on this topic confirms that land rights were central to the Bedouin's struggle for equal citizenship within Israel. The Prawer protests of 2013 and youth mobilizations of the "48ers" in Israel marked a significant departure from such strategy. The "48ers" of Israel, born around 1990, protested not as Bedouins or for Bedouin rights specifically. In my interviews with the activists, I was repeatedly reminded how unlike any other protests, this one brought various Palestinian groups of Israel together. These activists also pointed out how they had led this movement with no permission, guidance, or organizational resources from parties or formal civil society organizations within Israel. In the next section, focus shifts to how the dynamics of the youth mobilizations played out against the backdrop of the state of political activism for Palestinians of Israel, with a primary focus on 2011.

Protesting as "48ers" within Israel

Just as the torrent of the popular uprisings of 2011 was descending rapidly across the Middle East, a stream of laws concerning the political participation of Palestinian citizens in Israel was also passed in the Knesset, or Israeli Parliament (Mosawa, 2012). According to a study published in December 2012 by the Mosawa Center (The Advocacy Center for Arab Citizens in Israel), the Israeli government had drafted dozens of discriminatory bills aimed at disenfranchizing Palestinian citizens through their right to culture, land, politics, and more (Mosawa, 2012, p. 5).

Some of these laws were the Anti-Boycott Law and the "Nakba" Law. According to Adalah (The Legal Center for Arab Minority Rights in Israel),

The Anti-Boycott Law, passed on 11 July 2011, prohibits the public promotion of academic, economic or cultural boycott by Israeli citizens and organizations against Israeli institutions or illegal Israeli settlements in the

West Bank. It enables the filing of civil lawsuits against anyone who calls for boycott; it creates a new "civil wrong" or tort. It also prohibits a person who calls for boycott from participating in any public tender.

According to the same Center, the "Nakba Law" meant the following:

> The law authorizes the Finance Minister to reduce state funding or support to an institution if it holds an activity that rejects the existence of Israel as a "Jewish and democratic state" or commemorates "Israel's Independence Day or the day on which the state was established as a day of mourning." Palestinians traditionally mark Israel's official Independence Day as a national day of mourning and organize commemorative events. This law deprives Arab citizens of their right to commemorate the Nakba, an integral part of their history.

The passing of these laws, protested by various Arab legal centers in Israel, demonstrates the increasingly constrained political environment for the Palestinians of Israel.[23] The introduction and passing of these laws are brought into this analysis to point out the increased alienation of the young Palestinians of Israel from the Israeli political system. Resistance to such laws revealed another internal force at work that pushed these activists to see their issues no longer as separate but as common restrictions imposed on them because of their status in Israel: a "Palestinian minority."[24]

In my interview with the director of the largest youth NGO for the Young Palestinians of Israel, Mr. Nadim Nashif of Baladna concluded that the introduction of these bills severely damaged the ability of Palestinian parties, NGOs, and activists to freely express their opinions and protest Israel's restrictive state policies, both within and outside of the Green Line. According to him, resistance to these policies shaped the form and content of the protests of the young Palestinians of Israel, including their firmer grasping onto their Palestinian heritage and nationality.

One example was when, on March 15, 2011, the Nakba Law was passed in the Israeli Knesset. Ironically, this was the same day on which the Palestinians of Gaza and the West Bank took to the streets to protest political division and demand the unity of the political parties. While youth groups in Israel also took to the streets on March 15, 2011, they were opposing something different: The law that prohibited them to remember Nakba as part of their integral history in Israel. Resistance to this particular law may also explain the increased use by the Palestinians of Israel of highly visible Palestinian national symbols, such as flags, *keffiyeh*, and other symbols during the protests analyzed in this study.

At the very time when the images of the Arab Spring were diffused instantly in a world networked by Internet, most of my interviewees in Israel concluded that they were using the same digital networks primarily for two reasons: First, inspired by these regional events, they were following and supporting various protests taking place in the region. As a result, they forged new connections with activists by expanding their digital networks. Second, in my conversation with various activists, I learned that they traveled extensively in Jordan and Lebanon to receive training and particular advice on how to use social media to mobilize and advocate for a particular issue within their own communities.[25] Ultimately, the prime way that these activists raised awareness about these laws and the risks it posed for different groups of Palestinians was through the increased exposure of the Palestinian youth to social media platforms.

Determining the accurate figures of the percentage of Internet usage among the Palestinians of Israel is somewhat complicated. Technically, the data on Internet usage in the different areas of Palestinian residence is scattered between several bodies and split among Israeli and Palestinian service providers. Thus, there is not a single body that is able to provide this data in a unified form. Still, understanding how youth movements of the Palestinians of Israel have evolved, how do they relate to other similar movements in the Palestinian Territories, and to what degree social media has influenced their communication and mobilizing patterns remains crucial to understand increased awareness about these laws.

According to the Israeli Central Bureau of Statistics for 2015, 47 percent of Palestinians of Israel older than twenty years use the Internet. Over 56.3 percent of Palestinian households in Israel have a computer, while 74.4 percent of Palestinian households in Israel are connected to the Internet.

All this data illustrates the significant role of the social media networks as enablers of alternative platforms through which Palestinian youth of Israel receive their news, express their voice, and engage on newer forms of activism on issues that directly affect their daily lives. This is what one activist said about the role of social media for Palestinian youth activism in Israel:

> For me, before talking about social media as means to strategize and organize protests within Israel, we must above all focus on how social media

helped create a sense of awareness—that we: Druze, Muslims, Christians and Bedouins, are all treated unfairly by the State of Israel—simply for being Palestinians. I think that before the increased use of the SMNs, Palestinians of the North had no idea of what was going in the South of Israel, let alone what was going on with Palestinians in East Jerusalem, West Bank or Gaza. For the first time, these young "48ers" got their news in their personal social media sites, on their way to school, from their peers, in Gaza or West Bank, or Jerusalem, South or North of Israel. They see the reality not through the TV lenses anymore—but through social media.

I met Khaled in his office in East Jerusalem in his capacity as co-director at a Grassroots Jerusalem community organization. As illustrated in the above quote, Khaled's belief that social media helped connect the spread of awareness of the commonality of issues facing different groups of Palestinians of Israel is in line with that of the executive director of Baladna. Both of these NGO activists agreed that increased exposure to social media networks exposed the fragmentations between various groups of Palestinians of Israel, particularly at a time when affiliation of youth in relations to Parties and conventional organizations within Israel had been rapidly decreasing.

"Palestinian Youth Affairs in Israel," a study published in 2012 by Baladna, Association for Arab Youth in Israel, reported the results of a survey[26] on the basis of which they estimated that only 4 percent of Palestinian youth in Israel were associated with political parties and even less, 2 percent, with civil society organizations within Israel. The results of Baladna's report are also in line with another study produced by the Abraham Fund Initiatives and the Friedrich Ebert Foundation,[27] who reported a sharp decline in the Palestinian voter participation in Israel. The study revealed a deep level of distrust among Palestinians of Israel toward Israel's political system and skepticism regarding their ability to influence policy. While dissatisfaction with the government was the main cause for such decline, young Palestinians were also disappointed by their choices for Arab leadership, who often seem more interested in the Palestinian-Israeli conflict than their day-to-day social problems, such as education and health.[28]

These results are further confirmed by the executive director of Baladna: "Most of the political activities here are led by Parties, which rally youth in their activities or organizations, but there is not much space actually for youth to lead a movement like they did in Prawer." This quote exemplifies the situation of the Palestinians of Israel with regard to their political parties, as similar to those of their Palestinian peers across the Green Line. It points to the general disappointment and decreased affiliation of young Palestinians with Arab political parties. In my conversation about this particular topic, Khaled stated the following:

> One fact that makes me optimistic is that young people are moving away from their deep affiliations with their Political Parties. The politically unaffiliated are increasing in numbers, and are drawn in other movements outside political parties. While I am not sure how this will play in the long run, I believe that we should celebrate the fact that young people are more aware now about alternative ways of engaging politically. Once away from their family atmosphere, they start to drift away from the political affiliation they grew up to. (Personal Communication, November 20, 2016)

Khaled's quote illustrates the potential for the increased masses of unaffiliated youth to move from party-affiliated youth activism which prevents young Palestinians from seeing what is common in their political struggle within Israel. Khaled's personal story is an example in case. He identifies himself as a Palestinian Druze of Israel. Khaled's identification with his Palestinian identity became complete when he publicly refused to enlist in the Israeli Army and launched the movement "Urfod: Resist, your people will protect you."[29] "Urfod is my life story and therefore it's a movement that I am committed thoroughly. It is more than a movement about refusing to military conscription in the Israeli Army. It is a movement about the potential of the Druze community, flipping its approach, and unifying with the Palestinian political map."

The two major developments that affected the types of protests and mobilizing modes of Palestinians of Israel, which were discussed until now, are increased restrictions from the Israeli government on Palestinian youth activism and increased disappointment of Palestinians of Israel with their Arab political parties. At the nexus of these two quiet but simultaneously evolving developments, we can trace the spontaneous youth protests and the creation of independent youth groups or movements around issues of importance to them. We can also examine their choice to be nonpolitical and their growing reliance on social media networks in order to organize and coordinate.

At this time, we see the start of youth groups such as "Jaffa Movement,"[30] "Haifa Movement," and "Galilee Movement" as open venues to discuss issues that affected young people on a daily basis. Within these movements, we can also see youth from the north and south of Israel and from different ethnic and religious backgrounds coming together to affect positive change. My interviews with activists from Jaffa, as well as a combined number of eighty blogs, news reports, and in-depth articles covering the Prawer protests,[31] indicate that they were unaffiliated with parties and acting independently from official political agendas. Following is a brief account of a campaign in 2011, organized by such independent youth movements as an example of ongoing youth protests and mobilizations led by such independent youth networks, which paved the way toward the larger broad-based movement now known as "Stop the Prawer Plan."

The Arab Spring and the Palestinians of Israel

While the hasty winds of the Arab Spring blew briefly in the West Bank and Gaza, in the form of solidarity protests with the Tunisia and Egyptian revolutions and then under the mobilizing banner of the 15 March movement, scarce attention was paid to similar youth-led demonstrations taking place in Jaffa, Haifa, and Tel Aviv.[32] In this section, I bring into focus a collection of such seemingly isolated protests and movements taking place within Israel before the Stop the Prawer protests. Taken together, these protests demonstrate that the wave of the Arab Spring was also definitely felt within Israel, highlighting the identity struggle of the "48ers" and heightening their sense of being Palestinian. Often overlooked, these small, scattered protests were indicative of a nascent cross-Green Line Palestinian youth network that preceded the Prawer Movement, culminating in 2013.

The Israeli daily *Yedioth Aharnot* (Ynet) reported that several demonstrations took place as the Palestinians of Israel denounced the Mubarak regime.[33] In January 2011, protesters in Tel Aviv held a rally outside the Egyptian embassy, while hundreds demonstrated in the Palestinian village of Kfar Yassif in the Galilee region. In Haifa, dozens of young Palestinians held up Palestinian and Tunisian flags, chanting slogans in support of the Egyptian uprising, while slamming President Mubarak and (Israeli) Prime Minister Benjamin Netanyahu.[34]

In the meantime, another cycle of protests of the young Palestinians of Israel that took place in the wake of the Arab Spring was the 15 March Palestinian

Youth movement of 2011. Although on March 15, 2011, joint demonstrations took place by Palestinian Youth in Haifa and Jaffa, they were largely analyzed as isolated events, with primary focus on Ramallah. As already explained in the "the Forgotten Revolution" chapter the Gaza protests received much less coverage. In addition, the 15 March movement of Israel received less attention than the protests combined between the West Bank and Gaza (Burton, 2017; Maira, 2013; Nabulsi, 2014).

Yet, the active involvement of the "48ers"[35] was not limited to the 15 March movement. A series of campaigns, focusing on issues like prisoners and hunger strikers,[36] were organized by the same core network of activists. Each of the eight activists interviewed in Haifa explained directly how they had first met their peers on the other side of the Green Line through coordinating and participating in a series of protests between 2011 and 2012. Activists from Haifa, Jaffa, Gaza, Ramallah, Nablus, Hebron, and Bethlehem confirmed that while the coordination of these protests between the '48 and '67 Palestinians happened primarily online, their emotional bonds were forged in the physical sites of these protests whenever meeting in person was possible.

It is important to highlight this emerging youth network across the border because the interviewees confirmed their high levels of connections with various youth groups beyond the Green Line. In the words of one activist from Wadi Ara, Northern Israel,

> Because of those protests in 2011, the activists here know the same people from Gaza, Ramallah, Hebron. We supported their protests by organizing our own solidarity protests here in Israel. We shared these images via our digital networks. The next time we wanted to organize something here activists from these networks would organize similar protests in their own areas. When you decide to become a political activist, you enter this network and you are part of it—so it becomes easier to organize these protests. You can see how the protests may end, but the connections, the ties between us got stronger. (Personal Communication, November 15, 2016)

This quote illustrates how a small core group of Palestinian activist across borders had established a sort of bond and a set of emerging Palestinian issues as a result of this cycle of cross-border protests organized during 2011. A short analysis of one such protest may be analytically meaningful here because it demonstrates a set of lessons learned during this increased cycle of protests that were put to use in the youth mobilizations against the Prawer Plan.

Hungry for Freedom: Online and offline
lessons in political organizing

Majd, aged twenty-five, sits in his hometown Haifa, at a lively café, bustling with music and a relaxed atmosphere, filled with mixed sounds of conversations in both Hebrew and Arabic. Majd, unlike other activists in Haifa who were interviewees for this book, preferred to remain anonymous. Most of these activists accepted to the interviews primarily based on recommendations by other activists in the West Bank that participated in the study. Most of the initial connections between Palestinians on either side of the Green Line were established via social media networks, while tighter bonds were forged when the "48ers" would travel to the West Bank to attend demonstrations and protests at the wake of the Arab Spring. Majd was one of the main organizers of the "Hungry for Freedom" campaign and later of the "Prawer Movement."

Two major developments had touched Majd's heart and mind while studying political science at the Hebrew University of Jerusalem between 2010 and 2014. The first, he recalls, awakened his courage to protest and sparked his hope that ordinary people can affect positive change. The second event convinced him of the value of social media as an indispensable tool linking many Palestinian youth groups both inside and outside Israel and Palestine.

The first event was the Arab Spring: the inspirational and hopeful images on the Internet and TV of people occupying town squares and streets, demanding change and a better life from their authoritarian governments and corrupt institutions. He said, "Seeing some of the toughest authoritarian regimes in the region implode like that, it was powerful! I had this sudden realization to fear power no more."

The second event was the hunger strike by more than 100 Palestinian prisoners in Israeli jails, which began on September 27, 2011. "Hungry for Freedom" was a campaign in response to this event. "It is unacceptable that people are starving for their freedom and we do nothing about it," Majd said, when explaining why he felt emotionally compelled to do something about it. He met up with about a dozen of his friends from his hometown Haifa and started talking about visible ways (both online and offline) in which they could support this general hunger strike. Two weeks later, on October 15, 2011, their pictures flooded Palestinian digital networks and social media networks, both personal and organizational.[37] Blindfolded and hands-bound, holding banners with the slogan "Hungry for Freedom," these activists self-organized and staged solidarity sit-ins in the roads of Haifa, Ramallah, and Gaza City. The group also relied on their own Facebook pages, Twitter feeds, and blogs.

From the moment they met, Majd was clear about one advantage of the newly formed group called "Hungry for Freedom"[38]: The participants were not aligned politically with any party and they would disperse after this campaign. This was, in fact, in line with the formational dynamics of other youth groups at the time, not only in the Palestinian territories and Israel but also across the region (al-Shabaka, 2015; Policy Analysis Unit, 2012; Nabulsi, 2014.

Majd stated in his interview something that was later confirmed by other similar activists across the West Bank and Gaza: "Being unaffiliated with parties was an advantage and dissolving the group after merely one campaign was intentional." This statement contradicted much of the literature available on social movements and collective action. Scholars usually have pointed to their lack of organizational support and structure as the reason for the quick dissolution of these movements thereafter (Bayat, 2010; Ghonim, 2012; Herrera, 2014; Khatib and Lust, 2014). Other activists had spoken about a lack of strategy for what comes after a particular group organizes and successfully leads an online campaign, followed by a street protest.

But not in Majd's mind; he had also been present in the 15 March movement in the West Bank, and had participated in various similar protests in Haifa. He explained that in their context, being independent implied opening up a space for expressions around issues that pertained to their daily lives, which were not priorities in the parties' ideological agendas. According to him, these issues brought together young people from different groups within the Palestinians of Israel. Majd also stated that he had understood from previous protests, including the 15 March movement, that every group that extends its life beyond the goal of the campaign will sooner or later run into conflict with other groups/organizations/parties and will be crushed. In his own words,

There was an advantage to our insistence to being independent groups, not affiliated with any parties. We learned that being non-political made it easier for us to bring different groups of people together. And being non-confrontational with Parties meant that they did not interfere with our activities as long as we did not side with any particular ideological agenda. (Personal Communication, January 15, 2016)

This quote explains how the lack of political affiliations coupled with the new opportunities afforded by the SMNs generated the formation of multiple youth groups and increased the diversity of their composition. This strategic approach, according to Majd, accounts for the success of bringing together various similar independent youth groups across Northern and Southern Israel.

When it comes to the effect of social media in this campaign, Majd's reflections on its empowering as well as limiting capacity in coordinating and mobilizing are also important to mention here. Majd was initially very excited and aware about the powerful role of the social media for his generation: to express what is happening in the street, with no filter, from people to people. He admitted how creating a Facebook page and its first campaign "Hungry for Freedom" was a first easy step for him and the six other funding members of his group. The youth group, later composed of twelve members, published their first call for solidarity with the hunger strikers. Majd recalls how they did everything by themselves, even the T-shirts that they spray-painted black. Some members of the group took over the social media work—including networking with other Palestinian groups. Other groups focused on the logistics of organizing in the street. They deliberately chose public sites for their protests, some of the most prominent streets in Haifa, such as Ben Gurion Street, which is full of trendy cafés and popular restaurants.

Right here at the intersection of online and offline preparations for this campaign, Majd realized the first pitfall of a social media campaign. Despite the fact that the campaign had generated a lot of awareness online, Majd was surprised by the stark reality he discovered on the ground. His participation in this street protest in Haifa shocked him about a different reality—completely different from the political discussions in the Hebrew University campus in East Jerusalem, or from his friend network on Facebook, or from the 15 March demonstrations in Ramallah, where he had personally participated. There in the street, in Haifa, he met people that knew nothing about Palestinian political prisoners.

> On Facebook you express yourself with ease, you talk about support, you show solidarity, etc. But then you get out on the street. And you realize .. . people there don't know anything, they don't even know who is called a political prisoner and why. So much for the brave history of heroism and patriotic feelings we had shared on Facebook. But try getting that message in the street! They don't really care about your patriotic feelings, so you

realize that if you really want to talk to them, you need to know how to get their attention, because just national pride itself will not cut it. (Personal Communication, January 15, 2016)

This quote of Majd exemplifies the realization of the group about how social media was great to reach out to people, but primarily to people who believed or already shared similar opinions. Online, Hungry for Freedom's initial objective to express solidarity with the political prisoners in a hunger strike was successfully achieved. Yet offline, the young organizers realized the wide internal divisions within their own society.

Just a few kilometers south of the city of Haifa, lives Maysan, aged twenty-five, another participant from the Hungry for Freedom protest. When asked about her reasons for joining the campaign (she was twenty-one years old at the time), she shared a quite different story from that of Majd. Maysan stated that her motivation stemmed from her own personal background and life story.

Being a Druze and joining a group that was campaigning for Palestinian political prisoners, is quite a paradox—It just didn't make sense, neither to Palestinians nor to Israelis. This is a big problem that's keeping us from protesting effectively. So I decided to join. (Personal Communication, December 2, 2016)

This quote indicates that Maysan's decision, as a Druze, to join a political cause for Palestinians, was a concrete attempt to overcome internal divisions among the different communities in Israel. Maysan was born in Isfyah, a Druze village nestled on Mount Carmel in Northern Israel. In the previous section of this chapter, different minority groups living in Israel, including the Druze population and their relations with the State of Israel, were briefly explained. According to her, the Israeli government systematically undermines the cohesiveness of the Palestinian community in Israel, just like it did with the Druze population in 1956, at that time requiring their conscription into the army. As a consequence of that policy, Israel designates the Druze as a national group distinct from the rest of the Palestinian minority.

Now actively involved in campaigns against Druze conscription for military service, Maysan shared a vivid memory from her teenage years. It was an event that, according to her, marked the beginning of her quest for identity and belonging in the State of Israel. In 2008, at the time when Israel's Operation

Cast Lead was taking place in Gaza, Maysan was in high school. One day, to express her solidarity with the Palestinians of Gaza, she decided to go to school wearing a black and white *keffiyeh*. That day, Maysan was prohibited from stepping inside the school by her school principal because of her scarf. Her peers, other students who called her "a terrorist," also castigated her. "I was shocked," recalls Maysan, "This is my village, my people! They know me! How can they call me a terrorist?"

Maysan's sudden realization, as evident in the above quote, was that her action of wearing a Palestinian *keffiyeh* or not defined her relationship with her fellow friends and within her community. In many ways, Maysan's fight with the school principal became a recurrent theme in her quest for identity and loyalty vis-à-vis the Israeli state and her Palestinian-Arab identity. "To Israeli Jews, Druze, no matter what they do, no matter how they serve the country, will always be Arabs; and to the rest of the Palestinians, Druze, no matter what they do, will always be traitors."

Maysan's personal struggle and her activism are very much defined and shaped by the characteristics of the Druze community in Israel and the particular relationships of this group with the Israeli State. Her story serves here to explain her rationale for deciding to participate in "Hungry for Freedom," a campaign that focused on a "non-Druze" cause, such as the Palestinian Political Prisoners.

Likewise, Maysan admitted the influence of the events of the Arab Spring in the actions of the Palestinians of Israel. Still, like Majd, she seemed very clear about the opportunities and the limitations that social media presented for this group of activists:

> I believe in working directly with individuals—yes we can reach a lot of people on social media who like, share and support our activism here in Israel. But mostly these people already think like us, so they are not helping us to reach those that think differently from us. But when you meet individuals from very different groups—and you to talk to them not as an outsider, but make them understand what's happening, and discover that you are not that much different, despite being from another group, that's real success for me.

Both Majd and Maysan indicate that the lessons they had learned from their online and offline interactions taught them how to bridge the gap between online and offline realities and what issues should they rally around to best support this endeavor. Although interviewed separately, they both expressed that what they had learned from campaigns such as Hungry for Freedom was how to be more collective and not to forget to be inclusive of the different groups of the Palestinian society in Israel.

The Hungry for Freedom campaign was presented as a specific example here to demonstrate that a growing network of activists across the Green Line was active in a series of protests during 2011–12 in Israel. While the online success of this campaign is well documented,[39] the offline experiences of the activists involved directly in this campaign were presented here to explain how and why certain issues resonated better with these youth groups and to what degree did social media affect their mobilizing and coordinating efforts.

A common conclusion gathered from various interviews across Israel and Palestine is that their national identity and its expression are greatly shaped by living in the Jewish State of Israel. As a result, in reacting to Israel's government policies that imposed discriminatory divisions between the Arabs and the Jews in Israel, these young people appeared to grasp even more firmly onto their Palestinian heritage and nationality. While enabling connection across the border, social media networks had also exposed the vulnerabilities of these youth groups: reaching and talking to networks of like-minded people such as themselves across the border. This deeply influenced the extent of the reach of their offline campaigns, where these activists realized the immense barriers dividing different groups of Palestinians living in Israel.

In this context and building on previous protests such as Hungry for Freedom, we turn now to the analysis of the Prawer Movement.

Prawer Plan

Maysan received the news of the passing of the Prawer Plan into Israeli law via the Twitter feed on her mobile phone. In her interview with me, she explained that for almost two years she had been part of this network of Palestinian youth across borders: "Together for Change."[40] She told me that, to her, this was not a unique Bedouin challenge which called for Bedouin activism. She did not think that it was enough to mobilize only public advocates of Bedouin land rights issues, legal court files, or specialized NGOs on indigenous rights.

To her mind, everyone who is not Jewish in Israel is threatened by discriminatory policies of the State of Israel, so they should stand up together.

As explained in some earlier sections of this chapter, to Maysan the key to making a protest successful was its broad-based participation by various sections of the Palestinian-Arab communities in Israel. To her, Al Arakib was not a unique Bedouin village. Their house demolitions and status as "unrecognized" were not strictly a Bedouin issue either. Just as I indicated in another part of this chapter, she concluded that the refusal to comply with military conscription of Druze in the Israeli Army was not simply a Druze issue, hence a matter for only "Druze activism." In line with her conviction that state policies toward various groups of the Palestinians of Israel are designed to undermine the cohesiveness of a Palestinian community in Israel, Maysan rejected the notion of a purely "Bedouin struggle" and opted instead to define it as a "Palestinian struggle":

> Listen: The land appropriation, house demolitions, unrecognized villages- are not unique for those of us who live here. They (Israelis) are building settlements on Palestinian lands in the West Bank, while also pushing us out from our historic land here in Israel. They have destroyed so many houses in my village. I see house demolitions happening all over the country on a regular basis. In addition, about 200 Arab houses in my village don't have electricity, because the Israeli Housing Authority does not consider them as legal housing. (Personal Communication, January 2, 2017)

Maysan's quote indicates her awareness about the similar situation on the ground for various segments of the Palestinian community inside and outside of Israel and their common predicament. The path that led her to this Palestinian consciousness seemed gradual and characterized by increased personal and online contacts between her peers beyond the Green Line. This is indicated in the creation of a youth group "Together for Change" as an online project uniting youth from the West Bank, Gaza, and Israel to discuss and work together on problems facing Palestinian youth. About 250,000 young people shared and followed the activities of this group.[41]

This group, as reported by the Association for Arab Youth, Baladna, in its 2013–14 report, with its social media following from Palestinians of all regions, has helped to increase contacts between these various segments of the Palestinian population. Maysan integrated into this lively network of activists, facilitated primarily by the Internet, mobile phones, and social media platforms. She maintains that such online ties overcame the geographical divisions between the West Bank, Gaza, and Israel and strengthened their Palestinian nationalistic feeling.

This was evident particularly in the protests she organized and participated in against the backdrop of the Arab Spring. In 2010, coordinating primarily via SMNs, hers and other youth groups in Haifa had been staging solidarity protests with Tunisian and Egyptian revolutions. In 2011, she was helping various youth groups in the West Bank with their 15 March movement, and she was a key organizer and participant of a series of street protests in Haifa, including "Hungry for Freedom." In 2012, she was one of the key founders of the "Urfod" movement, aimed at refusing Druze military conscription into the Israeli Army.

Maysan's experiences from her life as an activist serve to explain how her participation in this campaign was not a reaction to the Prawer Plan alone. Maysan, Majd, and other activists I spoke to indicate the existence of a growing network of activists, who had organized a number of other protests in the period of 2011–13, primarily inspired by the Arab Spring. Their combined experiences in various protests across the Palestinian territories laid the groundwork for what turned out to be an impressive youth mobilization of Palestinians of Israel. The Prawer bill presented a great opportunity.

Maysan explained how she and her friends mobilized and coordinated their action in preparation for street protests. Initially, Maysan got directly involved in an online Facebook campaign called "PrawerShallnotPass,"[42] which called for every Palestinian to join the protests against "the biggest Israeli land grab since 1948."[43] Next, she led a small group of activists to stage a protest in their own Druze village, determined to tell their community what was going on in the Negev. With a group of friends, she waved a banner that they had quickly created together: "Stop the Prawer Plan! Today it is visiting the Negev; tomorrow it will be here. We are in this together!"

In the last week of June and the entire month of July 2013, groups of youth from established networks, such as the Haifa Movement stood at traffic roundabouts, entered cafés and restaurants, and talked to people in the street about what was happening in the Negev.[44] They also distributed leaflets in villages such as Sakhnin, Isfyah, and Wadi Ara. After midnight, they sprayed graffiti on the walls and other visible urban sites in Haifa. This outreach strategy of speaking to communities (both in urban areas and in villages), making videos, displaying posters, sharing tweets, and posting updates on their Facebook page demonstrates the grassroots groundwork that these activists did before the actual protests or the "Days of Rage."

This in-person coordination was also coupled with increased efforts to raise awareness through social media networks, particularly Twitter and Facebook. Widely shared hashtags, such as #StopPrawerPlan and #AngerStrike, spread the news and triggered solidarity among various Palestinian youth networks in the West Bank,[45] Gaza,[46] East Jerusalem, and those in the diaspora.[47] In the wake of these instantaneous online youth actions, initiated primarily via social media platforms, several major street protests soon followed.

As a result of such online and offline coordinating efforts, on July 15 and August 1, 2013, thousands of young Palestinian protesters from Southern and Northern Israel took to the streets to demonstrate against the Prawer Plan. About 1,000 activists demonstrated in Hura,[48] a Bedouin area in the Negev (Naqab) desert, where many Bedouin villages are located. Simultaneously, a protest in the city of Haifa[49] in Northern Israel took place. Next, the activists moved to Wadi Ara, all across the Upper and Lower Galilee in Northern Israel, spreading the geography of the protest sites as far as southern Tel Aviv, where they blocked traffic and marched through the streets of the City of Jaffa.

To quell such unexpected uprisings, Israeli police responded swiftly and with excessive force.[50] Images[51] of the Israeli riot police, Special Forces and Mounties, violently arresting hundreds of activists[52] went viral on various SMNs. In light of such a strong response by the State of Israel, the PrawerPlanShallNot Pass group called on their Facebook page for another "Day of Rage" on November 30, 2013.

This time, youth groups from Gaza, the West Bank and East Jerusalem coordinated their actions in a timely manner with the young Palestinians of Israel.[53] As planned, on November 30, 2013, dozens of Palestinians rallied in Gaza City's Palestine Square, joining a "Day of Rage" against the Prawer-Begin Plan. In Ramallah, the West Bank, over 100 Palestinians and international activists took part in the demonstration in solidarity with the Bedouins of the Negev Desert. In East Jerusalem, youth groups protested in front of the Damascus Gate of the Old City.

Two weeks later, on December 12, 2013, Prime Minister Benjamin Netanyahu's government decided to drop the draft of the bill to resettle nearly 30,000 Bedouin living in the Negev.[54] The reasons, as declared by various state actors, were unrelated with these youth-led movements of the Palestinians of Israel, which lasted for almost six months. Yet, in light of all formal internal and external efforts to stop the Prawer Plan, this spontaneous youth-led movement seemed to have temporarily succeeded in preventing the Israeli government from turning the controversial bill into a law. For the activists involved in the movement they had no doubt that it was their success.[55]

Concluding remarks

This chapter examined the efforts of Palestinian youth activists in Israel to organize and coordinate the Prawer Movement. Seen together as a collection of Palestinian protests in the West Bank, Gaza, and Israel, these protests fit well in the overall scope of this book: the emergence of networked Palestinian youth movements in the post–Arab Spring context.

While tracing the trajectory of this movement within Israel, I have also etched out the particular national and regional conditions that shaped their mobilization modes and motivated the framing of their protests. The Prawer protests marked a turning point in the political awareness of young Palestinians of Israel. It was the first broad-based youth movement that took place outside the controlling structures of the Arab parties of Israel while managing to transcend the fragmentations and internal division between various Palestinian groups of Israel. The movement started off as a matter of Bedouin land rights within Israel. But thanks to a growing network of activists with personal and online ties across the Green Line, it turned into a movement for Palestinian national rights.

Included in this analysis is a series of protests that were organized prior to the culmination of the youth mobilizations of the Palestinians of Israel in the Stop the Prawer Movement. In 2011 alone, these young Palestinians of Israel had organized street demonstrations in Tel Aviv and Jaffa in January 2011, on 15 March (2011) and the Hungry for Freedom campaign on October 15, 2011. By linking these seemingly isolated events and campaigns in a sustained chain of protests, against the backdrop of the Arab Spring, it demonstrates how a nascent-networked movement is taking place outside the controlling structure of the Arab Parties and the Government of Israel.

The organizers of these movements have been identified here as a group of activists whose tendency to grasp more tightly to their Palestinian identity seems in part a reaction to contemporary Israeli politics which severely controls and limits their ability to protest and demand their rights as citizens within Israel. Still, as this study shows overall, the ability of these activists to coordinate such massive youth mobilization, despite physical boundaries, geographical barriers, and the efforts of the Israeli government to control and crush their actions, is remarkable.

The evolving nature of the mobilizing patterns of Palestinians of Israel includes decreased affiliation with parties and increased reliance on digital networks for coordination and mobilization. These developments are also in line with an emerging mobilizing pattern that I have demonstrated throughout this book while examining different protests across different Palestinian geographical areas. Through direct interviews with a dozen Palestinian activists of Israeli citizenship, I have also suggested the potential of a growing network of activists across borders, whose strategic approach and coordination efforts culminated in the successful mobilization of the Prawer Movement.

7

General Conclusions

"If you disregard people's motives, it becomes much harder to foresee their actions."

George Orwell

My goal throughout this study was to explain the relationship between digital networks and new forms of youth activism within a Palestinian context, marked by territorial fragmentation, Israel's ongoing military occupation, and two divided Palestinian political systems in the West Bank and Gaza. I have sought to demonstrate in each chapter how some groups of Palestinian youth, politically marginalized and unaffiliated with parties, have taken it upon themselves to seek out new movements and to participate in new venues of activism through more informal, horizontal, and globally informed networks. SMNs have played a significant role in facilitating this networked activism and in propelling these protests from the margins toward the center of the Palestinian politics.

Some of the most recent developments in Palestine and Israel still unfolding at the time of writing this book, seem to reinforce the increasing relevance of the main topic of this book: the evolving role of digital networks and Palestinian youth activism in the era of Internet. Other ongoing protests, new and traditional forms of political mobilization, seem to raise new questions, depending on how they evolve from now. While events like the rise of Ahed Tamimi as an online symbol of Palestinian resistance in Nabi Saleh and the ongoing weekly protests known as the Great March of Return in Gaza were both initiated and spread via SMNs, their mobilizing outcomes and trajectories have been very different.

The example of Ahed Tamimi demonstrated how social media can shine a light on and amplify existing and ongoing non-violent and decentralized grassroots movements, empowering local leaders on the ground. The Great March of Return demonstrated how these movements can take a completely different turn when formal organizations with hierarchical forms of mobilization seek to control the on-the-ground evolution of these online calls from independent youth networks. In this context, the Nabi Saleh case has demonstrated that it can blend more successfully cases of digital activism due to their decentralized forms of grassroots organizing, without the party-driven activism in their weekly protests that have been going on for a decade by now.

This seems to back one of the claims of this book that the uses of social media for activism can be as different as their venues and political realities in which they originate and evolve. The contentious politics, the territorial fragmentation, and Israel's occupation affect in different ways the everyday lives and mobilization modes of these activists in the West Bank and Gaza. As such, this book has argued that digital networks alone cannot fully explain the mobilizing outcomes of these movements, unless they are studied at the intersection of the online activism and offline dynamics of the very different contexts in which they take place and evolve.

Regardless of the final outcomes of these movements, I have suggested against dismissing these movements as insignificant, just because they fail in the face of authoritarian Palestinian rulers or Israeli military violence and online surveillance. Such a dismissive approach to analysis severely underestimates the contextual constraints that these activists have to operate under and leaves unexamined the novel forms of resistance that emerge as they seek to overcome those obstacles. These youth groups operate in a political environment where they face direct sanctions from Hamas, the PA, and the Government of Israel for every movement that shows promise of evolving into an alternative to that of the post-Oslo political frameworks.

Various chapters in this book have given examples of the constant change of their mobilizations modes, their frequent occurrence in unexpected venues and formats of organizing, and the ongoing lookout for alternative and better ways of organizing. Alternating between online and offline modes of mobilizing and changing their organizing tactics frequently appears to be the only realistic choice for many of this activists toiling under Palestinian oppression and Israel's military occupation. I have proposed to view these protests instead as a growing and networked cycle of revolts and confrontations, alternating carefully between online and offline dynamics while seeking to resist both forces of oppression—internal and external.

Palestinian protests and new networked movements in the Internet age

In this study, I debated with a growing body of research that tends to analyze the potential impact of these protest movements primarily through the lenses of their connections to organized formal activism on the ground (Beinin and Vairel, 2011; Gelvin, 2012; Ajami, 2012; Council on Foreign Relations, 2011; Khatib and Lust, 2014; Herrera, 2014; Hoigilt, 2013, 2015). These scholars have focused primarily on the organizational and strategic deficiencies of these newer movements as the main reason for their inability to affect long-term political change. As a result, we know more about why these movements fail, but far less about why these young activists prefer loose networks of mobilization and under what conditions they might take off and eventually succeed.

In order to understand the evolution of these movements in the age of SMNs, this book applied a mixed theoretical approach. It employed Castells's theory of new networked social movements while grounding the analysis of these youth mobilizations in their own particular contexts and providing a broader backdrop of the history of collective Palestinian movements.

Of particular interest for my own analysis in this book is the role that these networks play in mobilizing diverse and previously unconnected youth groups within authoritarian contexts, which have been covered in recent publications that examine the role of SMNs for collective action in the Middle East. The theoretical insights of Faris and Tohamy, for example, can explain some mobilizing outcomes grounded in Palestinian authoritarianism, but cannot fully account for another layer of dynamics that envelop these movements in the double context of repression and occupation.

It was suggested in the previous chapters that there exists a growing rift between activists that prefer to organize and mobilize primarily using digital networks and traditional parties or social movement organizations that rely on older forms of mobilizing and utilizing top-down leadership, large organizational resources, and rigid ideological agendas. The central tension, at the core of the relations between newer forms of protests and more traditional forms of collective engagement, have overall transformed the Palestinian arena of youth activism and political mobilization in some unexpected ways.

First, it signaled the return of the Palestinian youth to the streets, on their own terms with their own ideas and political solutions. Despite ups and downs in mobilizing outcomes, errors in strategic calculations, internal group cohesion issues, and so forth, the youth presence in the streets of Gaza, the West Bank, and inside of Israel has resulted in a renewed spirit of community organizing and resistance that the parties had previously undermined. These newer forms of protests revealed an ongoing process of experimentation, always subject to adaptation and further evolution.

Second, more than convincing their parties or their society, these loosely coordinated youth groups were able to convince, above all, themselves about their power to organize outside the existing mobilizing structures of large organizations with broad resources. The case studies brought under analysis in this book demonstrated that with the right fusion of an innovative idea for action, the right social tool for spreading awareness, and the initial cohesion of a small collection of activists, they were able to achieve successful and at times massive youth mobilizations. Such large-scale youth mobilizations were previously possible only within the reach of the organizational structures such as the official parties or social movement organizations.

In spite of the differences in contexts, goals, and demands of youth activists, my research identified the persistence of key features in these Palestinian protests, as common to new social networked movements. These common features relate to the onset of mobilizations primarily on digital networks, their eventual transformation into street protests, and the tendency for themes to draw on the emotional hardships or everyday realities that shape the lives of activists and propel them to action. It is in these seemingly irrelevant daily events where increased feelings of distrust and cynicism toward the institutional actors—which do too little for the people—accumulate and then spread via digital networks. Finally, these Palestinian protests were led by masses of youth, unaffiliated with established political parties and distrustful of their political leadership.

Through the identification and study of these elements, this study has not only sought to include these Palestinian protests movements in the narrative of the Arab Spring but also positioned them in the expanding arena of ongoing globally networked movements in this digital age.

Key findings

I began by asking why and how, in the face of political intimidation, geographic segregations, and sheer violence, did these youth groups come together to protest and demand change, as is evident in their sustained chain of protests between 2011 and 2013. What propelled these young people to abandon the safety of their online dissent for the uncertainty of street mobilization? How did the organizers of these protests transform their emotional online calls into courageous street action and what did it mean to them to overcome their fear, knowing that they were risking everything and yet still choosing to participate in these protests?

To answer these questions, the chapters of this study drew on a number of important youth protests in the West Bank, Gaza, and Israel and their evolution beyond the events of the Arab Spring. In the Gaza Strip, I focused on the online and offline dynamics of the GYBO youth group. The developmental trajectory of this and other youth groups was chronicled from the global ripples caused by the call to action on their Facebook pages, to the sudden burst of the 15 March movement, where thousands of youth took to the streets of Gaza to demand the end of the division between the two main Palestinian parties. In particular this case study revealed the emotional and political repercussions that this movement experienced afterward in the daily lives of the founders of this group.

In the West Bank the book examined a wave of youth-led protests that took place between 2011 and 2013, organized by a youth group called "Palestinians for Dignity" (PFD), created in the aftermath of the 15 March movement. Evident in this chapter is the constant search of the activists for a renewed strategy of resistance and their desire to articulate a new vision for the Palestinian cause.

Inside Israel, the study shed light on the sudden explosion of youth mobilizations of young Palestinian citizens of Israel, as is evident in the "Stop the Prawer" movement, a Palestinian youth movement initiated within Israel that grew cross the border beyond the Green Line. I focused on their online and offline tactics to spread awareness and overcome their own internal divisions caused by internal dynamics of the different Palestinians groups, vis-à-vis the State of Israel.

Although each chapter presented different trajectories for the development of different protests, within the timeline of 2011–13, the analytical focus in this book remained consistent. I traced the online and offline formational dynamics of these youth groups—their intentions, motivations, and actions—as they evolved from the online space of digital networks where they first expressed dissent, to the offline challenges of street protests where they demanded change. In the process, I embedded the ups and downs of their movements in their own political and social contexts in Gaza, the West Bank, and Israel. Simultaneously, I examined their motivations for online and offline action, by intertwining within the narratives of their movements and their personal life stories. Ultimately, this book sought to provide a glimpse of the complex realities of the everyday political organizing of these Palestinian youth groups in the age of the Internet.

I argued that these online campaigns and offline protests signaled a turning point in the ways young Palestinians mobilize and organize, thus laying the groundwork for a new networked Palestinian social movement, developing outside the structures of official parties and formal political organizations. Particularly within a Palestinian context marked by segregation walls, military checkpoints, and internal political intimidation, social media networks and increased social media literacy among Palestinian youths enabled this collection of protest movements to move from the margins of the Palestinian society, after the Second Intifada, to its center.

In addition to the frequent use of social media networks to express political dissent and call for online and offline protests, they have made the work of activists more effective, particularly in their context of political repression and military violence. While the Israeli efforts to contain Ahed Tamimi's story was called "Israel's PR disaster," these digital tools have often saved these activists from prolonged time in jail as a result of global pressure put on the Palestinian or Israeli authorities for their release.

The findings in this study involve three key areas: (1) the internal and external conditions that determined the transformation of certain actions initiated on digital networks into street protests led by youth groups in Palestine; (2) the degree to which social media, online networks, and new forms of activism in this digital age affected the more traditional mobilization modes, as implemented by the official Palestinian parties and more conventional party-affiliated youth organizations in each separate geographic area; and (3) the long-term impact of these youth groups and their newer mobilization modes within their society and their current predicament and relations with existing grassroots movements within the occupied Palestinian territories.

Motivational factors for new Palestinian youth movements

Online dissent and offline social networks

The initial online actions of these youth groups were emotion-driven, expressed and accumulated primarily in the online digital platforms such as Facebook and Twitter and in the blogosphere. These emotional online expressions were consistently triggered by small events happening in small villages and towns, in the streets, offices, cafés, and other shared public spaces in Gaza, the West Bank, and Israel. Often, such triggering events are far from developments that indicate major shifts or crises in the relations between the Palestinian parties or in the Palestinian-Israeli conflict. In my analysis, they appear rather as abrupt episodes that disrupted the daily lives of some young people already living difficult lives.

Such recurrent and personalized online outbursts happened in tandem with the growing social media literacy by the vast majority of these Palestinian youth groups. Most of these personal emotions of discontent and outrage had been channeled in one particular digital platform or another. Also, the spark of the Arab Spring ignited a Palestinian blogosphere already seething in discontent and anger and lit a very different fire in the Palestinian context, evident in the 15 March movement in Gaza, the West Bank, and even inside Israel.

The story of GYBO was raised as an example in Gaza. The closure of an independent Palestinian youth NGO by the Hamas authorities triggered an outraged online response by a group of young people in Gaza. Feeling devastated, they reacted by writing an online manifesto, whose reverberations went viral instantly and were spread via global networks of action. Although they faced direct consequences for their online dissent against Hamas, some of GYBO's members went on and became the organizers of one of the biggest youth mobilizations seen in the streets of Gaza since the Second Intifada. Others opted to drop their association with GYBO.

To better understand how these shared experiences of discontent resonated emotionally with a broader number of young Palestinians and how they translated into widespread street mobilizations, I also referred to a broad online survey of Palestinian online engagement patterns, conducted during the period of 2011–13.

My study exposed a multiplicity of similar Palestinian youth groups who were experimenting, producing, and consuming personalized content in free online spaces—away from the control of their ruling governments. Taken together, these sites represented growing and solidifying digital communications networks, as well as the Palestinian youth's growing preferences for nonhierarchical communication forms and free exploration of new ideas.

I concluded that underneath this online ventilation of resentment in Palestinian society, a vast network of like-minded young people who were producing and sharing content expressing this discontent were finding each other online. This online dissent, however fraught with internal tension, became fundamental to the formation of a consciousness by a growing network of young Palestinians, who, although predominantly online, were still struggling to define a common set of norms that would bind them together under a new brand of Palestinian youth activism.

It is important to recognize here that the bitter realization of people like Abu Yazan (GYBO) about their complete inability to influence the "legitimate" political actors and structures is still relevant at the time of writing this book. Voices like the ones brought in this book are consistently muted, and the aspirations of individuals like these young activists that organized these protests are not recognized. It is this shared experience of invisibility that fuels such alternative Palestinian networks of engagement.

The Arab Spring and the Palestinian mobilizations of 2011

The production of Palestinian personalized content in the blogosphere, together with the multiplicity of these lesser known protests, evident in the three in-depth case studies analyzed in my research, gives credibility to one of the propositions of this study: that the Palestinian protests are not an exception, but an appropriate addition to the narrative of the Arab Spring.

Unlike some scholarly conclusions, which question the notion of a Palestinian Spring (Hillal, 2011; Hoigilt, 2013, 2015), I conclude in this book that there actually was a Palestinian Spring, but one, which took a different path due to the unique Palestinian context. Young Palestinians, for the first time in the history of Palestinian youth activism, rose publicly and collectively and took to the streets against their own leaders, parties, and establishment. The controversial 15 March youth movement, which took place simultaneously in Gaza, the West Bank, and within Israel, was inspired by the way other young Arabs rose up against their states' corrupt institutions and authoritarian regimes, demanding political change. These mobilizations demonstrated that these youth activists were not sitting on the sidelines, but were in fact at the frontline, in solidarity with the demands for change of their Arab peers. The new Arab demands for change left a deep impression in the young Palestinians' hearts and minds, propelling them to break the barrier of fear and assert their role in the Palestinian streets. By turning against their divided leadership, while simultaneously resisting Israel's occupation, they introduced the notion that the Palestinian struggle must be waged on two parallel fronts: internal and external.

This scattered collection of Palestinian youth movements may not have shown a clear political strategy or core vision, but it did reveal what lit the emotions and inspired the shift in the core demands of these youths. While it has not changed or affect the unity of the parties, it made clear the intention and commitment of a new group of activists in search of an alternative, more inclusive, and inspiring strategy. This foundational strategy, evident in the PFD protests and campaigns, rejected the sole emphasis on the occupation over that of authoritarian governance, thus undermining the ability of Palestinian ruling organizations to control and direct these newer forms of youth activism.

Palestinian youth between "old" and "new" forms of collectivity

The ways in which these new forms of Palestinian youth activism in this digital age affected the more traditional mobilization modes, as implemented by official parties and conventional organizations, are directly tied to the ongoing debate over the role of the digital networks for organizing, mobilizing, and achieving political change.

I have suggested in this study an ongoing decline in the ability of the Palestinian parties or more formal structures to direct and control the scope of these newer forms of Palestinian youth activism. The case studies in this book, demonstrate a series of youth protests taking place outside of their organizing structures, led by independent youth groups who intentionally bypass formal leadership and prefer to instead coordinate primarily through digital networks.

While conventional organizations like Hamas and Fatah and other key formal actors in the Palestinian context relied heavily on rigid organizational structures and top-down modes of mobilization, the young Palestinians I studied preferred loosely coordinated actions facilitated primarily online, far from those formal Palestinian actors. The cases of GYBO, PFD, and Hungry for Freedom revealed in detail how members of these youth groups were connected online with like-minded peers across the West Bank and Gaza and managed to circumvent the censorship and top-down authoritarian organizations of the main Palestinian factions.

The fundamental characteristics of the new communication technologies, with their most important functions of personalizing and sharing, enabled the GYBO, PFD, and "Stop the Prawer" movement activists to shake up the practice of "top-down communication as usual" by parties and NGOs. Young Palestinians from Gaza, the West Bank, and inside of Israel occupied this medium and created personalized messages as individuals fed up with the hierarchies of their political structures and the public narratives imposed by their leaders. This significant deviation in the communication patterns enabled alternative youth mobilizations in the form of online and offline cycles of protests. Because of the social media networks, these Palestinian youths were able to overcome their geographic separations and organize protests that were previously out of their reach and could not be orchestrated outside of traditional organizational structures.

The case of the PFD in the West Bank, as well as the way its members were able to share content and information about their actions instantly and raise awareness about their protests through their ties with global networks of action, confirms the same conclusion. I have described here how territorial fragmentation, military borders, and internal political divisions marked the Palestinians' everyday experience. Yet, coordination and exposure through social media networks played a crucial role in allowing youth to overcome these obstacles and organize impressive youth mobilizations across borders. Moreover, the "Stop the Prawer Plan" movement in Israel was also coordinated primarily online through digital networks, indicating the growing influence of a network of activists who were able to expand, maintain, and strengthen ties across borders between Israel and Palestine.

Long-term impact of new networked Palestinian movements

Often these youth groups have been criticized for their inability to move from a series of scattered protests into a massive sustained organized movement with potential to have tangible influence on the Palestinian sociopolitical landscape. To address the question of the long-term impact of these new forms of social movements in this digital age, I examined the actual impact of the protests of these joined networks in two ways: (1) the effect that they had on the personal lives of the youth and their formation and evolution as activists and (2) the effect on the relationships of these groups with existing grassroots movements within Palestinian society. The findings here are particularly important because they tie directly into my overall argument about the multiplicity of movements growing outside of formal parties and political organizations.

My interviews with seasoned Palestinian activists[1] of nonviolent popular resistance and pioneers of the First Intifada indicated that some of the newer groups of activists have in fact connected and aligned strategically with older existing non violent grassroots movements on the ground. The activists of the PFD in particular were active participants in the activities of the Stop the Wall campaign, which coordinates grassroots and nonviolent demonstrations against the Israeli construction of the separation barrier and land confiscation in the West Bank. The Stop the Wall movement, otherwise known as the "popular resistance," is a loosely coordinated commitee that has creatively and sustainbly fueled an enduring form of active and organized resistance to the Israeli presence in the West Bank since the end of the Second Intifada in 2005.

Another link that PFD developed with these grassroots committees was through their weekly demonstration in the Nabi Saleh protests against the expansion of settlements in the West Bank. Finally, a last example of the alignments of these groups with other broader networks of actions is their connections to the BDS movement. In the chapter on West Bank, I indicated how the "Freedom Rides" campaign was utilized by the BDS movement to push for divestment by Veolia—the French company that, at the time, provided bus transportation for Jewish Israeli settlers in the West Bank.

The case of PFD and the youth-led protests at the time marked a new phase of linking between the emerging group of actors who initiated their actions through online social networks and other existing decentralized grassroots activism, led by popular resistance committees across the West Bank. From their interaction with these other grassroots movements, youth groups also strengthened their links to broader Palestinian society by building intercommunity trust and by joining together in street protests. This enhanced mobilizing strategy significantly contributed to popular nonviolent resistance efforts, which have been occurring over the years in the West Bank.

I also examined whether the newer mobilizing forms of these youth groups affected these more traditional ongoing popular movements within Palestinian society. In my interviews with some eminent activists from the first and second intifadas, leaders of West Bank grassroots movements described some of the gains that had resulted from the linking of popular resistance with the efforts of these youth groups. One of these gains was a surge of creativity in the repertoire of Palestinian nonviolent resistance because of these young people and their ideas for protests.

As a result of the constant renewal and variation between online and offline tactics and the social media links that these youth groups brought with them, some grassroots movements in the West Bank received more attention in the form of international media coverage and global online exposure. The examples brought in my study were the Nabi Saleh protests, the "Bab al-Shams" campaign and the "Stop the Prawer" movement within Israel.

Another novelty that these youth groups introduced through their protests was an element of spontaneity and surprise, which often caught both Israeli and Palestinian authorities off guard. A direct consequence of such an approach is evident in their strategy of switching targets of protest between the PA and Israel, as seen in the systematic chain of protests that the Palestinians for Dignity organized between 2011 and 2013. This type of fluctuation in protests and unpredictability in targeting inhibited the ability of the PA and Israeli authorities to control or permanently stop these types of mobilization by the youth groups.

I also discussed with these youth activists and more traditional grassroots leaders the prevalent conclusions of scholars and analysts about how critical it is for youth groups to align with powerful institutional actors. These youth activists also persistently asked a question, that according to them, is left unanswered: Why are they criticized for trying something new that didn't work out? What, they ask have their parties done that has actually worked out? While they appeared very aware of the criticism, and somewhat concerned and uncertain, they mentioned that the point often missing in such analysis is the perspective of these activists about why they choose to remain apart, instead of falling in line behind one party or another. They are dissatisfied with the feeling of being caught in the ongoing "old guard" insistence that "you're either with us or against us."

In short, from the perspective of these young activists, the trust in their parties was lost the moment it became clear to them that they could no longer influence them. My research shows that Palestinian youths possess a strong desire to have a voice in the shaping of their present and future. This is why the youths so strongly demanded the political unity between the two main Palestinian factions. Until now, this demand has gone unacknowledged by their parties, and this is reflected in the dissipation of the emotional bonds and affinity of the youths to their parties.

New questions for further research

I now move to some anomalies that this study discovered but could not thoroughly explain. Such inconclusive results are worth mentioning here because they may suggest further areas of research. Having exposed a rupture between the mobilizing forms of the youth groups analyzed in this study, I also want to stress that the point of my study is not at all to conclude that the hold of the traditional Palestinian parties on Palestinian society is over.

The sudden and unexpected youth mobilizations examined in this book indicated not only an emerging group of young activists who shed their political affiliations. Its immediate results also revealed how deeply entrenched the Palestinian parties are in the fabric of the Palestinian society. On the one hand, the expectation that one is either with one political faction or with the other made these youth groups appear weak or unimportant to various groups within Palestinian society. On the other hand, the parties were constantly trying to put "sticks in their wheels" to upend progress by a series of tactics exposed in this study such as infiltrating the movements from within by youth affiliated with the parties, targeting specific individuals in these youth groups and particularly the community reputation of female members.

These conditions forced the activists of the movements analyzed in this book to invest much more energy to keep their nascent movements together in the face of these constant efforts to undermine them, rather than thinking about the way ahead. In addition, the fact that some members of these youth groups had previously been members of party-affiliated youth organizations meant they had prior experience with activism rooted in the structures of the parties. Through their personal life stories covered in this study, I have consistently described how hard it has proven for these activists to escape the factional labels assigned to them based on their own families' perceived political affiliations. This significantly restricted young activists' ability to act independently in a sustained way.

One example of the depth of the political affiliations in Palestinian society are on display at Palestinian universities, where student organizations strongly aligned with each of the parties create a highly politicized environment. Despite the focus of this study on newer forms of activism generally taking place outside of university campuses, I have also indicated what a major challenge it is for Palestinian youth activists to mobilize students en masse in a sustained manner from within the universities, as had happened before and during the First Intifada. However I also pointed out how other studies have also concluded that university elections do not really translate into political loyalties of the students toward the respective parties (Casati, 2016). Behind the façade of high student voter turnout lies a distrustful body of Palestinian students, aware of preselected groups of students being groomed for future political careers in one party or another—with the rest being left aside. In fact, even among student politicians I've persistently felt a palpable sense of resignation about the inability to exert political influence, notwithstanding the fervent activity connected with student elections each spring semester.

Another anomaly that this book did not cover is the disengagement with the Palestinian parties in some cases, but then solidarity with them under certain other circumstances. These activists' search for new forms of activism takes place simultaneously with an emotional attachment to symbolic imagery and icons of the First Intifada which is both in their protests and in their posts online. This ongoing paradox of simultaneous online and offline allegiances is thus deeply rooted in the particularities of the Palestinian context as a nation without a state. The quest to understand why certain calls for political actions expand certain solidarity networks and deflate some others must take into consideration the ways these youth activists negotiate and accommodate between these two intertwined layers of alliances and loyalties in their lives.

Online and even in their demonstrations, they often embrace the heroic images of Palestinian youth as the drivers of collective resistance against Israel's occupation: the Palestinian flag, the iconic black and white *keffiyeh*, the home keys, and the patriotic songs hold deep symbolic meaning, imparted on them by their grandparents and parents.

Such performances of allegiance online speak to a deep desire to re-inscribe the consciousness of a national identity in the online space.

This online and offline collective imagery continues to enable stateless Palestinians to present publicly their enormous efforts to resist Israel's occupation and to maintain their national identity[2] against such impossible odds. By using multiple digital media platforms to convey two seemingly exclusive positions, these youths are forging new models of resistance. This model accommodates contradictory positions and presents them as interrelated. Through the symbolic and political allegiance to the Palestinian cause, they define their identities in the face of Israeli occupation and other external political actors that deny their political and cultural existence. By contrast, through their counter-narrative resistance to the official political, they nurture personalized modes of expressions, which translate into new forms of activism. Seen in this context, the initial broad mass mobilizations of the Great March of Return can start to make more sense.

I present these conclusions here because I do not want to suggest that the hold of these parties on their youth is over. Instead, I want to emphasize that the sustained cycles of protests that I analyzed represent a serious alternative to the traditional forms for protesting and mobilizing, as represented solely by parties within a Palestinian context. While these parties continue to have significant power, I have demonstrated that their capacity to draw on these newer forms of mobilizations is significantly weakening. As more advanced alternatives for individual and group action arise, this may pose a serious problem for the mass-mobilizing capacities of these powerful formal actors in the future.

Final thoughts

What did these types of movements accomplish within the Palestinian context? This question is especially important when trying to determine the broader explanatory value of this study. Did they fundamentally change the internal relations between the two parties? Did they dramatically reshape the Palestinians' relations with Israel and the rest of the world? What is the alternative to the decaying political institutions in Palestine represented by the authorities in Gaza and the West Bank and the formal political organizations such as the PFLP, the Democratic Front for the Liberation of Palestine, Hamas, and Fatah?

This study has found some answers to these questions while leaving other questions for further research. The persistence and success of the sustained chain of protest movements, led by these leaderless youth groups, demonstrate first and foremost a group of young people not sitting on the sidelines as described by party leaders, but in actuality, sitting right on the very frontlines of a growing movement. My case studies demonstrate the growing influence of a network of young Palestinians, born around the historical period of the Oslo Accords, as well as their persistent efforts to have their voice heard and to make their ideas count. These new forms of protest, facilitated primarily via social media, provided a grassroots alternative to the top-down activities organized by the Palestinian political parties and the PA.

Due to increased authoritarianism and in the face of ongoing Israeli occupation, some lessons activists have learned are thus: to not become a fixed body, a political party, or an NGO, but rather to stay loosely organized with the goal of remaining in touch with Palestinian society while avoiding power struggles with their parties.

What these networks have done so far is to filter small successes from a series of impressive protests while continuing to innovate and stay active. They have also suggested a way forward, which involves cycles of confrontation on many different fronts. I have pointed out in this study the risk of overlooking these emergent movements within the Palestinian society. The questions of strategy, short- or long-term political goals, and generally viable ways to measure the impact and effectiveness of these emerging networked movements on a broad scale should not override the lasting impact that these protests had on the activists themselves and the ongoing potential of newly forged personal connections and meaningful organizing skills that could be harnessed in the future with the right spark.

Observing the formational dynamics of these newer movements, even within the larger background of the Palestinian-Israeli field, is important. What is happening in these Palestinian cities and villages may appear disconnected or as isolated episodes of protests on the surface; yet, when studied more deeply, all of these various initiatives are intertwined. These silent, yet growing movements may provide a loose framework for action with the ability to set many factors into motion at the right time. While policy makers, academics, and political pundits point repeatedly at the absence of a unified body to lead these movements, I emphasize the growing presence of a network, however loose, that binds these movements on the ground and seeks not to control their evolution on the ground but to empower it.

Finally, providing human context while exploring the formational dynamics of these newer forms of movements was essential in this study. There is substantial analysis and research on major developments that have affected the past and present shifts in the Israeli-Palestinian conflict, Palestinian youth activism, and Palestinian popular resistance and grassroots movements. However, the perspectives of these young Palestinians are often mentioned in these studies only as an afterthought. Bringing into the body of this analysis the voices and experiences of young Palestinians, who do not normally make it into the news or broader scholarly analysis on the subject of Palestine and Israel, I believe, is a valid contribution.

These online and offline campaigns enabled the accumulation and integration of the multiple efforts of young people who contributed their own ideas in support of issues that resonated emotionally with them. These ideas did not need to be sought out for approval from higher or deeper chains of command. Some of them took off in the form of impressive youth mobilizations and others died out. Moreover, while no one knew from the very beginning which of these ideas would succeed or which would fail, the tenacity of these young individuals to keep trying nevertheless is remarkable. Ultimately, the real liberating truth that these activists learned on their own, in the streets of Gaza, the West Bank, and even inside Israel, was the self-realization and renewed confidence in their ability to move forward without the need for acceptance or approval from the established power structures.

Notes

Preface

1 A close observation of Palestinians' immediate online responses to US President Trump's declaration on Jerusalem demonstrated how increased feelings of distrust, cynicism, and disappointment toward local and global actors were virally spreading via social media networks, triggering a range of reactions on Facebook and Twitter. The hashtag #Jerusalem is the eternal Palestinian Capital topped the global trends with more than 358K tweets, followed by #Jerusalem is ours and #Quds.[1] The online social activism platform, Avaaz, initiated a petition: "Defend our Dignity: Defend Jerusalem," which within a few days, had reached 80,000 online signatures, while another million signatures were secured through another online platform, Change.org.[1] At the moment of writing this book, the reaction on these various social media platforms suggests a growing feeling of discontent and anger among Palestinians permeating through the online space.

2 Statements and Releases (2017, December). Statement by President Trump on Jerusalem. Retrieved from: https://www.whitehouse.gov/briefings-statements/statement-president-trump-jerusalem/

3 The most recent interviews were conducted during the period of December 2017–January 2018 and August–September 2018.

4 Interview with Ahmed Abu Artema was conducted on August 28, 2018.

5 "Every Friday, security men and police are deployed to support demonstrators, facilitate their movement, secure their tents and properties in the eastern areas of Gaza," Iyad al-Bazm, a spokesman for the Hamas-affiliated Interior Ministry in Gaza, wrote on his Facebook page on April 28.

6 Every March 30, since 1976, Land Day is commemorated since 1976, when Israeli security forces shot dead six Israeli Arabs who were protesting the expropriation of Arab-owned land in Northern Israel to build and establish Jewish communities. About 100 others were wounded and hundreds were arrested during the protest.

7 These protests still continue at the time of this writing, but reached a momentum in the period between March 30 and May 14, 2018.

8	The demonstration that days reached the highest level of fatal developments where more attempts to breach the wall were made on the Gaza's side while Israel engaged in live fire exchanges with the unarmed populations in Gaza and brought up tanks to target Hamas. By the end of that day, 58 Palestinian had been killed and 2,771 wounded. This was a serious escalation and brought widespread condemnations internationally.

9	Zahar stated on May 12: "The protests are peaceful but are protected by our weapons and guns. Otherwise they would have been wiped out. The Zionist occupation soldiers are well aware that behind the demonstrators stand our men with their guns and rockets. That is why they did not cross the border."

10	Shehab News Agency (December 19, 2017).

11	Free the Tamimi Women (December 22, 2017).

12	Taghreeba (Free Palestine) (December 27, 2017).

13	Ahed Tamimi indicted on charges of assaulting a soldier and stone throwing (January 2, 2018). Retrieved from: https://www.maannews.com/Content.aspx?id=779712

14	Huwaida Arraf (@huwaidaarraf). (January 12, 2018).
	AVAAZ (December 19, 2017).

15	 https://www.haaretz.com/israel-news/italian-artists-barred-from-israel-for-10-years-after-tamimi-mural-1.6320442

16	Second interview with Issa Amro, a leading Palestinian activist again at his Youth Against Settlements Center in the West Bank city of Hebron.

17	IMEU (September 19, 2016).

18	Palestinian Authority arrests activist over Facebook post (September 4, 2017).

Chapter 1

1	http://www.theguardian.com/world/2011/jan/02/free-gaza-youth-manifesto-palestinian; https://www.youtube.com/watch?v=NKXL5fOXkws

2	http://www.pcbs.gov.ps/site/512/default.aspx?tabID=512&lang=en&ItemID=1701&mid=3171&wversion=Staging

3	According to the same source, the total population in the occupied Palestinian territory totaled 4.81 million in 2016.

4	Palestinian Youth Affairs in Israel (2012). Field Research conducted by Baladna: Association for Arab Youth in Israel.

5	Palestinian Youth Affairs in Israel (2012). Field Research conducted by Baladna: Association for Arab Youth in Israel.

6 Throughout this study I rely on a combination of several Israeli and Palestinian sources in order to address this obstacle.

7 http://mondoweiss.net

8 https://electronicintifada.net

9 https://972mag.com

Chapter 3

1 Together, these authors sought to explain how and why this transformation occurred. Their sound analysis in this study cautions the reader to veer away from seeing the new technologies as disconnected from their particular social contexts.

> It is a mistake to build a theory of democratization around a particular kind of software, a single website, or one piece of hardware. It is also erroneous to label these social events as Twitter, Facebook or Wikileaks revolutions. It does not make sense to argue that digital media causes civil society leaders or dictators to be more effective at their work. Technology tools and social actors who use them, together, make or suppress political uprising. (Howard and Hussain, p. 31)

2 With this term, Rinnawi refers to the ambivalent ways in which the government both enhance and restrain the use of Internet in their countries (Mellor, 2011).

3 According to this camp of scholars, attributing the uprisings to social media transforms the true heroes of uprisings—the participants—from protagonists into patsies who act not because they choose too but because they are somehow technologically compelled to do so (Gelvin 2012, p. 51).

4 Most of the early literature on the Arab Uprisings, reflects this trend of searching for "real activists" By focusing too much on the "real participants" from established political organizations on the ground, this scholarly approach may have underestimated how these choices for activism, are increasingly upsetting the existing organizational elements of long-established movements on the ground, indicating a major ongoing rupture in contemporary mobilization processes.

5 Definition: a body of literature on generations dating to the late 1990s draws directly on communication technologies for naming this generation, and on affirmation how generational change and technological change are perceived as intrinsically connected in this era. In addition to millennials and Generation Y (Talpit 2009)—FACEBOOK generation, Linda Herrera prefers the term "wired

generation" for it captures how communication behavior in this high-tech era leads to a rewiring of users' cognitive make-up which makes their relationship to political and social systems and their notions as citizens.

6   Definition: those born between 1977 and 2000, according to Cole. He defines them as more literate than their elders, more urban and cosmopolitan, more technologically savvy and less religiously observant than those aged over thirty-five. Cole contends that "a new generation has been awakened," more democratic, more tolerant and more secular.

7   Qawasmi and Othman (2016). For more data on this topic, see "# Palestine: Palestinian Social Media Activity during 2015." Retrieved from http://www.7amleh.org/en/article/62

8   During the same war, Israel also captured the Sinai Peninsula and Gaza Strip from Egypt, the Shebaa farms from Lebanon, the Golan Heights from Syria, and the West Bank and East Jerusalem from Jordan.

9   Some of the studies I consulted in the substantial literature on the history of the Israeli-Palestinian conflict are Quigley (1990; Shepherd 2000; Shlaim 2000; Kimmerling and Migdal, 1993; Khalidi, 2008).

Chapter 4

1   http://www.maannews.com/Content.aspx?id=338296

2   http://sharek.ps/en/?page_id=113

3   http://www.al-monitor.com/pulse/iw/originals/2013/01/palestine-ngo-economic-challenges.html

4   The director of Gaza's Branch was accused of "ethical corruption, encouraging non-veiling, mixing of the sexes, and teaching music and dancing."

5   Excerpt from the GYBO manifesto posted on their Facebook page.

6   http://cyberdissidents.org/bin/content6bfe.html?ID=503&q=3&s=24

7   This is the only opening paragraph of a 1000-word document, or what is now known as the "Gazan Youth's Manifesto for Change."

8   http://www.theguardian.com/world/2011/jan/02/free-gaza-youth-manifesto-palestinian; https://www.youtube.com/watch?v=NKXL5fOXkws

9   http://www.reuters.com/article/us-palestinians-chronology-idUSL1752364420070617

10   Today, their Facebook page counts 45,000 followers, with around 21, 000 followers on Twitter.

11   https://al-shabaka.org/roundtables/palestinian-youth-revolt-any-role-for-political-parties/

12 Dhillon and Yousef (2009).

13 Khaled Hroub (Summer 2006).

14 http://www.nytimes.com/2006/01/30/world/middleeast/rice-admits-us-underestimated-hamas-strength.html

15 http://www.washingtonpost.com/wp-dyn/content/article/2006/01/26/AR2006012600372.html

16 Most sarcastically, this dilemma is captured in this news report: Americans are saying "no, unless" to Hamas and the Europeans are saying "yes, if". "EU and US wait on Hamas," International Herald Tribune, January 31, 2006.

17 Middle East Report, nr 73 : Ruling Palestine I: Gaza under Hamas, March 2007.

18 Palestinian Public Opinion Poll No. 23, Palestinian Center for Policy and Survey Research, March 22–24, 2007, http://www.pcpsr.org/survey/polls/2007/p23e1.html

19 Human Rights Watch (June 2007).

20 International Committee of the Red Cross (ICRC) (June 2007).

21 https://www.iwmf.org/blog/2012/10/08/asmaa-al-ghoul-2012-courage-in-journalism-award/

22 http://www.motherjones.com/politics/2010/12/gaza-hamas-asma-al-ghoul

23 Amnesty International (July 2009).

24 United Nations (December 2009).

25 In her blog, Palinoia, Jihane, wrote in detail about the co-optation of the protest by the parties and various factions (https://palinoia.wordpress.com/2011/03/15/march-15th-movement-statement/)

Chapter 5

1 His most recent book on this topic is called *Popular Resistance in Palestine: A History of Hope and Empowerment* (Qumsyeh, 2011).

2 In my personal communication with Professor Qumsyeh, he did not reveal the name of the student. I found out through a different interview, but the student requested that his identity remain anonymous.

3 Interview with Fadi Quran, November 6, 2015.

4 Interview with Badia Dwaik, November 16, 2015.

5 http://www.freegaza.org

6 https://palsolidarity.org

7 Interview with Huwaida Arraf, October 22, 2015.

8 http://mondoweiss.net/2011/11/follow-the-freedom-rides/

9   https://www.facebook.com/PalestinianFreedomRides/

10 https://twitter.com/PalFreedomRides

11 http://palfreedomrides.blogspot.co.il/2011/11/palestinian-freedom-riders-on-their-way.html?view=classic

12 https://electronicintifada.net/content/us-south-palestine-freedom-rides-change-history/10599

13 https://www.theguardian.com/world/2011/nov/15/palestinians-protest-racist-bus-policy
    https://www.washingtonpost.com/world/middle_east/palestinian-freedom-riders-arrested-on-bus-to-jerusalem/2011/11/15/gIQAQfkcPN_story.html

14 https://bdsmovement.net/news/bds-marks-another-victory-veolia-sells-all-israeli-operations

15 I calculated this number through my personal research, amid various social media platforms where these events were announced and coordinated. I also followed their coverage through some independent online media news forums, such as *Electronic Intifada*, Mondoweiss, and +972. Through these online media sources, I sought to trace the frequency and duration of their protests. I also counted these events listed at the "Chronology," Journal of Palestine Studies. Finally I combined these findings with their local and international coverage in mainstream media. Therefore, I believe this number represents an accurate estimate.

16 Hoigilt (2013).

17 Institute for Applied Research.

18 http://www.nytimes.com/2011/01/26/opinion/26goldberg.html?_r=0

19 The term "Fayyadism" was coined by Friedman who wrote in 2009 that "Fayyad's is based on the simple but all-too-rare notion that an Arab leader's legitimacy should be based not on slogans or rejectionism or personality cults or security services, but on delivering transparent, accountable administration and services." The term also refers to Palestinian prime minister Salam Fayyad's program to build a Palestinian state despite occupation and internal division.

20 https://electronicintifada.net/content/salam-fayyads-cynical-party/7530

21 Palestinian National Authority. National Development Plan 2011-2013: Establishing the State, Building our Future. Palestinian National Authority, 2011.

22 Palestinian National Authority. Palestinian Reform and Development Plan: 2008-2010. Palestinian National Authority, 2008.

23 Friedman, Thomas. "Green Shoots in Palestine," *The New York Times.* August 4, 2009. http://www.nytimes.com/2009/08/05/opinion/05friedman.html

24 Friedman, Thomas. "Green Shoots in Palestine," *The New York Times*. August 4, 2009. http://www.nytimes.com/2009/08/05/opinion/05friedman.html

25 https://electronicintifada.net/content/politics-fear/7168

26 Measures Taken by Israel in Support of Developing the Palestinian Economy, the Socioeconomic Structure, and the Security Reforms. Report of the Government of Israel to the Ad Hoc Liaison Committee, State of Israel, 2010.

27 Measures Taken by Israel in Support of Developing the Palestinian Economy, the Socioeconomic Structure, and the Security Reforms. Report of the Government of Israel to the Ad Hoc Liaison Committee, State of Israel, 2011.

28 http://www.sahafi.jo/arc/art1.php?id=61361d83c5ff01b319a50a09a3c7b551a6021 89e

29 http://edition.cnn.com/2011/WORLD/africa/02/05/egypt.protests.palestinians/

30 http://www.democracynow.org/2011/2/3/headlines/palestinian_authority_shuts_ down_pro_egyptian_protest

31 From my interview that I conducted with this activist in Ramallah, on November 12, 2015.

32 http://www.maannews.com/Content.aspx?id=369077

33 https://al-shabaka.org/roundtables/achieving-palestinian-spring/

34 No exact date for the creation of this group is available.

35 http://english.al-akhbar.com/node/9267

36 Palestinians for Dignity: Saeb Erekat, Go Home.

37 https://occupiedpalestine.wordpress.com/2012/01/12/palestinians-for-dignity-demonstration-against-the-return-to-negotiations.

38 http://mondoweiss.net/2012/01/palestinian-youth-fed-up-with-illegitimate-representation-to-protest-negotiations/

39 https://electronicintifada.net/content/pa-repression-feeds-flames-palestinian-discontent/11456

40 https://electronicintifada.net/content/palestinians-reclaim-streets-despite-pa-police-repression/11474

41 https://electronicintifada.net/blogs/ali-abunimah/palestinian-youth-call-ramallah-protest-against-israeli-palestinian-negotiations

42 https://www.washingtonpost.com/blogs/blogpost/post/ramallah-protesters-attacked-by-pa-police-photos/2012/07/01/gJQAWExWGW_blog.html

43 https://www.facebook.com/note.php?note_id=256740551101634

44 http://www.maannews.com/Content.aspx?id=518957

45 http://english.dohainstitute.org/release/94454f0f-ed0b-40c1-b9b3-58c5b6f0b525.

46 http://stopthewall.org/2012/10/03/palestinian-youth-why-were-speaking-out-against-political-arrests

47 http://mondoweiss.net/2012/05/under-mounting-pressure-from-hunger-strikers-and-un-protest-ban-ki-moon-criticizes-administrative-detention-but-weakly/

48 http://www.maannews.com/Content.aspx?id=508726

49 http://www.voanews.com/a/west-bank-obama/1625603.html

50 http://www.nytimes.com/2013/01/12/world/middleeast/palestinians-set-up-camp-in-israeli-occupied-west-bank-territory.html

51 http://www.bbc.com/news/world-middle-east-21002450

52 https://electronicintifada.net/content/making-history-bab-al-shams/12098

53 http://stopthewall.org/2013/02/02/more-200-palestinians-build-village-bab-munatir-nablus-region

54 https://www.theguardian.com/world/2013/jan/13/isarel-evicts-e1-palestinian-peace-camp

55 https://www.facebook.com/pg/free.fadi.quran/about/?tab=page_info

56 https://electronicintifada.net/content/israel-jailed-my-friend-hassan-karajah-break-grassroots-struggle/12144

57 posted on the website http://www.stopthewall.org

58 http://972mag.com/amnesty-international-calls-for-release-of-bassem-tamimi-prisoner-of-conscience/59063/

59 https://nabisalehsolidarity.wordpress.com/about/

60 https://www.facebook.com/Nabi-Saleh-Solidarity-177013109017209/

61 https://www.youtube.com/watch?v=eQ9BLW2TEw0

62 https://twitter.com/nabisaleh

63 http://thelede.blogs.nytimes.com/2011/06/17/palestinians-film-west-bank-protests-with-israeli-supplied-cameras/

64 http://www.nytimes.com/2013/03/17/magazine/is-this-where-the-third-intifada-will-start.html?_r=0

65 https://electronicintifada.net/content/bassem-tamimi-our-destiny-resist/9894

66 Some of this literature included Qumsyeh, 2011; Kaufman-Lacusta, 2011; King, 2007).

67 The term "intifada" literally means "shaking off."

68 Israeli-Palestinian Interim Agreement 1995.

69 Ibid.

70 Ibid.

71 Sayigh, Y. (1997). Armed Struggle and the Search for State: The Palestinian National Movement, 1949–1993.

72 Foundation for Middle East Peace, 2012.

73 Rothsten, Robert L., Moshe Ma'oz, and Khalil Shikaki. The Israeli-Palestinian Peace Process

74 http://allegralaboratory.net/the-road-to-oslo-and-its-reverse-palestine/

75 Said, E. (1995). The Middle East Peace Process: Misleading Images and Brutal Actualities.

76 Hammami (2000).

77 Dana (2015).

78 One of the original Freedom Bus Riders discussed at the beginning of this chapter.

Chapter 6

1 Government Decision, *Confirming the Recommendations for Regulation of the Bedouin Settlement in the Negev*, September 11, 2011 (hereinafter Government Decision or GD). In approving the plan, the government also accepted amendments by National Security Adviser Yaakov Amidror, who was commissioned by the state to review the plan in June 2011 (Government Decision no. 3707, September 11, 2011).

2 The plan was prepared by a committee headed by Mr. Ehud Prawer, former deputy chairman of the National Security Council.

3 The numbers are different as represented by different sources, varying from 30,000 to 70,000. The numbers used in this study are in alignment with those used consistently by Adalah: The Legal Center for Arab Minority Rights in Israel.

4 Discriminatory Prawer Plan to evict tens of thousands of Bedouins from their communities in the Negev (July 11, 2013).

5 Demolition and Eviction of Bedouin Citizens of Israel in the Naqab (Negev)— The Prawer Plan. Retrieved from https://www.adalah.org/en/content/view/7589

6 Press Release: The Knesset Approves the Highly Devastating Prawer-Begin Bill in First Voting Round (June 25, 2013).

7 Israel: Halt Demolitions of Bedouin Homes in Negev (August 1, 2010).

8 https://www.facebook.com/prawershallnotpass

9 Balasubramanian and Vaid-Menon (August 19, 2013).

10 Schwarczenberg (November 30, 2013a).

11 Viscous crackdown on unarmed protesters against the Prawer Plan just outside Ramallah (December 2, 2013).

12 Palestinians rally in Gaza to stop Prawer Plan on International Day of Rage (December 3, 2013).

13 Kane (November 30, 2013).

14 Activists hold "day of rage" protests against Prawer Plan (November 30, 2013). Retrieved from: https://972mag.com/activists-stage-day-of-rage-protests-against-prawer-plan/82706/

15 Stop Israel's ethnic cleansing of Palestinian Bedouin! (November 30, 2013).

16 Bahour (September 26, 2016).

17 Palestinian Youth Affairs in Israel (2012). Field research conducted by Baladna: Association for Arab Youth in Israel.

18 Palestinian Youth Affairs in Israel (2012). Field research conducted by Baladna: Association for Arab Youth in Israel.

19 Majid Al Haj, in his article titled "The Status of the Palestinians in Israel: A Double Periphery in an Ethno-National State," uses the term "A Double periphery" to describe the status of Palestinians of Israel. The article is part of a series of articles published in the volume *Critical Issues in Israeli Society* (Dowty, 2004).

20 IsraelGovernmentEstimate, IsraelLandsAuthority, http://www.mmi.gov.il/static/HanhalaPirsumim/Beduin_information.pdf (accessed February 14, 2017).

21 The term is commonly used and originally borrowed from Legal Ottoman. It means "dead."

22 Demolition and Eviction of Bedouin Citizens of Israel in the Naqab (Negev)—The Prawer Plan. Retrieved from: https://www.adalah.org/en/content/view/7589

23 Mosawa (2012).

24 Al Saafin and Hassan Budour (September 7, 2013).

25 Two of the activists that I spoke to mentioned their training experiences with Ahel (http://ahel.org/en/what-do-we-offer/), a non-profit organization based in Jordan, specializing in community organizing and campaign coaching.

26 Palestinian Youth Affairs in Israel (2012). Field research conducted by Baladna: Association for Arab Youth in Israel.

27 The Abraham Fund Initiatives (2015).

28 Ben-Amos, 2012.

29 https://www.facebook.com/pg/urfod/about/?ref=page_internal

30 https://schwarczenberg.com/tag/jaffa-based-activists/

31 Balasubramanian and Vaid-Menon (August 19, 2013).

32 Al Saafin, L. (March 23, 2012).

33 Raved (January 29, 2011).

34 Dana (January 29, 2011).

35 Omer-Man (February 20, 2016).

36 Nieuwhof (October 11, 2011).

37 Haifa Youth Support Striking Palestinian prisoners (October 15, 2011).

38 https://www.facebook.com/pg/Hungry-For-Freedom-للحرية-جائعون-281161825235578/about/?ref=page_internal

39 Nabulsi (2014).

40 http://palvision.ps/en/project/mit7arkeen/

41 Baladna, Association for Arab Youth (2014).

42 (www.facebook.com/parwershallnotpass)

43 https://occupiedpalestine.wordpress.com/2013/08/01/live-blog-stopprawerplan-in-photos/

44 Kopty (July 13, 2013).

45 https://electronicintifada.net/blogs/linah-alsaafin/palestinian-national-strike-stop-israels-prawer-plan-ethnic-cleansing

46 Palestinians rally in Gaza to stop Prawer Plan on International Day of Rage (December 3, 2013).

47 https://ozcoalitionagainstisraeliapartheid.wordpress.com/2013/11/30/melbourne-against-the-prawer-plan-stop-israels-ethnic-cleansing-of-palestinian-bedouin/

48 Schwarczenberg (November 30, 2013b).

49 Ibid.

50 Viscous crackdown on unarmed protesters against the Prawer Plan just outside Ramallah (December 2, 2013).

51 Abunimah (December 1, 2013).

52 Adalah and ACRI: The Shabak is Trying to Sow Fear among Anti-PrawElectronic Intifada, Mondoweisser Plan Activists. (November 28, 2013).

53 Kopty (November 24, 2013).

54 Berman (December 12, 2013).

55 https://electronicintifada.net/blogs/maureen-clare-murphy/withdrawal-prawer-plan-bill-major-achievement-palestinians-israel

Chapter 7

1 I had a series of interviews with eminent activists such as Bassem Tamimi, Ali Abu Awad; Sami Awad, Mazen Qumsyeh, Isa Amro, Huwaida Arraf, and so on.

2 Khalidi, p. 223.

Appendix

List of interviewees.

No	Name	Position	Affiliation	Location	Interview Format	Date
1	Dr. Khalil Shikaki	Professor of Political Science	Director of the Palestinian Center for Policy and Survey Research	Ramallah	In Person	December 27, 2015
2	Dr. Ali Jarbawi	Professor of Political Science	Birzeit University	Ramallah	In Person	October 22, 2015
3	Sam Bahour	Writer, activist, businessman	Director of Applied Management Systems (AIM), and Al Shabaka Policy Advisor	Ramallah	In Person	September 4, 2015
4	Dr. Mazen Qumsyeh	Professor, Director & Activist	Bethlehem University and Palestine Natural History Museum	Bethlehem	In Person	October 22, 2015 and September 20, 2017
5	Issa Amro	Human rights activist	Cofounder and director of Youth Against settlements	Hebron	In Person	January 2016 and September 2017
6	Badia Dwaik	Activist	Founder and director of "Human Rights Defenders"	Hebron	In Person	September 9, 2015
7	Ali Abu Awwad	Activist	Activist, founder of "Tagheer" (Change) Palestinian movement	Gush Etzyon	In Person	September 16, 2015

(Continued)

No	Name	Position	Affiliation	Location	Interview Format	Date
8	Mariam Barghouti	Activist/journalist	Freelance writer	Ramallah	In Person	June 11, 2015
9	Fadi Quran	Activist	Senior campaigner for Avaaz	Ramallah	In Person	May 10, 2015
10	Ahmed Al Deir	Activist	Youth mobilizer for ActionAid	Bethlehem	In Person	October 12, 2015
11	Ibrahim Abdullatif Ashour	Activist	Youth Program Director, for Save Youth Future	Gaza	Skype	September 2016
12	Ayman Maghamish	Social media activist	Rapper	Gaza	Skype	
13	Moheeb Shath	NGO Executive	ex-Director of Sharek Youth Organization	Gaza	Skype, In Person	October 2015/ September 2016
14	Fadi al khoury	Activist	Youth organizer	Gaza	Skype	September 2015
15	Mohammed al Komboz	Social media activist	Cofounder of End the Division Youth group	Gaza	Skype	November 2016
16	Yousef al Jamal	Social media activist	Participant and organizer of many youth campaigns	Gaza	Skype	November 2016
17	Yousef al Noury	Activist	Participant in 15 March group	Gaza	Skype	October 3, 2015

18	Khaled Saad	Activist	Youth Coordinator	Gaza		November 2015
19	Huwaida Arrad	Human rights activist	Cofounder of ISM	Ramallah	In Person	October 2016
20	Imad Abu Shamsya	Citizen journali	Human Rights Defender Group	Hebron	In Person	December 2015
21	Imad Abu Fadi	Citizen journalist	Human Rights Defender Group	Hebron	In Person	December 2015
22	Yasmine Al Khoudary	Blogger/journalist	Researcher	UK	email	September 2016
23	Jehane El Farra	Blogger/journalist	Journalist	UK (from Gaza)	Skype	November 2015
24	Wasim Zaher	Blogger/social media activist	Internet	Canada (from Gaza)	Interview via email	September 2016
25	Mohammed Matter (Abu Yazan)	Social media activist	Founder of Gaza Youth Breaks Out	Germany (from Gaza)	Skype	September 2015
26	Tarek El Farra	Social media activist	Youth Coordinator	Gaza	Skype	November 2015
27	Hazem Abu Helal	Activist	Herak al Shebabi	Ramallah	In Person	September 2016
28	Asmaa Al Ghoul	Blogger/journalist/activist	Freelance writer	Gaza	Skype	December 2015
29	Sami Awad	Activist, Director of NGO	Holy Land Trust	Bethlehem	In Person	September 2015/November 2017
30	Majd Khalaj	Student/activist	Hungry for Freedom campaign	Haifa	In Person	January 2016

(Continued)

No	Name	Position	Affiliation	Location	Interview Format	Date
31	Basem Tamimi	Activist	Leader of the Nabi Saleh nonviolent popular committee	Nabi Saleh	In Person	October 2016/ December 2017/ January 2018
32	Nadim Nashif	Al Shabakah Policy Advisor	Former Director of "Baladna" youth organization	Haifa	In Person	December 2016/ December 2018
33	Khaled Farrag	Activist	Founder of Grassroots Jerusalem	Jerusalem	In Person	September 2016
34	Reem Omran	Blogger, NGO activists		Canada (from Gaza)	Skype	November 2017
35	Maisan Hamdan	Activist	Participant in "Stop the Prawer" movement	Haifa	In Person	November 2017
36	Eitan Alimi	Professor	Hebrew University of Jerusalem	Hebrew U	In Person	September 2016
37	Heba Hayek	NGO activist	Student	Gaza	Skype	September 2015
38	Noor (anonymous)	Activist	Participant in 15 March movement	Nablus	In person	September 2015
39	Ahmed Abu Artema	Activist	Great March of Return organizer	Gaza	Skype	August 28, 2018
40	Ahmad K	Activist	Great March of Return Participant	Gaza	Skype	September 2, 2018

References

Abu-Rabia, A. (2001). *A Bedouin Century: Education and Development among the Negev Tribes in the 20th Century*. New York: Berghahn Books.

Abu-Saad, I. (2008). "State rule and indigenous resistance among al Naqab Bedouin Arabs." *Hagar Studies in Culture, Polity and Identities*, Vol. 8, No. 2, pp. 3–24.

Ajami, F. (2012). "Five Myths about the Arab Spring." *The Washington Post*. Retrieved from: https://www.washingtonpost.com/opinions/five-myths-about-the-arab-spring/2011/12/21/gIQA32TVuP_story.html?utm_term=.0151613ea813

Al-Haj, M. (2004). "The status of the Palestinians in Israel: A double periphery in an ethno-national state." In Alan Dowty, ed., *Critical Issues in Israeli Society*, pp. 109–26. EBOOK 001734433.

Al-Haj, M. (2005). "Whither the green line? Trends in the orientation of the Palestinians in Israel and the territories." *Israel Affairs*, Vol. 11, No. 1, pp. 183–206.

al-Shabaka, the Palestinian Policy Network (August 2011). Achieving a Palestinian Spring [Policy Analysis]. Abunimah, A., Barakat, R., Doumani, B., Haddad, T., Hilal, J., al-Masri, H., Qato, M., and Youmans, W. Retrieved from: https://al-shabaka.org/roundtables/achieving-palestinian-spring/ al-shabaka

al-Shabaka, the Palestinian Policy Network (November 2015). Palestinian Youth Revolt: Any Role for Political Parties? [Policy Analysis]. Tartir, A., Shobaki, B., Juma, J., Hilal, J., Suleiman, J., Shaheen, K., Abu Samra, M., and Ali, N. Retrieved from: https://al-shabaka.org/roundtables/palestinian-youth-revolt-any-role-for-political-parties/

Alimi, E. (2012). "Occupy Israel: A tale of startling success and hopeful failure." *Journal of Social Movement Studies*, Vol. 11, No. 2–3, pp. 402–7.

Allen, L. (2013). *The Rise and Fall of Human Rights, Cynicism and Politics in Occupied Palestine*. Stanford, CA: Stanford University Press.

Allweil, Y. (2013). "Surprising alliances for dwelling and citizenship: Palestinian-Israeli participation in the mass housing protest of 2011." *International Journal of Islamic Architecture*, Vol. 2, No. 1, pp. 41–9.

Amram, Y. (November 30, 2013). "Grassfire: Outbreak of the social protest, its operation style and the results observed in the short time." *American Journal of Social Sciences*, Vol. 1, No. 1, pp. 1–12. Retrieved from: http://www.openscienceonline.com/journal/ajss

Anduiza, E., Jensen, M. J., and Jorba, L. (2012). *Digital Media and Political Engagement Worldwide*. New York: Cambridge University Press.

Aouragh, M. (2012). *Palestine Online: Transnationalism, the Internet and the Construction of Identity*. London: I.B. Tauris.

ASDA'A Burson-Marsteller (2017). *Arab Youth Survey 2017*. Dubai: ASDA'A Burson-Marsteller.

Awad, M. E. (1984). "Nonviolent resistance as a strategy for the occupied territories." *Journal of Palestine Studies*, Vol. 13, No. 4, pp. 22–36.

Barber, B. (2001). "Political violence, social integration, and youth functioning: Palestinian youth from the Intifada." *Journal of Community Psychology*, Vol. 29, No. 3, pp. 259–80.

Bauerlein, M., ed. (2011). *The Digital Divide: Arguments for and against Facebook, Google, Texting, and the Age of Social Networking*. New York: Tarcher/Penguin Group.

Bayat, A. (2010). *Life as Politics: How Ordinary People Change the Middle East*. Stanford, CA: Stanford University Press.

Bayat, A. (2017). *Revolution Without Revolutionaries: Making Sense of the Arab Spring*. Standford: Standford University Press.

Beck, U. (2006). *The Cosmopolitan Vision*. Malden, MA: Polity Press.

Beinin, J. and Vairel, F., eds. (2011). *Social Movements, Mobilization, and Contestation in the Middle East and North Africa*. Stanford, CA: Stanford University Press.

Beitler, R. (2004). *The Path to Mass Rebellion: An Analysis of Two Intifadas*. Oxford: Lexington Books.

Benkler, J. (2007). *The Wealth of Networks*. New Haven, CT: Yale University Press.

Bennett, W. L. (1998). "The uncivic culture: communication, identity, and the rise of lifestyle politics." *P.S: Political Science and Politics*, Vol. 31, No. 4, 741–61.

Bennett, W. L. (2008). *Civic Life Online: Learning How Digital Media Can Engage Youth*. Cambridge, MA: MIT Press.

Bennett, W. L. (2012). "The personalization of politics: Political identity, social media, and changing patterns of participation." *Annals- American Academy of Political and Social Science*, Vol. 644, pp. 20–39.

Bennett, L. and Segerberg, A. (2013). *The Logic of Connective Action*. New York: Cambridge University Press.

Berti, B. (2015). "Non-State actors as providers of governance: The Hamas government in Gaza between effective sovereignty, centralized authority, and resistance." *Middle East Journal*, Vol. 69, No. 1, pp. 9–31. HTTP://DX.DOI.ORG/10.3751/69.1.11

Bimber, B., Flanagan, A. J., and Stohl, C. (January 1, 2005). "Reconceptualizing collective action in the contemporary media environment." *Communication Theory*, Vol. 15, No. 4, 365–88.

Bimber, B., Flanagan, A. J., and Stohl, C. (2012). *Collective Action in Organizations. Interaction and Engagement in the Era of Technological Change*. NewYork: Cambridge University Press.

Brown, N. (September 2010). "Fayyad is not the problem, but Fayyadism is not the solution to Palestine's political crisis." *Carnegie Endowment for International Peace, Carnegie Papers.* Retrieved from: http://carnegieendowment.org/files/fayyad_not_problem_2.pdf

Brown, N. (June 2010). "Are Palestinians building a state?." *Carnegie Endowment for International Peace, Carnegie Papers.* Retrieved from: http://carnegieendowment.org/files/palestinian_state1.pdf

Brown, N. (2012). Gaza five years on: Hamas settles in. *Carnegie Endowment for International Peace, Carnegie Papers.* Retrived from: https://carnegieendowment.org/files/Hamas_Settles_In_Full_Text.pdf

Brynen, R. (2012). *Beyond the Arab Spring: Authoritarianism & Democratization in the Arab World.* Boulder, CO: Lynne Rienner Publishers.

Burton, G. (2017). "Building ties across the Green Line: The Palestinian 15 March youth movement in Israel and occupied Palestinian territory in 2011." *Third World Quarterly*, Vol. 38, No. 1, pp. 169–84. DOI: 10.1080/01436597.2015.1135398

Casati, N. (2016). "Political participation in a Palestinian university: Nablus undergraduates' political subjectivities through boredom, fear and consumption." *Ethnography.* DOI: 10.1177/1466138116649976

Castells, M. (1996). *The Rise of the Network Society.* Malden, MA: Blackwell Publishers.

Castells, M. (2009). *Communication Power.* Oxford: Oxford University Press.

Castells, M. (2010). *The Rise of the Network Society*, Volume 1 (2nd ed.)., Chichester, West Sussex, Malden, MA: Blackwell Publishers.

Castells, M. (2012). *Networks of Outrage and Hope: Social Movements in the Internet Age*, Rev. ed. Malden, MA: Polity Press.

Chadwick, A. (2013). *The Hybrid Media System: Politics and Power.* Oxford: Oxford University Press.

Challand, B. (2009). *Civil Society: Foreign Donors and the Power to Promote and Exclude.* London: Routledge Press.

Chehab, Z. (2007). *Inside Hamas: The Untold Story of the Islamic Movement.* New York: Nation Books.

Chorev, H. (2017). "The wave of lone-wolves attacks in Israel (October 2015–September 2016) and Palestinian social media." *Tel Aviv Notes*, Vol. 11, No. 20. Retrieved from: https://dayan.org/content/wave-lone-wolf-attacks-israel-oct-2015-sep-2016-and-palestinian-social-media

Christophersen, N., Hoigilt, J., and Tiltnes, A. A. (2012). "Palestinian youth and the Arab Spring." *Norwegian Center for Conflict Resolution.* Retrieved from NOREF website: http://noref.no/content/view/full/165634

Cole, D. (2003). "Where have the Bedouin gone?" *Anthropological Quarterly*, Vol. 76, No. 2, pp. 235–67.

Cole, J. R. (2014). *The New Arabs: How the Millennial Generation Is Changing the Middle East*. New York: Simon and Schuster.

Collins, J. (2004). *Occupied by Memory: The Intifada Generation and the Palestinian State of Emergency*, New York: New York University Press.

Collins, J. (2011). *Global Palestine*. Oxford University Press.

Couldry, N. (2015). "The myth of 'us': Digital networks, political change and the production of collectivity." *Information, Communication & Society*, Vol. 18, No. 6, pp. 608–26. DOI: 10.1080/1369118X.2014.979216

Çubukçu, A. (2005). "Can the network speak? [Review of the book *Multitude: War and Democracy in the Age of Empire* by M. Hardt & A. Negri]." *The Arab Studies Journal*, Vol. 13/14, No. 2/1, pp. 168–73. Retrieved from Stable URL: http://www.jstor.org/stable/27933949

Dana, T. (2015). "The structural transformation of Palestinian Civil Society: Key paradigm shifts." *Middle East Critique*, Vol. 24, No. 2, pp. 1–20.

Darcy, Sh. and Reynolds, J. (2010). "An enduring occupation. The status of the Gaza strip from the perspective of the International law." *Journal of Conflict and Security Law*, Vol. 15, No. 2, pp. 211–43. DOI: https://doi.org/10.1093/jcsl/krq011

Della, P. D. and Diani, M. (2006). *Social Movements: An Introduction*. Malden, MA: Blackwell Pub.

Dhillon, N. and Yousef, T., eds. (2009). *Generation in Waiting: The Unfulfilled Promise of Young People in the Middle East*. Brookings Institution Press.

Diamond, L. J. and Plattner, M. F. (2012). *Liberation Technology: Social Media and the Struggle for Democracy*. Baltimore: Johns Hopkins University Press.

Doumani, B. (2004). "Scenes from daily life: The view from Nablus." *Journal of Palestine Studies*, Vol. 34, No. 1, pp. 37–45.

Dowty, A. (2004). *Critical Issues in Israeli Society*. Westport, CT: Greeowood Publishing Group.

Earl, J. and Kimport, K. (2011). *Digitally Enabled Social Change: Activism in the Internet Age*. Cambridge, MA: MIT Press.

Falah, G. (1983). "The development of the 'planned Bedouin settlements' in Israel 1964–1982: Evaluation and characteristics." *GeoForum,* Vol. 14, No. 3, pp. 311–23.

Falah, G. (1989). "Israel State Policy towards Bedouin Sedentarization in the Negev." *Journal of Palestine Studies*, Vol. 19, No. 2, pp. 71–90.

Faris, D. (2008). "Revolutions without revolutionaries? network theory, Facebook, and the Egyptian blogosphere." *Arab media & society*, Vol. 6, pp. 1–11.

Faris, D. (2013). *Dissent and Revolution in a Digital Age: Social Media, Blogging and Activism in Egypt*. I.B. Tauris.

Gelvin, J. L. (2012). *The Arab Uprisings: What Everyone Needs to Know*. New York: Oxford University Press.

Gerbaudo, P. (2012). *Tweets and the Streets: Social Media and Contemporary Activism*. London: PlutoPress.

Gharrah, R. (2015). *Arab Society in Israel: Population, Society, Economy (7)*. Jerusalem: Van Leer Institute, Hakibbutz Hameuchad. Google Scholar.

Ghonim, W. (2012). *Revolution 2.0: The Power of the People Is Greater Than the People in Power: A Memoir*. Boston: Houghton Mifflin Harcourt.

Giddens, A. (1991). *Modernity and Self-Identity: Self and Society in the Late Modern Age*. Stanford, CA: Stanford University Press.

Golan, G. and Salem, W. (2013). *Non-State Actors in the Middle East: Factors for Peace and Democracy*. Routledge.

Grinberg, L. L. (2013). "The J14 resistance mo(ve)ment : The Israeli mix of Tahrir square and Puerto del sol." *Current Sociology*, Vol. 61, No. 4, pp. 491–509. DOI: 10.1177/0011392113479748

Hall, B. (2014). "Bedouins' politics of place and memory: A case of unrecognized villages in the Negev." *Nomadic People*, Vol. 18, No. 2, pp. 147–64.

Halverson, J. R., Ruston, S. W., and Trethewey, A. (2013). "Mediated martyrs of the Arab Spring: New media, civil religion, and narrative in Tunisia and Egypt." *Journal of Communication*, Vol. 63, No. 2, pp. 312–32.

Hamilton, S. F. (2003). *Coming of Age in American Communities* (The Youth Development Handbook). Sage Publications.

Hammack, P. L. (2010). *Narrative and the Politics of Identity:The cultural Psychology of Israeli and Palestinian Youth*. Oxford University Press.

Hammami, R. (2000). "Palestinian NGOs since Oslo: From NGO politics to social movements?" *Middle East Report,* No. 214, pp. 16–19.

Hanafi, S. and Tabar, L. (2005). *The Emergence of a Palestinian Globalized Elite*. Institute of Jerusalem Studies & Muwatin, The Palestinian Institute for the study of democracy.

Hart, J. (2002). "Children and nationalism in a Palestinian refugee camp in Jordan." *Childhood*, Vol. 9, No. 1, pp. 35–47.

Hart, J. (2008). "Dislocated masculinity: Adolescence and the Palestinian nation-in-exile." *Journal of Refugee Studies*, Vol. 21, No. 1, pp. 64–81.

Herrera, L., ed. (2014). *Wired Citizenship: Youth Learning and Activism in the Middle East.* New York: Routledge.

Herrera, L. and Mansour, A. (2015). "Arab Youth: Disruptive generation of the twenty-first century?" *The Oxford Handbook of Contemporary Middle-Easter and North African History*. DOI 10.1093/oxfordhb/9780199672530.013.19

Herrera, L. and Bayat, A., eds. (2010). *Being Young and Muslim: New Cultural Politics in the Global South and North*. New York: Oxford University Press.

Hilal, J. (May 6, 2011). *Palestinian Answers in the Arab Spring*. Institute for Palestine Studies. Retrieved from: http://www.palestine-studies.org/institute/fellows/palestinian-answers-arab-spring

Hoigilt, J. (2013). "The Palestinian spring that was not: The youth and political activism in the Occupied Palestinian Territories." *Arab Studies Quarterly*, Vol. 35, No. 4, pp. 343–59.

Hoigilt, J. (2015). "Nonviolent mobilization between a rock and a hard place: Popular resistance and double repression in the West Bank." *Journal of Peace Research*, Vol. 52, No. 5, pp. 541–58.

Howard, P. N. (2010). *The Digital Origins of Dictatorship and Democracy: Information Technology and Political Islam*. Oxford: Oxford University Press.

Howard, P. N. and Hussain, M. M. (2013). *Democracy's Fourth Wave? Digital Media and the Arab Spring*. Oxford: Oxford University Press.

Hroub, K. (2006). *Hamas, a Beginner's Guide*. Pluto Press.

Hroub, K. (Summer 2006). "A 'new Hamas' through its new documents." *Journal of Palestine Studies*, Vol. 34, No. 4, pp. 8–13.

Jensen, M. L. (2009). *The Political Ideology of Hamas: A Grassroots Perspective*. I.B. Tauris.

Juris, J. S. (2008). *Networking Futures: The Movements against Corporate Globalizations*. Duke University Press.

Juris, J. S. (2012). "Reflections on #occupy everywhere: social media, public space, and emerging logics of aggregation." *American Ethnologist*, Vol. 39, No. 2, pp. 259–79, ISSN 0094-0496, DOI: 10.1111/j.1548-1425.2012.01362

Kark, R. and Frantzman, J. (2012). "Empire, state and the Bedouin of the Middle East, past and present: A comparative study of land and settlement policies." *Middle Eastern Studies*, Vol. 48, No. 4, pp. 487–510.

Kaufman-Lacusta, M. (2011). *Refusing to Be Enemies: Palestinian and Israeli Nonviolent Resistance to the Israeli Occupation*. Reading: Ithaca Press.

Kedar, A. S. (2004). "Land settlement in the Negev in the international perspective." *Adalah's Newsletter*, Vol. 8. Available at SSRN: https://ssrn.com/abstract=909764

Khalaf, S. and Khalaf, R. S., eds. (2011). *Arab Youth: Social Mobilization in Times of Risk*. London: Saqi.

Khalidi, A. S. (April 2008). "The Palestinian national movement: What went wrong?" *Journal of Palestine Studies. Distinguished Lecture Series, no. 4*. Washington, DC: Jerusalem Fund for Education and Community Development. Retrieved from http://www.palestine-studies.org/institute/fellows/palestinian-national-movement-what-went-wrong

Khalidi, R. (1997). *Palestinian Identity: The Construction of Moderns National Consciousness*. New York: Columbia University Press.

Khalidi, R. and Sobhi, S. (2011). "Neoliberalism as liberation: The statehood program and the remaking of the Palestinian National Movement." *Journal of Palestine Studies*, Vol. XI, No. 2, pp. 6–25.

Khatib, L. and Lust, E., eds. (2014). *Taking to the Streets: The Transformation of Arab Activism*. Baltimore: John Hopkins University Press.

Kimmerling, B. and Migdal, J. (1993). *Palestinians: The Making of a People*. Cambridge, MA: Harvard University Press.

King, M. E. (2007). *A Quiet Revolution: The First Palestinian Intifada and Nonviolent Resistance*. New York: Nation Books.

Knutter, K. (2013). "Building a state on shifting sands: An evaluation of the Palestinian National Authority's policy reforms and performance in the West Bank, 2009–2011." Unpublished manuscript.

Kuttab, D. (1988). "A profile of the stonethrowers." *Journal of Palestine Studies*, Vol. 17, No. 3, pp. 14–23.

Lang, S. (2013). *NGOs, Civil Society, and the Public Sphere*. Cambridge University Press.

Langman, L. (2005). "From virtual public spheres to global justice: A critical theory of internetworked social movements." *Sociological Theory*, Vol. 23, No. 1, pp. 42–74.

Leech, P. (2012). "Re-reading the Myth of Fayyadism: A Critical Analysis of the Palestinian Authority's Reform and State-building Agenda, 2008–2011." *Arab Center for Research and Policy Studies*. Retrieved from: http://carnegieendowment. org/files/palestinian_state1.pdf

Lim, M. (2012). "Clicks, cabs, and coffee houses: Social media and oppositional movements in Egypt, 2004–2011." *Journal of Communication*, Vol. 62, p. 2.

Lockman, Z. and Beinin, J., eds. (1999). *Intifada: The Palestinian Uprising against Israeli Occupation*. South End Press.

Lustick, I. (1980). *Arabs in the Jewish State: Israel's Control of a National Minority*. Austin: University of Texas Press.

Lynch, M. (2006). *Voices of the New Arab Public: Iraq, Al-Jazeera, and Middle East Politics Today*. New York: Columbia University Press.

Lynch, M. (2012). *The Arab Uprising: The Unfinished Revolutions of the New Middle East*. New York: Public Affairs.

Maira, S. (2013). *Jil Oslo, Palestinian Hip-Hop, Youth Culture and Youth Movement*. Washington DC: Tadween Publishing.

Marom, N. (2013). "Activising space: The spatial politics of the 2011 protest movement in Israel," *Urban Studies*, Vol. 50, No. 13, pp. 2826–41.

Mason, P. (2012). *Why It's Kicking Off Everywhere: The New Global Revolutions*. Brooklyn, NY: Verso.

Mazawi, A. E. (1994). "Palestinian Arabs in Israel: Educational expansion, social mobility and political control." *Compare: A Journal of Comparative and International Education*, Vol. 4, No. 3, pp. 277–84.

McKee, E. (2015). "Demolitions and amendments: Coping with cultural recognition and its denial in southern Israel." *Nomadic Peoples,* Vol. 19, No. 1, pp. 95–119.

Mellor, N. (2005). *The Making of Arab News.* Lanham, MD: Rowman & Littlefield Publishers.

Mellor, N., ed. (2011). *Arab Media: Globalization and Emerging Media Industries.* Cambridge: Polity Press.

Merz, S. (2012). "'Missionaries of the new era': Neoliberalism and NGOs in Palestine." *Race and Class,* Vol. 55, No. 1, pp. 50–66.

Morris, B. (1987). *The Birth of The Palestinian Refugee Problem, 1947–1949.* Cambridge: University Press.

Mulderig, C. M. (2013). "An uncertain future: Youth frustration and the Arab spring." *The Pardee Papers,* No 16. Boston University.

Nabulsi, M. (2014). "'Hungry for freedom': Palestine youth activism in the era of social media." In L. Herrera and R. Sakr (eds.), *Wired Citizenship: Youth Learning and Activism in the Middle East,* pp. 105–20. New York and London: Routledge Taylor and Francis Group.

Natil, I. (2012). Palestinian youth movement and "the Arab Spring". Retrieved from: https://www.academia.edu/36752949/Palestinian_Youth_Movements_and_the_Arab_Spring_

The New Arab Revolt (2011). New York: Council on Foreign Relations.

Parker, C. (1999). *Resignation or Revolt? Socio-Political Development and the Challenges of Peace in Palestine.* I.B. Tauris.

Peled, Y. (2013). *The Challenge of Ethnic Democracy: The State and Minority Groups in Israel, Poland and Northern Island.* Routledge.

Postill, J. (2011). *Localizing the Internet: An Anthropological Account.* Oxford and New York: Berghahn.

Pressman, J. (2006). "The Second Intifada: Background and Causes of the Israeli-Palestinian Conflict." *Journal of Conflict Studies,* Vol. 23, No. 2 Retrieved from: http://journals.hil.unb.ca/index

Qawasmi, H. and Othman, D. (2016). *# Palestine: Palestinian Social Media Activity during 2015.* Retrieved from: http://www.7amleh.org/en/article/62

Quigley, J. (1990). *Palestine and Israel: A Challenge to Justice.* Durham, NC and London: Duke University Press.

Qumsiyeh, M. (2011). *Popular Resistance in Palestine, a History of Hope and Empowerment.* London: Pluto Press.

Rabinowitz, D. (1997). *Overlooking Nazareth: The Ethnography of Exclusion in Galilee.* Cambridge: Cambridge University Press.

Rabinowitz. D and Abu-Baker, K. (2005). *Coffins on Our Shoulders: The Experience of the Palestinian Citizens of Israel.* Berkeley: University of California Press.

Rouhana, N. and Ghanem, A. (1998). "The crises of minorities in ethnic states: The case of Palestinian citizens in Israel." *International Journal of Middle East Studies*, Vol. 30, No. 3, pp. 321–46.

Roy, S. (2006). *Failing Peace: Gaza and the Palestinian-Israeli Conflict*. Pluto Press.

Roy, S. (2011). *Hamas and Civil Society in Gaza: Engaging the Islamist Social Sector*. Princeton University Press.

Said, E. (1995). "The Middle East Peace process: Misleading images and brutal actualities." In: Moustafa Bayoumi and Andrew Rubin (eds.), *The Eduard Said Reader*, 382–98. London: Granta Books.

Salem, W. (2012). "Civil society in Palestine: Approaches, historical context and the role of the NGOs." *Palestine-Israel Journal*, Vol. 18, No. 2 and 3. Online source: https://pij.org/app.php/articles/1437/civil-society-in-palestine-approaches-historical-context-and-the-role-of-the-ngos

Sayigh, Y. (1997). *Armed Struggle and the Search for State*. Washington DC: Institute for Palestine Studies and Oxford, Clarendon Press.

Sayigh, Y. (2007). "Inducing a failed state." *Survival: Global Politics and Strategy Autumn*, Vol. 49, No. 3, pp. 7–40. DOI 10.1080/00396330701564786

Sayigh, Y. (2010). "Hamas rule in Gaza: Three years on." *Middle East Brief*, No. 41, pp. 1–8.

Sayigh, Y. (2011). "Policing the people, building the state: Authoritarian transformation in the West Bank and Gaza." *Carnegie Endowment for International*, pp. 1–28.

Sayre, E. and Al-Botmeh, S. (2010). *Youth Exclusion in the West Bank and Gaza Strip: The Impact of Social, Political and Economic Forces* (Middle East Youth Initiative working paper No.10). Retrieved from: Wolfenson Center for Development, Dubai School of Government website http://www.meyi.org/uploads/3/2/0/1/32012989/sayre

Schipper, S. (2015). "Urban social movements and the struggle for affordable housing in the globalizing city of Tel Aviv–Jaffa." *Environment and Planning A*, Vol. 47, pp. 521–36.

Scobbie, I. (2007). "An intimate disengagement: Israel's withdrawal from Gaza, the law of occupation and of self-determination." In: E. Cotran and M. Lau (eds.), *Yearbook of Islamic and Middle Eastern Law*, Vol. 11. Brill, pp. 3–31. Retrieved from: http://eprints.soas.ac.uk/3493/

Shafir, G. and Peled, Y. (2002). *Being Israeli: The Dynamics of Multiple Citizenship*. Cambridge Middle East Studies, Cambridge University Press.

Shamir, R. (1996). "Suspended in space: Bedouins under the law of Israel." *Law & Society Review*, Vol. 30, No. 2, pp. 231–57.

Shechter, A. (2013). "On the corner of Rothchild and Tahir." In: Michaela Birk and Steffen Hagermann (eds.), *The only Democracy? Zustand und Zukunft der israelischen Demokratie*. Berlin: AphorismA.

Shepherd, N. (2000). *Ploughing Sand: British rule in Palestine 1917–1948*. New Jersey: Rutgers University Press.

Sherrod, L. R., Torney-Purta, J., and Flanagan, C. A., eds. (2010). *Handbook of Research on Civic Engagement and Youth*. New Jersey: John Wiley & Sons Inc.

Shiqaqi, K. (2006). "Sweeping victory, uncertain mandate." *Journal of Democracy*, Vol. 17, No.3, pp. 116–30. DOI: 10.1353/jod.2006.0053

Shirky, C. (2008). *Here Comes Everybody: The Power of Organizing without Organizations*. New York: Penguin Books.

Shlaim, A. (2000). *The Iron Wall: Israel and the Arab World*. Penguin Books.

Simanovsky, N. (2011). "The Fayyad Plan: Implications for the State of Israel." *Palestine-Israel Journal*, Vol. 17, No. 12. Retrieved from: http://www.pij.org/details.php?id=1317

Sonay, A. (2017). *Making Revolution in Egypt: The April 6th Movement in a Global Context*. I.B. Tauris.

Swirski, Sh. (2016). "Invisible citizens: Israel government policy toward the Negev Bedouin." *Ben-Gurion University of the Negev*. Retrieved from: http://www.bgu.ac.il/bedouin

Tamimi, A. (2007). *Hamas: A History from Within*. Massachusetts: Olive Branch Press.

Taraki, L. (1990). *Intifada: Palestine at the Crossroads*. New York: Bir Zeit University & Praeger Publishers.

Tilly, C. and Tarrow, S. (2005). *Contentious Politics*. Oxford University Press.

Tohamy, A. (2016). *Youth Activism in Egypt: Islamism, Political Protest and Revolution*. I.B. Tauris.

Usher, G. (2006). "The democratic resistance: Hamas, Fatah, and the Palestinian Elections." *Journal of Palestine Studies*, Vol. 35, No. 3, pp. 20–36.

Yiftachel, O. (2012). "Naqab Bedouins and the (internal) colonial paradigm" In: Ahmad Amara, Ismael Abu-Saad and Oren Yiftachel (eds.), *Indigenious (In)Justice: Law and Human Rights among the Bedouins in the Naqab/Negev*, pp. 281–310. Harvard Human Rights Press.

Yiftachel, O., Roded, B., and Kedar, A. (2016). "Between rights and denials: Bedouin indigeneity in the Negev/Naqab." *Environment and Planning A*, Vol. 48, No. 11, pp. 2129–61.

Zaru, J. (2008). *Occupied with Nonviolence: A Palestinian Woman Speaks*. Minneapolis, MN: Fortress Press.

Zureik, E. (1979). *The Palestinians in Israel: A Study in Internal Colonialism*. London: Routledge.

Zweiri, M. (2006). "The Hamas victory: Shifting sands or major earthquake?" *Third World Quarterly*, Vol. 27, No. 4, pp. 675–87.

Online Organizational Resources

The Abraham Fund Initiatives (2015). The Political Participation of Arab Citizens in Israel. Retrieved from: http://www.abrahamfund.org/webfiles/fck/Election%20 Survey%20Full%20Report%20%20-%20English%20-%20January%202015.pdf

Adalah and ACRI (November 28, 2013). The Shabak Is Trying to Sow Fear among Anti-Prawer Plan Activists. Retrieved from: https://www.adalah.org/en/content/view/8224

Amnesty International (July 2009). "Israel- Gaza; Operation 'Cast Lead', 22 days of death and destruction." *Amnesty International Publications*. Retrieved from: https://www.amnesty.org/en/documents/MDE15/015/2009/en/

Arab Center for Research and Policy Studies (September 2012). *The Palestinian Protests of September 2012: The Birth of a Social Protest Movement*. Policy Analysis Unit. Retrieved from: http://english.dohainstitute.org/release/94454f0f-ed0b-40c1-b9b3-58c5b6f0b525

Arab World for Research and Development (AWRAD) (2012). Results of a specialized opinion poll among Palestinian youth. Retrieved from: www.awrad.org

AVAAZ (December 6, 2017). Defend Our Dignity, Defend Jerusalem. Retrieved from: https://secure.avaaz.org/campaign/en/jerusalem_mena_loc_en_my/

AVAAZ (December 19, 2017). Free Ahed Tamimi. Retrieved from: https://secure.avaaz.org/campaign/ar/free_ahed/

AWRAD (2015). Current Protests: An online study of Palestinian Youth (16–35 Years old), Ramallah Gaza, Arab World for Research & Development, December 2015.

AWRAD (2016). Youth Survey: Political Activism and Awareness. (18–25 years old), April 2016.

Baladna, Association for Arab Youth (2012). *Palestinian Youth Affairs in Israel, Field Research.*

Baladna, Association for Arab Youth (2014). *Annual Activities Report 2013–2014.* Retrieved from: https://issuu.com/baladnashbab/docs/interactive_report

Ben-Amos, A., ed. (2012). Political Participation of Arab Citizens in Israel—Attitude Survey ahead of the Elections to the Nineteenth Knesset.

Farsakh, L. (2011). Searching for the Palestinian Spring. Retreved from: https://www.jadaliyya.com/Details/25295

Farsakh, L. (February 21, 2012). "Searching for the Arab Spring in Ramallah." *Jadaliyya*. Retrieved from: www.jadaliyya.com/pages/index/4438/searching-for-the-arab-spring-in-ramallah

Foundation for Middle East Peace (2012). *Report on Israeli Settlement in the Occupied Territories, July–August 2012*. Foundation for Middle East Peace, 7. Retrieved from: http://www.fmep.org/reports/ archive/vol.-22/no.-4/PDF

Human Rights Watch (June 2007). "Gaza: Armed Palestinian groups commit grave crimes." *Press Release*. Retrieved from: https://www.hrw.org/news/2007/06/12/gaza-armed-palestinian-groups-commit-grave-crimes

Human Rights Watch (2010). *Reports of Torture in Palestinian Detention*. Retrieved from: http://www. Hrw.org/en/news/2010/10/20/west-bank- reports-torture-Palestinian-detention.

Institute For Applied Social Science [FAFO]. (February 2012). *Palestinian Youth and the Arab Spring in NOREF* (Norwegian Peace building Resource Centre). Retrieved from: http://www.peacebuilding.no/Regions/Middle-East-and-North-Africa/Israel-Palestine/Publications/Palestinian-youth-and-the-Arab-Spring/%28language%29/eng-US

Institute For Applied Social Science [FAFO]. (June 2013). *Palestinian Youth Activism: New Actors, New Possibilities? in* NOREF (Norwegian Peace building Resource Centre). Retrieved from: https://noref.test.vpdev.no/Publications/Regions/Israel-Palestine/Palestinian-youth-activism-new-actors-new-possibilities

International Committee of the Red Cross [ICRC]. (June 2007). "Latest report on ICRC activities in the field." *Gaza- West Bank. ICRC Bulletin* no 21. Retrieved from: http://reliefweb.int/report/occupied-palestinian-territory/opt-gaza-icrc-bulletin-no-21-2007

International Crisis Group (March 2007). "Ruling Palestine I: Gaza under Hamas." *Middle East Report No. 73*. Retrieved from: https://www.crisisgroup.org/middle-east-north-africa/eastern-mediterranean/israelpalestine/ruling-palestine-i-gaza-under-hamas

International Crisis Group (July 2008). "Ruling Palestine II. The West Bank model?" *Middle East Report No. 79*. Retrieved from: https://www.crisisgroup.org/middle-east-north-africa/eastern-mediterranean/israelpalestine/ruling-palestine-ii-west-bank-model

International Crisis Group (2010). "Squaring the circle: Palestinian security reform under occupation." *Middle East Report 98*.

The International Institute for Strategic Studies (2007). *Hamas coup in Gaza*, Vol. 13, No. 5, ISSN: 1356-7888.

Khalil, O. (March, 2013). "'Who are you?': The PLO and the limits of representation." *Al Shabaka Policy Brief*. Retrieved from: https://al-shabaka.org/wp-content/uploads/2013/03/Khalil_PolicyBrief_En_Mar_2013.pdf

Mosawa (2012). The 2013 Israeli Elections: Consequences for the Palestinians Arab Citizens in Israel. Retrieved from: http://www.mossawa.org/uploads/2013%20Israeli%20Elections%20(1).pdf

Palestinian Center for Policy and Survey Research (PCPSR). Public opinion polls on youth activism, youth and social media and youth and political parties from 2011–2016. Retrieved from: http://www.pcpsr.org

Palestinian Central Bureau of Statistics (PCBS) (2016). Annual statistics: Current estimated population in the Palestinian territories. Retrieved from: http://www.pcbs.gov.ps/site/lang__en/803/default.aspx

Palestinian Independent Commission for Citizen's Rights (PICCR) (October 2007). Retrieved from: http://www.imra.org.il/story.php3?id=36576

Sharek Youth Forum (2009). *Sharek Youth Forum Annual Report: Promise or Peril? The status of Youth in Palestine.* Retrieved from: http://sharek.ps/en/1/17

Sharek Youth Forum (2011). *Sharek Youth Forum Annual Report: Winds of Change: The Status of Youth in Palestine.* Retrieved from: http://sharek.ps/en/1/17

Sharek Youth Forum (2013). *Sharek Youth Forum Annual Report: The Future is Knocking: The Status of Youth in Palestine.* Retrieved from: http://sharek.ps/en/1/17

Spark (2013). *Spark Annual Progress Report.* Retrieved from: http://www.spark-online.org

Think Marketing (December 6, 2017). Twitter Explodes against Trump's Jerusalem decision. Retrieved from: https://thinkmarketingmagazine.com/twitter-explodes-trumps-jerusalem-decision/#mm

United Nations (UN) (December 2009). "Human rights in Palestine and other occupied Arab Territories." *Report of the United Nations Fact-Finding on the Gaza Conflict.* Retrieved from: http://www2.ohchr.org/english/bodies/hrcouncil/docs/12session/A-HRC-12-48.pdf

Social Media Sites (Facebook, Twitter, Blogs)

Bab Al-Shams (March 24, 2013). Update: The number of military and police vehicles raiding AhfadYounis now exceeds the 50!BabAlshams. (Facebook status update). Retrieved from: https://www.facebook.com/Babalshams2013/posts/514843315228241

Free Fadi Quran (February 27, 2012). Tomorrow, on the 27th, a court hearing for Fadi at Ofer Prison. (Facebook status update). Retrieved from: https://www.facebook.com/free.fadi.quran/

Free the Tamimi Women (December 22, 2017). Women and Girls: No Cooperation with the Occupation. (Facebook status update). Retrieved from: https://www.facebook.com/FreeTamimiWomen/

Gaza Youth Breaks Out (GYBO) (2011). Manifesto 1.0. (WordPress Blog Post). Retrieved from: https://gazaybo.wordpress.com/manifesto-0-1/

Hungry For Freedom (October 15, 2011). In support of the general hunger strike of the political Palestinian prisoners as part of the their struggle against the occupational authorities. (Facebook status update). Retrieved from https://www.facebook.com/Hungry-For-Freedom--281161825235578للحرية-جائعون/

Huwaida Arraf (@huwaidaarraf) (January 12, 2018). I wake up at night and I start crying because I feel she is cold. I am warm and she is called. # FreeAhedTamimi #NoWAYToTreatAChild. (Tweet). Retrieved from: https://twitter.com/huwaidaarraf/status/951916711149699075

IMEU (September 19, 2016). *Human Rights Defender Isa Amro on Trial.* (Video File). Retrieved from: https://www.youtube.com/watch?v=tZH6xOHXxB0

Kopty, A. (November 24, 2013). Schedule of worldwide actions to Stop Prawer on Nov. 30th Day of Rage. (Blog Post). Retrieved from: https://abirkopty.wordpress.com/2013/11/24/schedule-of-actions-worldwide-to-stop-prawer-on-nov-30th-day-of-rage/

Matter, M. (Mohammed Matter) (October 20, 2012). Two years ago we said "Fuck Israel. Fuck Hamas. Fuck Fatah. Fuck UN. Fuck UNWRA. Fuck USA!" We want to be free. We want to be able to live a normal life. We want peace. Is that too much to ask? (Facebook status update). Retrieved from: https://www.facebook.com/abu.yazan.gaza/posts/282214681898444

Nabi Saleh Solidarity (November 24, 2011). Nabi Saleh invaded last night. (Facebook status update). Retrieved from: https://www.facebook.com/search/top/?q=nabi%20saleh%20solidarity

Nabi Saleh Solidarity (March 2, 2012). Palestinian human rights defender Bassem Tamimi is a prisoner of conscience, detained solely for his role in organizing peaceful protests against the encroachment onto Palestinian lands by Israeli settlers, and should be released immediately and unconditionally, Amnesty International said today. (WordPress Blogpost). Retrieved from: https://nabisalehsolidarity.wordpress.com/2012/03/09/amnesty-international-israel-must-release-palestinian-prisoner-of-conscience-bassem-tamimi/

Palestine Freedom Rides (March 2, 2011). Emulating the freedom riders that helped carry the Civil Rights movement to a new and much more advanced stage. (Facebook status update). Retrieved from: https://www.facebook.com/PalestinianFreedomRides/posts/263832810335617

Prawer Wont Pass Campaign- International Page (December 13, 2013). Israel's government seems to be heading towards shelving the Prawer plan due to the decreased support for it among members of the Knesset (Israeli Parliament) and new revelations that the Plan was not presented to the Palestinian-Bedouins of Al-Naqab. However, it is important to highlight our campaign does not end here, even if the plan is shelved. (Facebook status update). Retrieved from: https://www.facebook.com/prawershallnotpass

Shehab News Agency (December 19, 2017). Video of the occupying forces arrested the 17-Year-old girl from the village of Nabi Saleh in Ramallah for slapping two Israeli soldiers in front of her family house. (Facebook status

update). Retrieved from: https://www.facebook.com/ShehabAgency.MainPage/
videos/2240962579279483/

Taghreeba (Free Palestine) (December 27, 2017). Till yesterday Ahed's twitter account
was online (@ahedAlTamimi), today @twitter decided to delete the account. (Tweet).
Retrieved from: https://twitter.com/Taghreeba/status/945984501502676992/
photo/1?ref_src=twsrc%5Etfw&ref_url=https%3A%2F%2Fwww.rt.com%2Fusa%
2F414396-twitter-delete-ahed-tamimi%2F

Blog-Based Magazines and Online
News Publications Cited

Abunimah, A. (December 1, 2013). Video: Israel police brutalize child amid
anti-Prawer protests. Retrieved from: https://electronicintifada.net/blogs/ali-
abunimah/video-israel-police-brutalize-child-amid-anti-prawer-protests

Activists hold 'day of rage' protests against Prawer Plan (November 30, 2013).
Retrieved from: https://972mag.com/activists-stage-day-of-rage-protests-against-
prawer-plan/82706/

Aderet, O. and Lis, J. (December 12, 2013). Israeli Government Halts Controversial
Plan to Resettle 30,000 Bedouin. Retrieved from: http://www.haaretz.com/israel-
news/1.563200

Al Saafin, L. (March 23, 2012). Imperfect revolution: Palestine's 15 March movement
one year on. Retrieved from: https://electronicintifada.net/content/imperfect-
revolution-palestines-15-march-movement-one-year/11092

Al Saafin, L. and Hassan Budour, Y. (September 7, 2013). Resist Israel's unjust system,
don't operate within it. Retrieved from: https://electronicintifada.net/content/
resist-israels-unjust-system-dont-operate-within-it/12751

Al Sukkar, N. (December 6, 2017). Jerusalem must remain the capital of Palestine.
Retrieved from: https://www.change.org/p/world-leaders-jerusalem-must-remain-
the-capital-of-palestine

Bahour, S. (September 26, 2016). Don't call us "Israeli Arabs": Palestinians
in Israel speak out. Retrieved from: http://www.haaretz.com/opinion/.
premium-1.744398

Balasubramanian, J. and Vaid-Menon, A. (August 19, 2013). A new wave of
Palestinian Youth Activism in Response to Israeli Prawer Plan. Retrieved from:
http://www.momken.org/?mod=articles&ID=5693

Berman, L. (December 12, 2013). Government shelves Prawer Plan on Bedouin
settlement. Retrieved from: http://www.timesofisrael.com/government-shelves-
prawer-plan-on-bedouin-settlement/

Chacar, H. (March 11, 2015). A new activism, a new generation of Palestinians in Israel. Retrieved from: https://972mag.com/a-new-activism-a-new-politics-a-new-generation-of-palestinians-in-israel/103837/

Clashes break out in Negev as police disperse anti-Prawer protest (November 30, 2013). Retrieved from: http://www.maannews.com/Content.aspx?id=652688

Dana, J. (January 29, 2011). From Jaffa to Cairo all people power is revolutionary. Retrieved from: https://972mag.com/from-jaffa-to-cairo-all-people-power-is-revolutionary/9701/

Demolition and Eviction of Bedouin Citizens of Israel in the Naqab (Negev)—The Prawer Plan. Retrieved from: https://www.adalah.org/en/content/view/7589

Discriminatory Prawer Plan to evict tens of thousands of Bedouins from their communities in the Negev (July 11, 2013). Retrieved from: http://www.eccpalestine.org/discriminatory-prawer-plan-to-evict-tens-of-thousands-of-bedouins-from-their-communities-in-the-negev/

Haifa Youth Support Striking Palestinian prisoners (October 15, 2011). Retrieved from: http://mideastnews-danmike.blogspot.co.il/2011/10/haifa-youth-support-striking.html

Israel: Halt Demolitions of Bedouin Homes in Negev (August 1, 2010). Retrieved from: https://www.hrw.org/news/2010/08/01/israel-halt-demolitions-bedouin-homes-negev

Julie, C. (October 14, 2013). Druze Israeli citizens serving Israel: Part reconstruction, part invention. Retrieved from: http://palestinemonitor.org/details.php?id=hmzw0ua5285ymuphucb65

Julie, C. (October 23, 2013). Stop the Prawer Plan: Palestinian Youth in solidarity with the Bedouins. Retrieved from: http://palestinemonitor.org/details.php?id=klvnbta5337y8j3cpex4e

Kane, A. (November 30, 2013). Thousands across Palestine protest against efforts to uproot Bedouin. Retrieved from: http://mondoweiss.net/2013/11/thousands-palestine-efforts/#sthash.zDzD0aY3.dpuf

Kopty, A. (July 13, 2013). July 15th: Anger Strike to stop Prawer Plan. Retrieved from: https://abirkopty.wordpress.com/2013/07/13/july-15th-anger-strike-to-stop-prawer-plan/

Moskowitz, J. (July 9, 2014). The Next Generation of Israeli-Palestinian Conflict. Retrieved from: https://www.theatlantic.com/international/archive/2014/07/the-next-generation-of-israeli-palestinian-conflict/374184/

Murphy, M. C. (December 13, 2013). Withdrawal of Prawer Plan bill "major achievement" for Palestinians in Israel. Retrieved from: https://electronicintifada.net/blogs/maureen-clare-murphy/withdrawal-prawer-plan-bill-major-achievement-palestinians-israel

Nashif, N. (January 13, 2016). Palestinian Citizens in Israel: A Fast-Shrinking Civic Space. Retrieved from: https://al-shabaka.org/commentaries/palestinian-citizens-in-israel-a-fast-shrinking-civic-space/

Nashif, N. and Naamneh, R. (January 13, 2016). Palestinian Citizens in Israel: A Fast-Shrinking Civic Space. Retrieved from: https://al-shabaka.org/commentaries/palestinian-citizens-in-israel-a-fast-shrinking-civic-space/

Nieuwhof, A. (October 11, 2011). Hunger strike movement for Palestine develops rapidly. Retrieved from: https://electronicintifada.net/blogs/adri-nieuwhof/hunger-strike-movement-palestine-develops-rapidly

Omer-Man, M. (February 20, 2016). From Haifa to Beirut: 48 Palestinians challenge regional isolation. Retrieved from: https://972mag.com/from-haifa-to-beirut-48-palestinians-challenge-regional-isolation/117210/

Palestinian Authority arrests activist over Facebook post (September 4, 2017). Retrieved from: http://www.middleeasteye.net/news/palestinian-authority-arrests-activist-over-facebook-post-1362138628

Palestinians Rally in Gaza to stop Prawer Plan on International Day of Rage (December 3, 2013). Retrieved from: https://palsolidarity.org/2013/12/photos-palestinians-rally-in-gaza-to-stop-prawer-plan-on-international-day-of-rage/

Police, Protesters Clash Across Israel at Rallies Against Bedouin Relocation. Retrieved from: http://www.haaretz.com/israel-news/1.560995

Press Release: The Knesset Approves the Highly Devastating Prawer-Begin Bill in First Voting Round (June 25, 2013). Retrieved from: http://www.dukium.org/press-release-the-knesset-approves-the-highly-devastating-prawer-begin-bill-in-first-voting-round/

Raved, A. (January 29, 2011). Arab Israelis back Egyptian protestors. Retrieved from: http://www.ynetnews.com/articles/0,7340,L-4020862,00.html

Schwarczenberg, H. (November 30, 2013a). Day of Rage against the Prawer plan: Yafa. Retrieved from: https://schwarczenberg.com/day-of-rage-against-the-prawer-plan-yafa-30-11-2013/

Schwarczenberg, H. (November 30, 2013b). Day of Rage against the Prawer plan, Hura. Retrieved from: https://schwarczenberg.com/day-of-rage-against-the-prawer-plan-hura/

Schwarczenberg, H. (November 16, 2013c). Jaffa demonstration against the Prawer plan. Retrieved from: https://schwarczenberg.com/yaffa-demonstration-against-the-prawer-plan-16-11-2013-2/

Stop Israel's ethnic cleansing of Palestinian Bedouin! (November 30, 2013). Retrieved from: https://ozcoalitionagainstisraeliapartheid.wordpress.com/2013/11/30/melbourne-against-the-prawer-plan-stop-israels-ethnic-cleansing-of-palestinian-bedouin/

Update on Detained Anti-Prawer Demonstrators in the North and the Naqab (December 3, 2013). Retrieved from: https://www.adalah.org/en/content/view/8226

Viscous crackdown on unarmed protesters against the Prawer Plan just outside Ramallah (December 2, 2013). Retrieved from: https://palsolidarity.org/2013/12/viscous-crackdown-on-non-violent-protestors-against-the-prawer-plan-just-outside-ramallah/

White, B. (March 29, 2012). Palestinians forge new strategies of resistance. Retrieved from: http://www.aljazeera.com/indepth/opinion/2012/03/20123297836253440.html

International and Regional Media Sites and Newspapers Cited:

+972 Mag
Al Jazeera
Al Monitor
The Atlantic
BBC
Electronic Intifada
Felesteen
The Guardian
Haaretz
Ma'an
Mondoweiss
The New York Times

Index

www.ingramcontent.com/pod-product-compliance
Lightning Source LLC
Chambersburg PA
CBHW050434280326
41932CB00013BA/2116